Structure of Language
Spoken and Written English

Structure of Language

Spoken and Written English

by

JANET TOWNEND MA, DipCST, AMBDA
Head of Training, the Dyslexia Institute, Egham

and

JEAN WALKER BA, AMBDA
Training Principal, the Dyslexia Institute, Sheffield

W
WHURR PUBLISHERS

Other Wiley Editorial Offices

John Wiley & Sons Inc., 111 River Street, Hoboken, NJ 07030, USA
Jossey-Bass, 989 Market Street, San Francisco, CA 94103-1741, USA
Wiley-VCH Verlag GmbH, Boschstr. 12, D-69469 Weinheim, Germany
John Wiley & Sons Australia Ltd, 42 McDougall Street, Milton, Queensland 4064,
Australia
John Wiley & Sons (Asia) Pte Ltd, 2 Clementi Loop #02-01, Jin Xing Distripark,
Singapore 129809
John Wiley & Sons Canada Ltd, 22 Worcester Road, Etobicoke, Ontario, Canada
M9W 1L1
Wiley also publishes its books in a variety of electronic formats. Some content that
appears in print may not be available in electronic books.

A catalogue record for this book is available from the British Library

ISBN -13   978-1-86156-429-0
ISBN -10   1-86156-429-5

Printed and bound in Great Britain by TJ International Ltd, Padstow, Cornwall

This book is printed on acid-free paper responsibly manufactured from sustainable
forestry in which at least two trees are planted for each one used for paper production.

Contents

Acknowledgements

Grateful acknowledgements are made for permission to reproduce the illustrations in this volume:

Figure 11.2 McCrum R, Cran W, MacNeil R (1986/1992) The Story of English. London: BBC Books and Faber & Faber. (permission pending)

Figure 11.4 Crystal D (1995) The Cambridge Encyclopaedia of the English Language, Cambridge University Press, reproduced with permission from the publisher and author.

Figure 11.8 The British Library, and Crystal D (1995) The Cambridge Encyclopaedia of the English Language, Cambridge University Press, reproduced with permission from the publisher and author.

Table 12.3 Crystal D (1995) The Cambridge Encyclopaedia of the English Language, Cambridge University Press, reproduced with permission from the publisher and author.

Figure 12.4 Resources for Studying *Beowulf* www.georgetown.edu/irvinemj/english016/beowulf/beowulf.html

Figure 12.6 The Huntingdon Library, San Marino, California. Crystal D (1995) The Cambridge Encyclopaedia of the English Language, Cambridge University Press, reproduced with permission from the publisher and author.

Introduction

At the time of writing, anyone between the ages of 15 and 50 may be coming to grammar here for the first time. You will be too old to have benefited from the National Literacy Strategy and too young to have been taught grammar traditionally, before the 'modernizations' of the 1960s deprived our school pupils of learning how language works. This aside is a professional, not a political one.

Having, between us, nearly half a century of experience of working with people who struggle with language and literacy, we are both convinced of the importance of a structured, analytical, sequential and cumulative approach to the teaching of reading, writing and spelling. We are offering you just that kind of approach to how language works by means of this book. It is our hope that you find language as wonderful, and as wonderfull as we do. We still find language amazing, exciting and often very funny; if we have imparted a tiny bit of that to you, our aim has been achieved.

It is quite unusual to combine spoken language and written language in the same book; those who need one perhaps consider they are unlikely to need the other. It is our contention that the two are so closely interdependent that it is amazing that no one has thought of doing it before. Why is an equal allocation of space given to spoken language? One reason is that spoken language – sounds, words, sentences – are our primary, biologically determined means of expressing ideas and information. Writing is a symbol system representing the spoken form. There are important differences between spoken and written language, which are explored in these chapters; that is why it has two parts.

There are huge differences between spoken and written language, and between how each is governed; we explore these themes, but the differences are the reason why this book has two distinct parts. However, by considering spoken language and written language side by side, we come to understand more about the essential characteristics of each. You will find the first part more descriptive, the second part more prescriptive; that is the nature of the essential difference between the two language systems.

An important reason for a closer look at spoken language is that many individuals with literacy difficulties, especially but not exclusively those with dyslexia, are late and poor talkers. Some will have speech sound difficulties, limited vocabulary or word retrieval problems. Others may have weaknesses at the level of sentences and grammar, others at the level of language meaning and use (often misdiagnosed as behaviour problems). Some will have more than one area of difficulty in spoken language. Many of these problems are significant, but subtle, and impede real progress in literacy, especially beyond the early, decoding stages.

There are all kinds of intrinsic and environmental reasons why some children attain spoken language competence slowly or with difficulty. Many of the factors that influence the acquisition of literacy skills are substantially the same ones as those that influence spoken language development.

Janet Townend is Head of Training at the Dyslexia Institute, Egham. She is a speech and language therapist, specialist dyslexia teacher and teacher trainer, and has written the first part of the book. Jean Walker is a Training Principal at the Dyslexia Institute, Sheffield. An English teacher, specialist dyslexia teacher and teacher trainer, she has written the second part. The content started life as a series of lectures, forming one module of a postgraduate certificate in dyslexia and literacy. The module included a number of activities for the student, and these have been retained to encourage you to interact with the text. We urge you to complete the written tasks and oral exercises to facilitate your understanding and, we hope, your interest. In particular, you need to join in saying the sounds out loud in the exercises in Chapters 4 to 6. When reading a chapter you are advised to have paper to write on (a small space in the task will indicate that action is needed, but there is not room to write in the book). You should also have a separate piece of paper with which to mask the answers. The following symbols show at a glance when your equipment will be required:

 This indicates that there is a written task to do at this point.

 This symbol indicates that you will need to mask the answers.

 This symbol is placed beside the answers, so you can quickly see which part of the page to mask, and then uncover to check your own answers.

A note about the symbols used in this book

We have assumed that most readers will not be familiar with the International Phonetic Alphabet (IPA), and therefore we have used mainly diacritical markings to denote vowel sounds (see the table below). In Chapters 4 to 6, about phonetics and phonology, some IPA symbols are used, and there is a 'clue word' for each one. The most frequently occurring symbol, and the one we think you will find most useful, is /ə/, the unstressed English vowel, or schwa, which is used in the unstressed syllable in many words. Examples include *a* at the end of *vanilla*, *er* at the end of *mother*, *o* in the first syllable of *tomato*. You need to say them aloud and listen! There is much more about this within the pages of the book.

We have followed the convention of putting IPA symbols between slanting brackets /p/, and diacritical markings between square brackets [ā] or round brackets (ă). Readers who are interested in the full International Phonetic Alphabet may like to visit the website of the International Phonetic Association, or refer to any good introductory text on phonetics.

Diacritical markings

ă	Short vowel sound of letter a	cat
ā	Long vowel sound of letter a	lake
ĕ	Short vowel sound of letter e	egg
ē	Long vowel sound of letter e	see
ĭ	Short vowel sound of letter i	ink
ī	Long vowel sound of letter i	pipe
ŏ	Short vowel sound of letter o	off
ō	Long vowel sound of letter o	open
ŭ	Short vowel sound of letter u	cup (RP* only)
ū	Long vowel sound of letter u	music

*See Chapter 4 for a definition of RP (Received Pronunciation)

The subject matter of this book is essential core knowledge for teachers of language at any level, including those teaching English as an additional language. This is not a book about teaching, though we expect to number many teachers among our readers. The purpose of this book is to develop the knowledge base about how language works for anyone who has anything to do with language, whether teaching it, reading it, writing it, speaking it, listening to it, or communicating in any other of its rich variety of media. That seems to include all of us.

Janet Townend, Egham
Jean Walker, Sheffield

PART 1
SPOKEN LANGUAGE

CHAPTER 1

Human communication

Introduction

Before considering the details of the structure and development of spoken language, we will explore the wider topic of human communication as a whole. What is it? What forms does it take? What, if anything, makes talking different from other forms of human communication?

This chapter looks briefly at whether language plays an essential part in thought; the mechanisms of spoken language – neurological, anatomical, physiological and social – are examined; and finally we touch on how language may have come about. Compared with spoken language, written language is, of course, a recent development. In evolutionary terms, even spoken language has been around for a relatively short period.

How do humans communicate?

In many and various ways, as you will see.

Task 1.1

Take a large sheet of paper (A4 or similar) and write 'Human communication' in the middle. Now write down as many ways as you can think of in which people communicate with each other. Be prepared to think creatively, and do not limit yourself to verbal communication. Here are a few words to start you thinking.

Words	Eye contact
Writing	
HUMAN COMMUNICATION	
Dance	Road signs

Task 1.1
continued

When you have run out of ideas, look at Figure 1.1 for an amalgamation of ideas I have collected from teachers over several years. I have also added a few suggestions of my own.

A

LANGUAGE-BASED	NON-VERBAL: BODY
words	eye contact
writing	gesture
talking	touch
Braille	body language
sign languages	sex
finger spelling	laughing
hieroglyphs	facial expression
Morse code	crying
semaphore	posture
	position of body

HUMAN COMMUNICATION

VISUAL SYMBOLS	ACTION/EMOTION
road signs	action (e.g. kindness)
rebuses (e.g. ladies/	violence (slap/punch)
gentlemen picture signs)	affection (kiss/hug)
flags	

CREATIVE/ARTISTIC	NON-VERBAL: OTHER
colour	computer languages
painting and visual arts	chemical formulae
dance	equations
mime	mathematics
music	electronics
drama	sounds: bells/horns
performing arts	
clothes/décor	

Figure 1.1

Task 1.2

Now take either your own list, or mine, or a combination of the two, and try to group the different kinds of communication under headings. What criteria would you apply to combine or separate, say, emails and poetry? When you have finished, compare your list with mine.

I have chosen to have five category headings, but as you will see, some fit into more than one. This turned out to be a very tricky table to fill in! It is not an exhaustive list, and the

Task 1.2
continued

headings are my choice – yours are equally valid. I hope it demonstrates what a complex subject this is.

Electronic	Word-based	The Arts	Non-verbal: visual	Non-verbal: physical
email	talking	music	fashion (clothes, furnishing, etc.)	eye contact (or lack of)
text messages	listening	drama	road signs	gesture
computer languages	writing	dance	logos	posture
Morse code	reading	painting	information signs	touch
television	email	drawing	photographs	giving (gifts or service)
radio	text messages	sculpture	musical notation	sex
	sign language	architecture	numbers	facial expression
	finger spelling	photography		movement (e.g. walking away)
	braille	literature		laughing
	Morse code	poetry		crying
	semaphore			screaming
	hieroglyphs			non-words (e.g. 'shhh!')
A	numbers			

Why do humans communicate?

It is a small step from this exercise to considering the different purposes of human communication. Why do we need to be in touch with one another? First, because we are social beings, living in groups. Communication bonds us, and conveys information and feelings between individuals and groups. It may be considered the cement of society.

Task 1.3

Now make a short list of headings of things that can be communicated. My list is overleaf: cover it up until you are ready to check. Then go back to the list of means of communication, and think about which means are best suited to which content. For example, would semaphore be a good way to communicate emotion? Is poetry or music an effective way to communicate information? There are no right answers for this one; it is discussed in the text overleaf.

Task 1.3
continued

A

We may wish to communicate:

ideas	information	emotions	instructions
relationships	self-image	rules	warnings
entertainment			

any combination of the above ... and many more.

Because we are thinking individuals, communication may be used as a substitute for action (and, of course, vice versa). You may express outrage powerfully in words in a situation where, without words, you might have taken violent action. On the other hand, we have all experienced situations in which non-verbal messages such as a smile or a press of the hand may be more eloquent than words. Sometimes words are best, sometimes actions, sometimes both.

Some kinds of communication, such as music, can convey emotions; others, such as mathematical symbols, can convey information; words can do both. Of course, words can be represented by a range of symbols: sounds, letters on the page, raised dots in Braille, bleeps in Morse code, flags in semaphore, and so on. As thinkers, we can use communication, especially verbal communication, to express and share our ideas. It is arguable (and you would no doubt expect me to argue) that many abstract ideas are communicated most effectively through words.

The obvious limitation of spoken language, which is not shared by mathematics or music, is that we use different languages, depending on where we live or the society to which we belong. Some historical linguists (more orthodox academics might be tempted to call them *hysterical* linguists) have tried to show that all languages have a common origin. It is an attractive idea, but one on which we can only speculate. It is certainly true that the languages we use now can be grouped according to their common antecedents, and it is extremely likely that in pre-history there were far fewer languages in use than at present. This book is about the English language, so there will be very little reference to comparative linguistics, except to clarify points about English. As global communications now make it possible to speak to someone anywhere in the world in seconds, the need for a lingua franca becomes more urgent. At the present time, English seems to be aspiring to that role.

Language and thought

Do you think in words, or pictures, or both? Next time you are out for a walk or sitting on a train, think about it and try to come up with an answer for yourself. I know that I think in words, phrases and complete sentences, and if I am struggling with difficult ideas I often think out loud. For you it may be different, or vary according to circumstances.

What is the role of language in the development of concepts? Are words the labels we put on ideas, or do we need words for the concepts to develop? Before you decide where you stand on this question, consider the following example.

> Some years ago my husband and I were on a game drive in east Africa. As we drove through the national park we could see a vast landscape with birds and animals going about their business; it was beautiful, and quite interesting to watch. After a while we stopped and our guide began to point things out, telling us the names of the creatures we could see, describing their behaviour patterns and explaining how to tell one sort of gazelle from another. As we talked and listened, and as the day progressed, something happened; we began to see more in the landscape. We noticed details, differences, patterns, things we had not seen before. This was due entirely to the fact that we had labels for what we were looking at. What had been one thing (a landscape with fauna and flora) was now a huge number of different things, which could be differentiated.

Names of things are a sort of shorthand for describing their attributes. It is much easier to store names than sets of attributes, and this is why naming is an important aspect of conceptualization. Some labels are very specific, such as 'elephant', while others, such as 'cat', are more generic and require additional information.

The problem of labelling

Think for a moment about colours; we all know what blue looks like and those of us who are not colour-blind know what green looks like. We have the concepts, and the concept labels for blue-ness and green-ness. As we move towards turquoise or aquamarine on the spectrum, the line between blue and green begins to blur, and we may talk about 'greeny-blue' or 'bluey-green', but we will not all cross the dividing line at the same shade. We have all had, or at least heard, conversations in which people discuss the correct name label for a colour: 'It's a sort of pinky colour'; 'I'd say it was more of a mauve', and so on. Language labels are not absolute. Yet, finding the correct label for a colour is simple, when compared to finding the right words to describe an emotion.

The classification of things is a fascinating area for the linguist. A label is a powerful tool, carrying with it a whole package of attributes. Many plants and animals have had to be re-classified in the light of new scientific evidence, making it apparent that superficial similarities were misleading and erroneous.

For many years, the inert gases were believed by chemists not to react with anything; that is why they were called inert. As time went on, their inertia was called into question, but at first people were reluctant to believe that these gases had reacted with other elements because they were supposed to be inert. Their label had got in the way of new scientific thought, an erroneous label as it turned out. Giving a name to something is an awesome responsibility, for that name can take on a life of its own and become more important than the concept it was meant to label. The servant can become the master.

How does spoken communication happen?

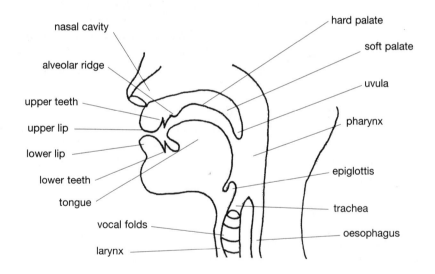

Figure 1.2 Lateral section through the head and neck.

The vocal tract

The diagram of a lateral section through the head and neck (Figure 1.2) shows the anatomy of the organs of speech. The first thing to happen is that air is breathed in and fills the lungs (not shown).

Towards the bottom of the diagram is the trachea. This is the 'windpipe', a flexible tube through which air travels to the lungs. A little way below where the diagram stops, the pipe divides into two, one half going to each lung. The tube behind the trachea is the oesophagus, through which swallowed food travels to the stomach.

The top part of the trachea is called the larynx. It is a semi-rigid tube, made up of a stack of rings of cartilage. The vocal cords, or more properly, the vocal folds, are membranes stretched across one of these rings. The next diagram (Figure 1.3) shows the vocal folds stretched across the larynx, viewed from above. These membranes can open and close, stretch tight or lie slack, making for different kinds of sounds. The diagram on the left shows the vocal folds open; that on the right shows them closed, during swallowing, for example.

VOCAL FOLDS VIEWED FROM ABOVE

vocal folds open
(breathing)

vocal folds closed
(swallowing)

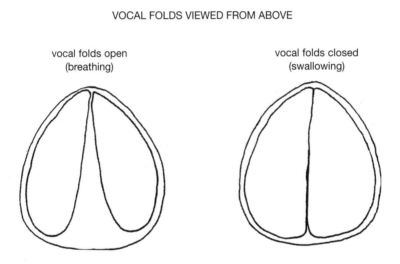

Figure 1.3 The movement of the vocal folds.

The primary function of the vocal folds is to protect the airways from foreign bodies. On swallowing, the glottis, which is the gap between the vocal folds, closes tightly so nothing can enter the lungs. There is an additional protection in the form of a flap called the epiglottis, situated above the larynx, which folds down to steer food and drink into the oesophagus. If some material heads down the wrong way, the resulting coughing and choking is the action of the vocal folds attempting to expel the foreign matter by forcing it upwards. During this process it is difficult to breathe; this is why a persistent fit of coughing leaves the sufferer gasping for breath.

In order to speak, the lungs expand and air rushes in; then they contract, pushing air out. This can be felt by placing the hands on the ribs. When about to speak, this column of air travels up until it reaches the larynx, where a decision has to be made. The secondary function of the vocal folds is speech, and the vocal folds can vibrate, producing voice, which is necessary for all vowel sounds and some consonant sounds (see Chapters 4–6 for detailed coverage of speech sounds). It is possible to feel whether a sound has voicing by cupping your hands over your ears, then say the sound /s/ followed by the sound /z/. They should be pure sounds, not the letter names, and without an 'uh' sound at the end. The /s/ should just be a hiss, and the /z/ a buzz. With your hands cupped over your ears, you should be able to feel vibrations in your head on /z/, which is voiced, but not on /s/, which is unvoiced.

The column of air, vibrating or not, continues up past the pharynx, the part of the vocal tract between the larynx and the back of the mouth. We are not normally very aware of the pharynx, unless about to get a cold, when it can be very painful. When you are not sure if it is the back of your nose or your throat that hurts, then you are feeling pain in your pharynx. The diagram shows that it is connected to the nasal cavity and the larynx.

When the column of air reaches the pharynx, the next decision has to be made. Is the sound to be made through the nose (in English that would be the nasal sounds /m/, /n/, or /ng/, as in *mail*, *nest* and *ring*), or through the mouth, which in English would be all the other speech sounds? The sounds made through the mouth are called oral sounds.

For nasal sounds, the uvula stays down and the air goes into the nasal cavity and out through the nostrils. A closure is made at some point in the mouth to prevent the air escaping that way. Try this: open your mouth wide with your head tilted slightly back, in front of a mirror and with the light behind you, and say 'ah'. You can see the uvula. It is the very back of the roof of the mouth, and dangles down, coming to a slight point above the back of the tongue.

The uvula is raised when the soft palate, or velum (the fleshy part of the roof of the mouth), is raised during oral sounds. This is to ensure that all the air is released through the mouth. In front of the soft palate is the hard palate, the bony roof of the mouth. This is formed by the two halves, left and right, fusing together *in utero*, in the early months of pregnancy. If you explore the bony roof of your mouth with your tongue you may be able to feel the join, in the form of a groove or a ridge, running from front to back.

A cleft palate is an incomplete fusion of these two halves, so there is a hole from the mouth up into the nasal cavity. This means that the nasal cavity cannot be sealed off, and air escapes down the nose during all speech sounds, giving the speech its characteristic nasal quality. A repaired cleft palate may leave an individual with a short or relatively immobile soft palate. The speech may still be nasal, even though there is no longer a hole, because the soft palate is not capable of lifting far enough up and back to make a good seal against the back wall of the pharynx.

Assuming an oral sound is to be made, and the structure and function of the organs of articulation are intact, the soft palate and uvula are raised to make a seal against the back wall of the pharynx, so the column of air is forced into the mouth. The tongue, an incredibly flexible organ, is made up of muscles running from front to back, from top to bottom, and from side to side. It moves into a variety of shapes and positions to form different speech sounds. The teeth, lips and palate may also be involved. There are different places to make sounds, and different ways to make them; we will look at all of these in later chapters.

It sounds like a relatively straightforward sequence of movements, until one considers how many different speech sounds there are in a word, in a sentence, in Shakespeare's *Hamlet*. A huge number of rapid movements is being made by the organs of speech, controlled by the motor cortex in the brain, in order to speak. There are at least nine distinct positions for the organs of articulation in the simple greeting 'Hello, Mum', which is over in less than a second.

The brain: the speech control centre

The understanding of language, and speech and language production is controlled by the brain. Look at Figure 1.4.

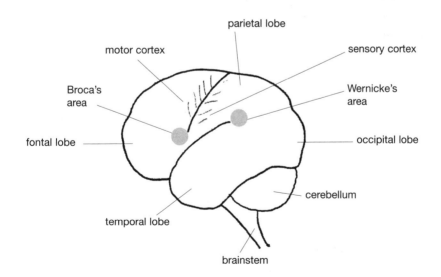

Figure 1.4 Language areas of the brain: the left cerebral hemisphere.

The cerebral cortex is the surface layer of the brain, grey in colour and with a surface area of almost one metre squared. It may be helpful to imagine it as a small tablecloth, spread out to about a metre square, then crumpled to fit into a container (the skull). It has very many folds, ridges and fissures to accommodate a huge surface area in a small space. The cortex is where the highest levels of brain function take place. The brain is divided into two halves, the cerebral hemispheres, joined by a 'bridge' called the corpus callosum. Each hemisphere is divided into several lobes, and at the lower part of the back of the brain both hemispheres are connected to the spinal cord by the brainstem. Adjacent to the brainstem is the cerebellum, which looks rather like a small cauliflower. The cerebellum is responsible for many automatic functions, such as balance (keeping the body upright) and co-ordination. We are mainly concerned here with some of the functions of the cerebral cortex, the surface layer of grey matter, and in particular those areas connected with spoken language.

The precise functioning of the brain is not, even now, completely understood, and new research findings are emerging all the time. One major development of recent years has been the introduction of scanning techniques such as MRI (magnetic resonance imaging) and PET (positron emission tomography). In the past it was possible to deduce function from studying form only by dissecting brains *post mortem*. These new scanning techniques now make it possible for scientists to look at live, healthy, working brains in action, and to study their function.

Each hemisphere is divided into four areas, or lobes. Very broadly speaking, the frontal lobes lie behind the forehead; the parietal lobes lie beneath the skull, on top of the head; the temporal lobes are at the sides, inside the part of the skull that lies above the ears; the occipital lobes are inside the skull at the deepest part of the back of the head. The left hemisphere is usually dominant for language functions, in both left-handed and right-handed people. It was formerly believed that left-handed people had their language centres in the right cerebral hemisphere; this is true of only a very small proportion of people.

One of the main spoken language areas is Wernicke's area, in the upper back part of the temporal lobe. This is involved in the comprehension of language and the structuring of spoken language output. The other main area is Broca's area, in the lower back part of the frontal lobe. This is involved in the production of spoken language, maybe formulating it into words and sentences. Another important area is the motor cortex, running along the back of the frontal lobes; this controls the movement of the speech organs that we looked at earlier. These organs, as we have seen, are a precision tool (as are the hands), and both the speech organs and the hands occupy a huge proportion of the motor cortex, far in excess of their relative size in the body.

Recent work has demonstrated that other areas of the brain are involved in language processing, and for each task, more than one area is active.

Different combinations of areas of the cortex are active, depending on the precise nature of the language task being carried out. It has also been suggested that the areas involved in language tasks are subject to gender differences. Neurophysiology is still a young science; one important outcome of the new scanning techniques is the discovery that the areas associated with specific functions are not as discrete as was once thought.

The subject matter of this chapter can be studied in more detail. Two very accessible books in the Bibliography are *The Human Brain: A Guided Tour* (1997) by Professor Susan Greenfield, and David Crystal's excellent *The Cambridge Encyclopaedia of Language* (1985b). This wonderful book has 450 large-format pages, all of them fascinating.

The communication process

We will now consider the communication process between speaker and listener. This is illustrated in Figure 1.5.

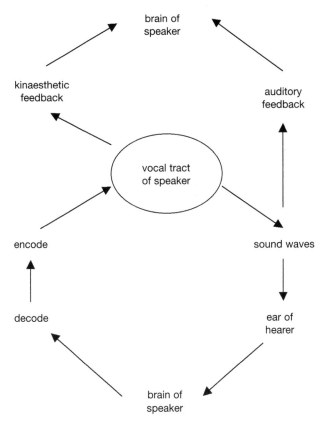

Figure 1.5 The articulatory loop.

Let us suppose someone walks into a room and speaks to a person already in the room. The utterance is initiated in the brain of the speaker, encoded and produced by the organs of speech, as we have seen. What emerges from the mouth are sound waves, which are transmitted through the air to the ear of the hearer. These waves then travel through the middle and inner ear, where they are converted to electrical impulses, via the auditory nerve to the brain, where they are decoded, and a response is encoded (remember Wernicke's and Broca's areas). The response travels by electrical impulses, via the motor cortex and the cranial nerves, to the muscles of the organs of speech. The sound waves produced travel in the same way to the other person, and a cycle of communication is set up.

Meanwhile, as the first utterance was being produced, the speaker could feel the movement of her own organs of articulation and could hear her own speech via her hearing and decoding ear-to-brain system. This perception of one's own utterance is called the feedback loop. Auditory feedback comes about via hearing, and the feedback from the vocal tract comes about through kinaesthetic and proprioceptive feedback, the sensation of movement and the position of the body in space.

Through this feedback, instant self-monitoring can take place; pitch and tone, speed and volume can be controlled. You will have noticed how the speech of a deaf person often lacks variety in pitch and tone, and may not be delivered at an appropriate volume. This is because the feedback loop is not intact and self-monitoring is unable to take place. Even those whose deafness is acquired later in life (profound deafness rather than the normal partial hearing loss that often comes with age) will gradually lose the subtleties of pitch, tone and volume control. The speech may increasingly take on the characteristics of the deaf speaker. Lord Ashley, the former MP Jack Ashley and champion of disability rights through a long parliamentary career, lost his hearing in middle age. Gifted speaker though he was, the lack of feedback caused his speech to sound increasingly like that of a deaf person. After an operation to restore his hearing many years later, the variety began to creep back and he started to sound like his former self again.

When I was a speech therapy student, there was a machine at college that was sometimes used in the treatment of stammering. Called a Delayed Auditory Feedback machine, it recorded speech through a microphone and delivered it back via headphones a fraction of a second later. The effects on speakers of having late feedback were very interesting: some stammerers became fluent. The speech and language therapy students' responses varied: some began to speak very slowly and deliberately; a small number stammered; a few spoke in a monotone; and I re-acquired the accent of my childhood. My Liverpool origins had by this time been skilfully overcome by my speech and drama teacher! The fact that almost no one was unaffected demonstrates the importance of feedback in the speaking process.

How did language come about?

One question that has never been answered, and probably never will be, is how spoken language came into being. A recent and rather colourful suggestion that I have heard is that we sang before we talked! There are many theories, none of them supported by any real evidence. There does not seem to be a gradual increase in spoken language skill as we move up through a list of mammals, or even through a list of primates. We do know that some mammals, dogs and horses, for example, respond to tone of voice and can be trained to obey human commands. It has also become apparent that some primitive linguistic skills are found in chimpanzees, and that chimps can be taught some sign language.

However, to teach a chimpanzee to sign is a long process requiring much patience and perseverance. Compare that to the expedition with which a human infant begins to talk, and it becomes obvious that we are dealing with an altogether different level of skill. Spoken language, speech, is a skill for which human anatomy, physiology and neurology are uniquely adapted.

The evidence of palaeontology would suggest that speech developed some time between 100,000 and 20,000 BC, and this can probably be narrowed down further to between 50,000 and 30,000 BC. It is possible that as primates began to walk on two legs, the arms and hands could have been used for sign and gesture. This would have been of limited use, as tools began to be used and the hands would be needed for wielding them.

It is important to remember that speech did not happen as an accidental additional faculty of the organs of eating and breathing. In fact, the adaptation of the oral tract to speech is at the cost of some efficiency in breathing, chewing and swallowing. The structure of a monkey's larynx is such that it cannot choke on food, whereas humans can. There must be considerable survival benefits in being able to speak to compensate for the sacrifice of the effectiveness of these basic life functions.

Conclusion

This chapter has provided an opportunity to stand back and think about the wider aspects of human communication. It has introduced a physical and cognitive framework in which to learn about language. The rest of the book is about the detail.

Summary

In this chapter we have looked at:

- the means and purposes of human communication
- language, thought, labels and concepts
- the physical process of speaking
- the role of the brain in spoken language
- the communication process and the importance of feedback
- the possible origins of language
- how humans are physically adapted for speech

CHAPTER 2
The structure of language

When is a sentence not a sentence?

It is important to remember that when the term **sentence** is used in spoken language, it does not necessarily mean a perfectly formed, grammatically correct sentence. It may be the kind of sentence that has only one word: 'Hello', for example, or 'Help'. It could be a one-word response to a question: 'What's for dinner?' 'Fish'.

The spoken sentence does not have to have a subject, a verb and an object, a beginning, a middle and an end, a capital letter or a full stop. The linguist *describes* what happens in an utterance; linguistics is essentially descriptive, not prescriptive (and that is a phrase you will encounter again!). In the second part of this book, dealing with written language, things will be different, because written language is rule-governed and subject to prescription.

So the answer to the question 'When is a sentence not a sentence?' might be 'When it is being discussed in the first part of this book'.

Models of language structure

This topic forms an introduction to and an outline of the spoken language part of the book. It demonstrates how the different topics in the subject fit together.

First, we will consider three models of spoken language structure. Models are ways of breaking down language into its constituent parts. They can be very simple, with broad categories and few headings, or enormously detailed, with a great deal of terminology, strands, layers and levels, or they can be somewhere in between. The first model is very simple, with only three main categories; the second is more detailed, and based on concentric circles. The third model has five parts, and is the one we shall use throughout the rest of the spoken language part of the book.

Task 2.1   Take a few minutes to think about how you would break
                  language up into its parts. After you have done so, look at the
                  first model (Figure 2.1), then review your model if you wish, in the
                  light of what you have learned.

                  Cover Figure 2.1 until you are ready to continue.

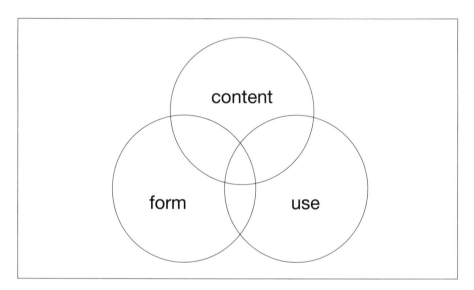

Figure 2.1 The first model.

The first model

Figure 2.1 is adapted by Borwick and Townend (1993) from the Bloom
and Lahey model of spoken language. Bloom and Lahey were two
American linguists who used this model to show the interrelationship
between the different aspects of language. They considered that language
consists of three related areas: **form**, **content** and **use**. You can see that
the three circles overlap each other, so there is an area of commonality
between all of them. All these areas are needed for language to be developed for competent use. The circle on the left, form, has in it phonology,
which is the sound system of language, and syntax, the sentence system;
these are the working parts or the structural framework of the language.
The content circle represents the words, which are the units of meaning;
these are fitted into the structural framework. The third circle is language
use, which is the most difficult of the three; it is the social communicative

aspect of language, incorporating meaning, subtlety and flexibility. The easiest way to appreciate the importance of all these areas is to consider what would happen if any one of them was missing.

Form

Imagine that you were learning a foreign language, but you were not being taught the form of that language; you would not know the grammatical rules, nor would you know the sounds. It would be like arriving in a foreign country, not knowing the language, but armed with a dictionary (one lacking a pronunciation guide!). You could find the words, but you could neither pronounce them nor string them into sentences. It would be impossible to express your ideas or your needs.

Content

If you know the grammatical rules and the pronunciation, but you do not have the words, you will have difficulty in getting your meaning across. This is what would happen if the 'content' circle was missing. Imagine that you are in a country where you speak enough of the language to travel, and you are taken ill. You would find it difficult to conduct a detailed conversation with a doctor about your symptoms and treatment options. This difficulty is experienced in mother tongue by many dyslexic individuals, who often have a word-finding difficulty, by some individuals who have had a stroke, and by all of us with increasing age.

Use

If the 'use' circle was absent, a speaker might have a very good knowledge of the sounds and grammar of the language and its vocabulary, but would be unable to use the tools appropriately. They would be unable to adapt language according to the person being spoken to, would have no idea of, for example, tact, and would not conform to the conventions of communication. A difficulty of this kind is found in some people with specific language impairment or autistic spectrum difficulties, and can be found in some kinds of mental illness.

It is clear that all three interlocking circles need to be present for verbal communication to be effective. This is a very simple model, but it does manage to encompass the whole of spoken language.

The second model

The next model is described in a book called *Teach Yourself Linguistics* (Aitchison, 1987a). It is a sequence of concentric circles, with **phonetics** in the centre, moving out to **phonology**, **syntax**, **semantics** and **pragmatics**.

Phonetics is the study of speech sounds. In her book, Aitchison states that phonetics is not a real part of linguistics, though a knowledge of phonetics helps understanding of linguistics. She is making an important distinction between phonetics and phonology; only phonology is related to languages. Other linguists will treat phonology as a subset of phonetics. See Chapter 4 for a discussion of this distinction.

Phonetics and phonology

Phonetics is the scientific study of speech sounds, which is needed in order to understand how speech sounds are made; we looked at this in Chapter 1. It also encompasses the range of speech sounds that is possible, the physics of sound (acoustics) and the technical aspects of speech production.

The next circle is phonology, which is the way sounds behave in language, so this is the point at which sounds become part of linguistics in this model. Phonology is the study of sounds in language, relationships between sounds, and how they influence each other. It also covers possible and impossible sound combinations in any given language, pronunciation, and the adaptations of pronunciation depending on the phonological and linguistic context. This is something we will return to in Chapters 4–6. Phonology is very relevant to the development of literacy.

Syntax and semantics

Aitchison's next circle is syntax. This is a broad circle, because it contains the whole area of words and sentences; in other words, it is made up of most of what we are doing when we speak, apart from the sounds. It covers the way words are built, and their order in the utterance.

Semantics, the next circle, is the term used for the meaning of language. The important function of language is to convey meaning: information, emotions, instructions and so on, as we discussed in Chapter 1.

Grammar and pragmatics

Aitchison suggests that the term **grammar** involves phonology, syntax and semantics (meaning). This is a broad definition, and many linguists would use the term grammar in a narrower way. It is suggested that the narrow use of the term is to be found mainly in older books. For non-specialists, however, we consider the narrower definition is more helpful, and in the later chapters you will find grammar used to cover word order and word structure, with phonology, vocabulary and semantics discussed under their own headings.

The last circle is pragmatics, or language use. This has been encountered already in the Bloom and Lahey model; it is the social,
communicative function of language.

The third model

We now come to the third model (Figure 2.2), which divides language
into five different areas, and this is the model we will be using as the basis
for the remaining chapters in Part 1. There are many overlaps with the
models we have already considered.

Figure 2.2 A five-part model of language structure.

Phonology

First comes phonology, which, as we know, is the study of speech sounds
within language. It includes the selection of individual sounds used in any
language (in this case, the sounds of English); the pronunciation of those
sounds; the way sounds go together in combination, what combinations
are possible and what combinations are impossible. For example, we recognize that the consonant blends /sp/, /st/ and /sn/ are acceptable in
English, but that /sr/ and /sd/ are not. Also to be considered is the position
in the word in which a sound can occur; in English, /h/ always appears at
the beginning of the syllable, and never at the end.

A very important aspect of phonology is how sounds behave when they are put together, the influence of context. This makes the relationship between sound and letter very complicated in some cases.

Example: the letter *a*

This can be pronounced [ă] or [ā], as in *pan* or *taken*, but in some situations it is pronounced [ah], as in *bath* or *can't*. This most commonly occurs when the letter *a* is followed by two consonants, in writing, but it is not a hard rule. In the north and Midlands, the *a* would be [ă], as in *cat*. In the south west, the sound is [ă:], as in *cat*, but lengthened. If a *w* comes before the *a*, the vowel sound becomes [ŏ], as in *was* or *want*. Occasionally, the letter *a* makes the sound [or] when following *w*, as in *water* and *walk*, and sometimes it remains [ă], as in *wax*.

Prosodic features

Under the heading of phonology come the prosodic features of speech, also known as supra-segmental phonology, because it deals with the features above and beyond the segments. The segments are the phonemes, or individual speech sounds within the language. In addition to these sounds, there are features that change the way in which we use the sounds, combine them, and even say whole words to change the meaning. These are:

- pitch
- tone
- stress
- intonation
- volume
- speed

The meaning of a sentence can be changed, depending on the pitch and tone we use to say it. For example, say the word 'tea'; that means black, dried leaves used to make a hot drink, or it means a meal in the late afternoon. However, if you say it with rising intonation at the end, it means 'Would you like some tea? Or 'Have you made some tea?' With an extension to the vowel, and an exaggerated fall in intonation at the end, it may be a huge sigh of relief at the appearance of a cup of tea when you are exhausted, or a demand for someone to bring you one. A high, rising intonation at the beginning could indicate surprise at the appearance of the tea. So much from one word!

Similarly, if we say the sentence 'Look out', meaning 'Look out of the window' because there's a nice view, or it has started to rain, or someone is walking up the path, the intonation is very different from 'Look out!', which means 'Take care!', and carries urgency, danger, a warning. In both cases, the sounds are the same, but how you say them in terms of stress, volume and intonation pattern is very different, and this changes the meaning.

In Chapter 6 we will look at prosody, and its effects upon continuous speech. We will also look at the effect of continuous speech on prosody. This area of study repays careful attention, because it adds to our understanding of how we use language to convey meaning, which, of course, is what language is for.

Lexicon

Lexicon, from the Greek, means words; we could as easily have used the term **vocabulary**. The less common term has been used to get away from the idea that the concept of the word is a straightforward and familiar one. I want to suggest that this area is broader than just words in the way we understand the term. In Chapter 7, we will be considering words and part-words under the collective term morphemes. Morphemes are units within words; they may be whole words in their own right, or they may be parts of words that cannot stand alone and have meaning only when attached to a whole word. They can be built together to make new words: *help* + *ful* = *helpful* or *cup* + *s* = *cups*, for example.

It is necessary to understand word structure in order to understand grammar. We also need to understand word structure to see how spelling works. Consider how you might count how many words an individual has in their vocabulary: do you count *cup* and *cups* as one word or two?

Syntax

Grammar can be divided into two: morphology, or word structure, which was mentioned above, and syntax, which is the arrangement of words, or word order. These two make up much of the stuff of our grammatical rules and structure in English.

Remember that when we talk about clustering words into what we rather loosely refer to as a sentence, we are really talking about an utterance, which may or may not be grammatically correct, as we understand it. The key to acceptability of an utterance is its intelligibility and therefore its usefulness in conveying meaning. However, there are also features that we recognize as 'incorrect' even in spoken English, such as putting the words in the wrong order. Linguistics has to be capable of describing any utterance, written or spoken, from a newspaper headline, or a curse, through to a complex piece of prose, a poem, a Government report, or a conversation between two people on the top of a bus. It needs to be very broad, and very embracing, so our definition of a sentence has to be a loose, unstructured and certainly non-judgemental one.

Acceptable spoken English	Unacceptable spoken English
• Ready?	• You ready are.
• Put it – let me see – erm – no – yes, there – that'll do.	• I putted it there.
• What's 'e up to? Dunno.	• Him's busy.

In written language, of course, things are very different, because the rules become important. Even in spoken language there have to be rules of acceptability and non-acceptability; you will recognize the kind of speech that has errors in it. For example, a non-native speaker of English, who has limited mastery, will make errors of the kind that no native speaker would make, even when using informal and abbreviated grammatical structures. Similarly, the language of young children can be full of errors. Many of the errors made by young children would never occur in adult speech; they have not copied erroneous patterns, which raises interesting issues about how language develops (this will be addressed in Chapter 3). Children do get a feel for the rules at a surprisingly early age and many of their errors are therefore over-regularization of the rules. They will try to apply a regular rule to an irregular word, hence infantilisms such as *bringed* or *sheeps*.

> **Example**
> 'I do not know' (acceptable, formal, correct)
> 'I don't know' (acceptable, informal, correct if spoken)
> 'I know not' (acceptable, correct, but archaic, or possibly poetic)
> 'Dunno' (acceptable if very informal, spoken)
> 'I not know' (not acceptable: young child, or non-native speaker)

The whole area of grammar is, in the context of spoken language, very far removed from what we used to think of as learning grammar at school. When you read the second part of this book, about written language, you will find that, too, quite different from what you remember from your school days (if you are old enough – as both the authors are – to remember the teaching of grammar in school!). An understanding of how language works has to be *useful*; it has to help people to use language to communicate more effectively, and to highlight where language is going wrong.

Semantics

Semantics is the study of the meaning of language. It is particularly interesting because it is possible to have a perfectly constructed but meaningless English sentence with the phonological aspects intact (all the sounds are right); the vocabulary correct (all the words are right); the syntax correct (the words are properly constructed, and in the right order). In short, everything is lined up properly, but still the sentence is meaningless. We will be looking in more detail at semantics in Chapter 9.

Noam Chomsky is an American linguist, a leader in the field of modern thinking about language. He could be described as the 'father of psycholinguistics' as a result of his groundbreaking work, which was mainly done in the 1960s and 1970s. He used, as an example, the sentence.

Colourless green ideas sleep furiously.

This sentence demonstrates how it is possible to have a perfectly constructed, but totally meaningless sentence. It has been suggested that the sentence is a piece of poetry, but so far no one has managed to interpret it to me satisfactorily. It is unlikely that, if you close your eyes, a picture appears to you from that string of words, despite its undoubted grammatical correctness. It would be possible to parse it, that is, to subject it to grammatical analysis; you could identify the subject, verb and (if there was one) the object; you could identify the determiners and the modifiers, but it still would lack any real meaning.

Similarly, you could take a series of non-words, string them together in a recognizable grammatical pattern, ask and answer questions from the resulting prose, but still have no idea what the sentence meant.

Example

The zob brendled in the lep.

Q. Who brendled in the lep?	A. The zob.
Q. What did the zob do?	A. Brendled in the lep.
Q. Where did the zob brendle?	A. In the lep.

This example makes points about word order and word structure in English.

We have already learned in the section on prosodic features (see page 22) that the same sentence can have more than one meaning, depending on how it is uttered. It is equally possible to convey the same meaning by a range of different utterances. As skilled speakers we do this all the time; we adapt our language to the social situation and to the person or group being addressed.

Semantics is about the meaning of words, the meaning of sentences, the meaning of utterances, and the way meaning can be changed. The whole point of spoken and written communication is to convey and receive meaning; the word is a conveyor of messages, ideas, information and emotional signals. We use language to express our needs, to have our needs met and to meet other people's needs. For teachers, language is their stock-in-trade, with meaning very much at the heart of it. It is therefore surprising that semantics, as an aspect of linguistics, came on to the scene relatively late, long after people had begun to study grammar, words and sounds.

Pragmatics

Pragmatics is an even later entry on to the linguistics scene. It is the study of language use, the social and interactive aspect of language. It looks at how we use language to communicate and cooperate with other people, including issues such as turn-taking, questions, appropriateness and the social rules of language. In general, language is a collaborative act, played by certain rules even with total strangers, and the study of how we know and obey (or do not obey) these rules is the subject of pragmatics. It is also concerned with language and emotion, language as a substitute for action, and language as action itself. A closer look at pragmatics will be taken in Chapter 9. One of the pleasures of studying semantics and pragmatics, language meaning and use, is the opportunity it gives to collect examples of how we play with language: jokes, puns, witticisms, *double entendres* and all kinds of verbal humour.

A summary of the model

Phonology:
sounds of a language
pronunciation
sound combinations
sounds in context
prosodic features

Lexicon:
vocabulary
word structure (morphology)

Syntax:
morphology
word order
sentence structure

Semantics:
meaning
inference
homonyms, etc.
ambiguity

Pragmatics:
use of language
social language
cooperation
turn-taking
appropriateness.

When language goes wrong

When an individual sustains brain damage due to head injury (birth trauma or a road traffic accident, for example), or through illness, such as a stroke (cerebral haemorrhage or thrombosis) or infection (meningitis or encephalitis), this can result in the loss or impairment of one or more aspects of language function. In such a case, breakdown in any, or all, of the areas we have looked at can occur.

Some adults who have suffered a stroke will be able to produce well-formed sentences, but which are apparently meaningless because the wrong words have been selected. Others can only communicate in 'telegrammatic speech', which is a string of words, not arranged into a sentence. The content words (nouns, verbs, maybe adjectives) will be there, but without the grammatical words that make it a cohesive utterance. In the first example, the affected area is vocabulary, with consequential effects upon meaning; in the second, it is the area of syntax that is affected, with similarly detrimental effects on meaning. A breakdown in any aspect of language has adverse effects upon the whole communication process.

When language is developing

In the very young child who is acquiring spoken language, the acquisition of all the spoken language skills is interdependent. As one skill develops, it helps to bring along the others; the skills move forward hand in hand, so to speak. The child does not learn phonology first, then words, then put them together into sentences, in the way he may learn to read or speak a foreign language or any other non-natural new skill. They develop in parallel and at an enormously rapid rate; consider, for a moment, how soon after birth a small child is using language in an effective way.

The development of spoken language is the subject of Chapter 3. We will be looking at the factors that affect language acquisition. The intrinsic factors include underlying cognitive ability, physical attributes such as hearing and motor skills, and perceptual skills to facilitate learning. A desire to communicate is another important factor. Extrinsic factors are those within the child's environment; language will not develop in a vacuum. The child needs a rich linguistic environment to feed in the raw material from which they can build a language system.

Language input and output

When considering language at any level and in any context, it is important to remember that we are talking about both input and output: receptive and expressive language; comprehension and expression; understanding and speaking; reading and writing. In any individual there is not one single level of linguistic skill, but two; each person is able to deal with a higher level of language on the input side than on the output side. This is the case at any level of skill, and continues no matter how many languages an individual may acquire. In foreign language learning, we can all attest to the fact that we can understand more than we can say. In mother tongue, the vocabulary we can comprehend is always larger than that which we can use; we can understand in spoken and written language more complex grammatical structures than we can use in speaking or writing.

This input, or knowledge of the language, is referred to by Chomsky (1965) as 'competence' and the output, or that which is used in expression, as 'performance'. The infant begins to understand spoken language before she can use it; the young child can always understand more words and more structures than she can use; the schoolchild can read more words than she can spell, and this difference continues throughout life and at all levels of ability.

As you read the following chapters in Part 1 you may find it helpful to refer back to this chapter to see how each of the aspects of language you are reading about fits into the whole picture.

Summary

In this chapter we have looked at:

- linguistics as descriptive not prescriptive
- the Bloom and Lahey model of language structure
- the Aitchison model of language structure
- the five-part model of language structure
- phonology, including prosody
- lexicon (words)
- grammar (syntax)
- semantics (meaning)
- pragmatics (use)
- what happens when language goes wrong
- a first look at developing language
- the importance of considering language input *and* output

CHAPTER 3
Language development

Introduction

In this chapter we will consider some theories of the acquisition of spoken language in the infant and young child, then we will look at the 'ages and stages' through which the child passes. Finally, we will consider some of the factors affecting speech and language acquisition.

A remarkable transformation

What is happening as an infant learns to speak? Remember that it takes place over a very short time span. A newborn baby boy cries only if he needs to indicate discomfort (too cold, too hot, hungry, wet, in pain) but by the time he goes to school, five years later, he can communicate needs, ideas, feelings and information efficiently and in great detail. He can understand much of what is being said; he has mastered all the common grammatical structures of his mother tongue (or even two mother tongues), including some of the irregularities; he has a vast vocabulary, which continues to grow daily. It is indeed a remarkable transformation. We have been describing a small boy; some researchers have suggested that small girls are even more skilled at spoken language in its early stages.

How does it happen?

Is language learned by imitation? Does the child have an innate blueprint for language? Is it something in between, or a combination of the two?

Task 3.1

Make a note of any ideas you have about how language may be acquired by young children. You may have ideas of your own, or from reading, or from experience of being with children.

Language acquisition has fascinated scholars – and others, including kings and rulers – for hundreds of years. Stories are told of experiments, carried out several centuries ago, in which some groups of children were brought up in a silent environment to see what language they would speak. Some suggested it would be Ancient Hebrew, believed to be the language spoken by the first man and woman, Adam and Eve, in the Garden of Eden, and even by God himself! One experiment ended in failure when all the children died. It was supposed that they could not live without the comfort of hearing the human voice. None of the experiments reports that their subjects ever spoke at all. They certainly did not grow up to speak Ancient Hebrew, High Dutch or even English. Needless to say, such an experiment is unlikely ever to be repeated.

There have, in more recent times, been a small number of children who have been brought up, for various reasons, in a silent environment. Even when these children have been taught intensively when they have been returned to society, they have not acquired language to the full, rich extent that they might have been expected to, if they had been exposed to language at the proper time. This suggests that there is an optimum time for acquiring language, and that, once it has been missed, it is not possible to develop language fully and normally. This optimum period seems to cover the first five years of life. This coincides with a period when the brain is at its most plastic.

Theories of language acquisition

We will consider four main theories of language acquisition and whether any one of them can stand alone.

The behaviourist model

The first is known as the behaviourist, or Learning Theory, model. This theory was in the ascendant for many years, since it was developed in the 1920s, and was still current, though increasingly challenged, in the late 1960s when I was learning about language. This theory suggests that children *learn* language; they do so by imitating the adult model, at first very approximately, and gradually with more precision, as they mature. At first this seems quite sensible and reasonable; children who do not hear, do not speak. Children are surrounded by the adult model, and those who are talked to a great deal tend to make very good progress. Children's speech does gradually get closer to the adult version. So maybe this model has some merit; maybe it is what happens, you may think.

As a theory to explain everything, I am afraid it will not do, for several reasons. The evidence against it is that children use linguistic structures they cannot have heard from an adult. You and I can make up our own, new sentences; we are not dependent on pulling one out from a file of sentences we have heard before. Language is essentially creative and dynamic. Chomsky used the term 'generative'. Even very young children can generate their own sentences. The evidence for this is powerful: children use their own grammar, not an imitation of, or even an approximation to, the adult model.

There is some evidence that young children are not good at precise imitation of sentences *until* they have mastered the grammatical structure in question for themselves.

For example, if asked to repeat the sentence:

The dog who is under the table is asleep.

the young child who has not yet mastered embedded clauses in his own speech may substitute a less sophisticated construction, such as:

The dog is under the table and he's asleep.

Similarly, a child who tells her mother 'I bringed Teddy downstairs', may be corrected, 'I *brought* Teddy downstairs' and respond with the mystified comment, 'That's what I said – I bringed him because I wanted to play with him'. Clearly, she has not learned the word *bringed* from anyone, but she has learned how to make a past tense. If she was learning by imitation, surely she would imitate first and learn to apply the rule later. She has had to learn the word to label the concept of bringing, but she has worked out for herself how to move it around by the rules. It is not her fault the rules do not always apply!

Language and cognition

The next theory to consider is that language acquisition is a direct outcome of cognitive development. As the child develops intellectually, so language comes along, riding on the back of that intelligence as a cognitive function. Jean Piaget, the Swiss cognitive–developmental psychologist who was working earlier in the twentieth century, was a leading exponent of this model. It is suggested that as intellectual, cognitive powers develop with maturation, increasingly sophisticated language develops as part of a natural skill progression. This is an attractive theory, linking, as it does, language skills with underlying ability; the greater the cognitive powers, the greater the linguistic ability. We know that verbal skills, and vocabulary in particular, are the best predictor of eventual academic success.

However, it fails to take account of the fact that some children with high levels of underlying ability may have poorly developed spoken language, for a variety of reasons. Similarly, people who sustain brain damage through head injury or illness may lose some spoken language function without losing underlying intellectual ability. Or they may lose some specific aspects of cognitive function without losing linguistic ability. There is therefore some separation between language and cognition; language development is not just clinging to the coat-tails of intellect, though aspects of this theory have something to recommend them.

Process theory

Process theory suggests that children have an innate capacity for processing linguistic data. Along with this, it is suggested that 'motherese', the simplified language adult carers use when talking to babies, is universal, and well suited to the needs of infants. It seems to be the case that the way we speak to babies is the same the world over: we slow down, we make sentences very simple, we repeat, we exaggerate our intonation patterns (listen, next time you are in a supermarket queue). Clearly this is a good thing, and helps the language acquisition of the young child.

But is that all there is to it? It is suggested by those who adhere to process theory that language develops as a result of the social interaction between carer and child, working and building on the innate problem-solving capacity for linguistic data, with which the child is born. It is a combination of a language-shaped space in the child, and the carer adapting her language to fit into it. The fact that this development depends upon some innate capacity to process the language to which the child is exposed, places this theory at one end of a continuum of those who believe that the infant has some biological capacity for language.

The biological capacity theories

The fourth theory we are to consider is at the other end of that continuum. Some linguists (of whom Chomsky was the early leader and Steven Pinker is the best-known recent exponent) believe that the innate capacity for language that all humans have is much more structured than mere problem solving. They suggest that the blueprint for language, maybe even a universal grammatical framework, is innate and biologically determined.

In the Pinker model, language evolves from Darwinian natural selection. This is a view not shared by Chomsky, who did not find Darwinian evolutionary theory sufficient to cover the development of spoken language. This school of thought believes that language is a phenomenon waiting to happen, because the child is born with a highly developed, biologically determined capacity for language.

Most linguists nowadays would subscribe to the belief that there is some innate, biological factor at work in the faculty of human infants to acquire language. Without it, it is very difficult to explain the incredible rapidity of language acquisition. Most of us would find it impossible to learn at the rate at which the small child acquires the phonology, vocabulary, grammar and semantics of his mother tongue, and the subtleties of pragmatics. Some, but not all linguists who do subscribe to the theory of innate capacity equate it with the capacity for physical development, such as learning to walk.

If asked how children learn to talk, most linguists would suggest that there is an element of all the theories described above at work.

How can we make sense of it?

A sensible way to look at language acquisition is as a combination of pre-determination and opportunity, or nature and nurture. I like to think of it as nature, under the influence of nurture: biological capacity worked on by environmental factors. Increasingly the nature–nurture debate has come down squarely right on the fence, or with one foot on either side, because many things are a combination of biologically determined (genetic) factors and environmental influences. Spoken language acquisition must surely be one of these.

For evidence, let us look at the characteristics of emerging language, say between the ages of 1 year and 4 years, the period when most language acquisition takes place. (However, we do need to remember that a great deal goes on during the first year of life and after the fourth birthday.)

Child language is rule governed.
- First of all, children speak according to strict grammatical rules, but, interestingly, not the adult rules. (We will go on to consider infant grammar later.)

Child language is full of generalizations.
- When children do start to learn the adult rules they do not learn the exceptions immediately, but they must learn the rules, or how could they make the generalizations? When a child says 'I rided my bike', he must know that this ending denotes past tense, and he adds it to make a grammatically acceptable sentence, according to his framework.

Child language is gradually assimilated to the adult form.
- It is not assimilated immediately, or all in one go. Gradually, the child's language becomes similar to the adult form and less like the infant form. This process is influenced by environmental factors, and this is where imitation becomes very important. People talk to the child, she imitates and receives positive feedback for her efforts, which motivates her to imitate more closely.

Child language is subject to rapid and dramatic growth.
- As we have already established, child language grows more rapidly and more dramatically than would be possible if it depended solely on the capacity of the adult to teach it. Parents and carers do not really teach infants to speak; they provide a model, they stimulate, encourage and reward, and language, normally, comes pouring from the child's lips.

As a young speech and language therapist I worked with a 3-year-old who had almost no expressive language, and with his parents. He made excellent progress. When I met the family some years later, the father said, 'We will never forget how you started John talking – he hasn't stopped since!' Even in that situation, I did not really teach John to speak; I fertilized the ground, by working on his listening, attention, phonological awareness, auditory sequencing and other perceptual skills. His mother and other key people in his life watered the ground by providing constant good models, positive feedback and something to talk about, and gradually, language grew. John acquired vocabulary and sentence structures none of us had taught him and began to enjoy using them, understanding and being understood; eventually he could hold his own in the family.

The interaction of influences

These four characteristics of child language would suggest that there is an interface between the biological, innate influences and the environmental, acquired influences. According to some linguists, the innate capacity is a general biological predisposition, a readiness to learn language. At the other extreme it is a universal grammar, common to all languages, a ready-built framework upon which can be hung the specifics of the language of the society into which the child is born. This innate capacity for language, whatever it may consist of, has been called the 'Language Acquisition Device'. Into it is fed raw linguistic data from the environment: the words, sounds and grammar of the mother tongue. Gradually, the child's language becomes more like the adult model, as the language-specific rules and the exceptions are learned, the vocabulary increases and the sound system matures. The sound system is probably the most obviously physical aspect of developing language. As we have established, at every stage in development, as in adult language, understanding is ahead of what can be expressed.

The sequence of language acquisition

We will look at the sequence of language acquisition in the early years, from the earliest, non-verbal sounds, to the mature model. It is very important to remember that the ages at which children develop each skill vary enormously; stages may last for a few days or several months, or be missed out altogether. This will be a rapid and very superficial coverage of a vast and fascinating subject. If it captures your interest, you may like to read *The Language Instinct* by Steven Pinker (1995).

Language in the first year of life

In the first few weeks of a baby's life, he makes only discomfort sounds; these are basic, biological sounds. He cries because he is uncomfortable.

Somewhere around the middle or the end of the second month a new sound appears, which is a comfort sound. These sounds are usually made in the back of the mouth, by the back of the tongue articulating with the soft palate, which is itself moving up and down. There is a nasal, vowel-like quality to these sounds; the nearest written representation I can manage is 'ngya, ngya, ngya'. The nature of the sounds probably has something to do with the position of the tongue at rest when the infant is lying on her back. If you want to hear it for yourself, you will have to find a clean, dry, recently fed young baby and exercise patience! These sounds will be made when the baby is awake and content. They do not appear to have any communicative or linguistic function, though, of course, they are a source of joy to the doting parents. Even at this early stage, communication is taking place, in that a fretful baby will be soothed by the sound of the mother's voice.

Sometimes, these sounds are strung together, and the baby appears to be making 'cooing' sounds. While this is not yet language, or even communication, the infant is moving the organs of speech in coordination, in the way that will be needed in the production of words.

Somewhere in the middle of the first year, between 5 months and 8 months in most babies, the parents will begin to hear more vocal play: smacking the lips together, squealing or babbling. While not all children will make all the possible noises, these sounds are universal, appearing in every language. Babies from different linguistic environments are likely to make the same kinds of sounds at this stage, and they will not be specific to any language.

Of course, the babies receive a reward for making sounds, because, as they vocalize, the parents make sounds back to them, smile, make eye contact or touch, and the infants learn that there is a prize for making sounds. They are beginning to learn that oral communication is a good thing. It is possible already to see the influences of the environment working on naturally occurring sound making. If the child does not receive positive feedback at this stage, normal language acquisition is put at risk.

Much of the second half of the first year, the period from 6 to 9 months, is characterized by increasing babbling patterns. These are usually very repetitive: 'abababa' or 'dadadada', for example. As they babble more and more, the parents respond more and more, using mother tongue sounds. Gradually, the sounds used by the infant become more like the sounds of the mother tongue, and the sounds that do not occur in the mother-tongue phonological system begin to disappear. Some linguists make a distinction between vocal play, which includes the more universal groups of sounds, and babbling, which is more language-specific.

The bilingual child

Many children are brought up in a completely bilingual environment, and a small number in an environment where more than two languages are used. In this case they will be internalizing the sound systems of all the languages they are acquiring. Young children who are fully bilingual normally reach each stage of language acquisition slightly later than they would have done if they were acquiring only one language. This is understandable in view of the fact that they are learning two or more sound systems, vocabularies and grammars.

When language acquisition is at risk

If babies do not receive any response from their significant adults, they stop doing it, so at this point babbling is taking on a communicative function. Profoundly deaf babies may gradually stop babbling because they are not getting the immediate feedback of people babbling back to them. However, if the parents sign to them, they will begin to babble with their hands and arms. Of course, touch and the use of mirrors can compensate for lack of hearing. Happily, it is very rare nowadays, at least in the developed world, for a deaf baby to remain undiagnosed for long, so provision can be made early for compensatory strategies to be put in place. As we know, there is a critical time for the acquisition of spoken language, so late diagnosis of a severe hearing loss can have very serious consequences.

Communicative language may be delayed or, in the most severe cases, non-existent, in children with difficulties on the autistic spectrum. Specific language impairment is a congenital difficulty in spoken language development, which may affect one or more aspects of language. Many children with moderate, severe or profound learning difficulties develop language late, and it may always be limited. Children who go on to be diagnosed as dyslexic are frequently late and poor talkers.

The arrival of words

It used to be thought that real words took the place of babbling, but it now seems more likely that babbling carries on after real words have begun to be used. We have all experienced children using non-words, making up their own words for things, using what is called 'jargon', which is the technical term for nonsense words. They chatter to themselves, but they are not making any sense as far as the rest of us can understand. This is a normal phase in language acquisition, usually occurring during the second year of life.

Often simultaneously, they will be developing real vocabulary. Around the turn of the first year words will start to emerge; they become real words at the point at which they acquire meaning. If a 1-year-old says 'adada', that is babble, unless she says it consistently when Daddy walks into the room, when it becomes a real word, used with meaning. Before this happens, she will have turned towards her father when someone says 'Here's Daddy' or 'Where's your Daddy?' Already we are seeing an example of comprehension being ahead of expression; she is understanding words at 8 or 9 months that she will not be using before her first birthday.

A child of this age has limited experience and limited opportunities to develop concepts. If there is a pet dog at home, *dog* is likely to be an early word in his vocabulary, but if there is a pet cat, this is a more likely early word. The child, having *dog* in his vocabulary, may believe it is the label only for one particular dog, or he may use it to label next door's cat, the sheep in his picture book and any other four-legged animal. Somehow he has come to understand that a table (four legs) is not a dog, and nor is a hen (animal). The concept is developing, but there is some refining to be done. Many mothers will have had the experience of their 1-year-old shouting 'Daddy' to a passing stranger in the street. My daughter only called out to dark-haired men with beards (like her father) so at least we could put it down to mistaken identity!

When does it become a sentence?

At first, the child's meaningful utterances will be confined to one word, so it would be easy to conclude that she is using single words, and will begin to use sentences later in the second year of life. However, some of these one-word utterances may actually be sentences, because young children use single words to convey a whole raft of meaning. They do not yet have the linguistic structures to string several words together, but they can use one word to mean many things. For example, 'milk' may mean 'I want some milk', 'I don't want this milk' or even 'I've spilled my milk'.

Putting two words together

Early infantile grammar is explained by David Crystal, in *The Cambridge Encyclopaedia of Language*, Chapter 4. Young children in the second year of life, at the time when they are starting to use two-word utterances produce the grammatical structures used only by children of this age. We are reminded of what we have already heard about children using sentences they cannot possibly have heard from an adult. This grammatical structure consists of two words: a pivot word and an open-class word. One pivot word may be used with a variety of open-class words to produce several different sentences. Just as one word can be used to mean several things, so can these primitive sentences be used in the same way. Let us take as an example *allgone* as the pivot word. Adult speakers know that there are two words, *all* and *gone* here, but in infant language, allgone is often used as a single unit. It can be put with a series of different open-class words to form a variety of utterances:

'Allgone milk'

'Allgone Daddy'

'Allgone car'

These are three good examples of pivot + open-class word sentences, each of which may have several meanings:

'Allgone milk' may mean	'I've finished my milk' 'I want some more milk' 'Take the milk away' 'I've dropped my cup'
'Allgone Daddy' may mean	'Daddy's gone' 'Goodbye Daddy' 'I can't see Daddy' 'Daddy's hiding' 'We're playing peekaboo, and Daddy has his hands over his face!'
'Allgone car' may mean	'The car has gone' 'We are going in the car' 'Someone has got into their car'

One of the interesting things about this structure is that it is very common among children who are around 2 years old, or slightly younger. They have never heard an adult using it, so where does it come from? This structure is also to be found in other languages. The vocabulary is, of course, language-specific, but the infantile grammar, with its own rules, is a framework into which newly learned vocabulary can be fitted. This reinforces the persuasion that language comes from within the child, and is not learned entirely by imitation.

Tackling longer words

One interesting thing about the second year of life is the way in which children attack words of more than one syllable. Sometimes one syllable, usually the first or the stressed syllable, will be repeated, or a syllable will be repeated using a phoneme that the child has mastered. One little girl in a group called herself 'Nuh-nuh' (Fiona), Eleanor called herself 'Luh-luh', Richard called himself 'Did-did' and Peter was 'Pee-pee'. Repeating a syllable or group of syllables is a less sophisticated phonological task than producing a series of different syllables, so Arabella became 'Ballabella'.

Another device for tackling words with more than two syllables is to omit one or more of the syllables, often the unstressed syllables. So, in the group of children introduced above, Fiona was, a little later, called by another child 'Ona' (the stress, of course, is on the second syllable). Others in the group had words such as 'ambance' (ambulance) and 'marlade' (marmalade), in which the unstressed syllable has disappeared.

Consonant blends are a problem at this stage and are often changed to a different one, simplified to a single consonant sound or omitted altogether. This is nicely exemplified by my mother-in-law (Grandma) who was called 'Brommar', 'Mummar' and 'Ommar' by a succession of two-year-old grandchildren. Grandad learned to answer variously to 'Gaga', 'Daddad' and 'Ad-dad'. The patterns of simplification resemble each other, even if the resulting words are different. In all these cases the problem sound is /gr/, which includes two relatively late-developing consonants.

Emerging longer sentences

As sentences develop, start to resemble mother tongue structures and become longer, they are at first telegrammatic. They resemble the language used in telegrams. They normally consist of the concrete, concept-bearing parts of the sentence, with meaning taking precedence over structure. A typical sentence will consist of nouns and verbs, and, soon, adjectives may be added, but words which have a purely grammatical function will be omitted. For example, 'Ben go bed' means 'Ben [wants to] go [to] bed [now]'. The meaning is quite clear, though only the bare bones of the sentence are present. Some telegrammatic sentences are less transparent. When 2-year-old Max looked out of the kitchen window one morning he exclaimed:

Oh no! Happen – garden.

It had been snowing in the night, for the first time in his life, and he was saying:

Oh no! (a favourite expression of his mother's) [What has] happen[ed] [in the] garden?

or possibly:

[Something remarkable has] happen[ed] [in the] garden!

The essential core of meaning is present, and the grammatical words are unnecessary for comprehension. To understand why this should happen, we need to consider two issues: one is that the words used are linked to identifiable concepts, for which the child has the verbal labels. The other is that these are the words that we stress in utterances, and the grammatical words (the ones in square brackets above) tend on the whole to be unstressed in connected speech. We will look at this again in Chapter 6.

Learning the rules

Gradually, this language assimilates to the adult model. One of the interesting features of this process is how quickly the children learn the rules, and learn to generalize them. Soon they are using such constructions as 'I bringed it', 'I rided my horse', they are talking about 'sheeps' and 'mouses', and they know, without being able to explain it, what they are doing. They are selecting a plural or a past tense morpheme and tacking it on to the end of a noun or a verb, correctly following the rule. This demonstrates that they have mastered the rule, but have not yet got to grips with the exceptions.

This is a very interesting stage, for two reasons. First, as Steven Pinker, in his book *Words and Rules* (1999), points out, children can be using correct irregular past tenses before they start generalizing and apparently getting it wrong. What seems to be happening is that the younger child imitates an irregular word as a whole, without being aware of how it is constructed. Later, she learns the rule, and at this point begins to apply it across the range of appropriate and inappropriate situations. It seems as if, linguistically, the child is going backwards. As Pinker observes, linguistic deterioration does not happen until much later in life! It is, in fact, a well-disguised progress.

The other thing that makes this stage particularly interesting is the way children deal with parental attempts to correct them. There is some evidence that between the stage of learning the rule and the stage of learning the exceptions, they will continue to apply the rule even if asked to imitate the correct version. Take this conversation, between a little girl and her mother, as an example:

C: I rided my horse.

M: Yes, you rode your horse, didn't you?

C: Yes, I rided him very fast.

Even a direct attempt at correction is unlikely to be any more successful:

C: I bringed Teddy in.

M: Say, 'I brought Teddy in.'

C: I bringed Teddy in.

The girl's grammatical rules take precedence over the requirement to imitate, so rule governance is a very powerful feature of child language at this stage. Once the exceptions are learned, the child will automatically begin to use them. Again we have an example of the child generating her own grammar, not imitating the linguistic structures of her environment.

Moving on in language

By the time he or she goes to school, the child has acquired all the common grammatical rules and many of the exceptions. It used to be thought that by the time the child was five years old, language structure was completely intact and the only subsequent development was in the area of increasing vocabulary. It is now known from more recent studies that some language acquisition is taking place in children throughout their primary school years. For example, around the age of seven they will begin to use such forms as *though, anyway, for instance, actually, of course*. At this time they will start to distinguish different underlying meanings for sentences that have the same surface structure. For example,

Ask him where the library is.

Tell him where the library is.

These sentences are structurally identical, but they are completely different in meaning. A fairly sophisticated level of linguistic processing is required to sort them out.

Another late acquisition is the fine-tuning of intonation patterns, and children of 10 and 11 years will still be gaining that skill (Cruttenden, 1974). Many adults never attain mastery of this, and misunderstandings between people can arise through erroneous interpretation of a perceived 'tone of voice'. You may be able to think of examples of this from your own experience; I know I can!

Vocabulary growth

One area of language that grows at an enormous rate during the early years at school, and at a more moderate rate throughout secondary and tertiary education, is vocabulary. Indeed, this continues throughout life; no doubt you have learned some new words as you have read this book. Some new vocabulary will be learned, which is to say stored in long-term memory. For example, an adult reading a book, listening to the radio or watching a television programme about an unfamiliar subject will hear many new words. Some will be learned, while others will be heard, understood for the duration of the time spent attending to the topic, then dismissed (forgotten, but not consciously) as not useful or relevant.

In the early stages of vocabulary acquisition, children will generalize words, so for example, they will use the word *dog* to refer to all four-legged animals, or they will operate on limited concepts, so they may only use the word *dog* to refer to the dog that lives in their own house. Gradually, they will learn to broaden the vocabulary and to broaden the concepts, so that concepts, groups and sub-groups have the correct labels.

During the early years, language content is largely concerned with the 'here and now', with things the child can reach out and feel, and with day-to-day experience in the immediate environment. Vocabulary and experience grow and expand in parallel, each feeding the other.

Vocabulary size

The question of the size of a child's vocabulary has been the subject of a number of studies. One very imaginative study in the mid-1980s put radio microphones on children ranging in age from under 2 to almost 11 years old, for 12 hours at a time. The surprising result was that the range of utterances used by these children in a day was absolutely vast; for example, a 2-year-old may use something like 1800 different words, and an 11-year-old may use up to 5000 words. This made linguists think differently about traditional beliefs concerning vocabulary size; children's vocabulary turned out to be much larger than had been thought.

One important consideration, of course, is how the words are counted. In this study, *book* and *books*, for example, were counted as two different words. However, by any method of counting, it was a remarkable result, and valuable new information.

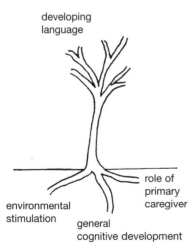

Figure 3.1 Early influences.

Factors affecting language development

To illustrate the factors that influence the acquisition of spoken language, I am using three diagrams based on the analogy of a growing tree, taken from *Developing Spoken Language Skills* (Borwick and Townend, 1993). The three key factors may be summarized as: general cognitive development, the role of the primary caregiver, and environmental stimulation.

Early influences

Figure 3.1 shows a sapling. It has a small number of branches, showing that there is not yet much language. But let us look at the roots of the tree at this stage. What are the important things that are going to nourish and nurture the emerging language; what is going to put leaves on the tree?

General cognitive development

First, we need to consider the general cognitive development of the child. The child has to be at a stage where he or she is intellectually capable of developing spoken language. That is a maturational, age-related issue, but it is also related to an extent to intellectual ability, which, of course, varies very much between individuals. We know that children with greater cognitive skills learn to speak more effectively and often earlier than children who have less overall ability, and that is very much what one would expect.

The role of the primary caregiver

The second root of the tree is the role of the primary caregiver; this may be the mother, but will be whoever looks after the child most of the time. This is a very important role. We have seen the essential role of positive feedback to the child's early utterances, social interaction between carer and child, and the use of what we have called 'Motherese', the special kind of language used by carers to talk to infants and young children.

Environmental stimulation

Building on the crucial role of the primary caregiver is the issue of environmental stimulation. If the child is not surrounded by a rich source of language, he or she will not have good models of language structure on which to build his own language, or plentiful vocabulary to build it with. No matter how good the innate predisposition for language may be, the potential cannot be realized unless the data are there to be fed in. These data come from the environment: vocabulary; good models of language, things to look at, things to talk about; things to label, and the encouragement in developing the concepts to which to attach those labels.

We will now look at the other factors that need to be considered.

Influences on developing language

In the second tree (Figure 3.2), things have been moved around slightly. The soil has become the general cognitive development, or underlying ability, of the child, into which the tree is rooted. Environmental stimulation and the role of the primary caregiver have been moved up to the sky, and are represented by the sun and the rain, the external influences on growth. They are the external factors affecting the child's acquisition of

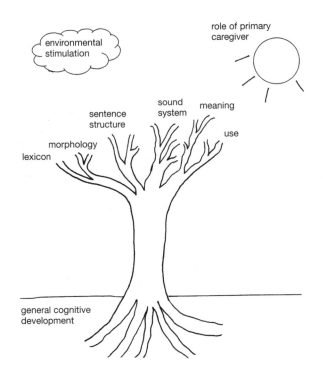

Figure 3.2 Influences on developing language.

language. The branches now have labels, which will be familiar from your reading of Chapter 2 on the structure of language. They are: phonology, the sound system; lexicon and morphology, the word system and word structure; syntax, the sentence structure, or grammar; semantics, language meaning; pragmatics, language use. These five aspects of language that need to develop are rooted in general cognitive development.

Physical factors

In Figure 3.3, the tree is in full leaf. Look first at the trunk; this is where the analogy breaks down, because in our tree, the 'sap' goes up and down! Motor competence has to be intact for speech to develop; the structure and function of the organs of speech are essential to the production of sounds. If a child has, for example, cerebral palsy, the neurological control of the speech muscles may be impaired, and speech production will be difficult. How difficult it will be depends on the location and severity of the cerebral lesion. For the articulatory loop to be completed, the child's hearing has to be adequate. Satisfactory articulation enables the child to rehearse verbally his or her emerging language skills and facilitates effective communication between the child and his or her 'significant others'.

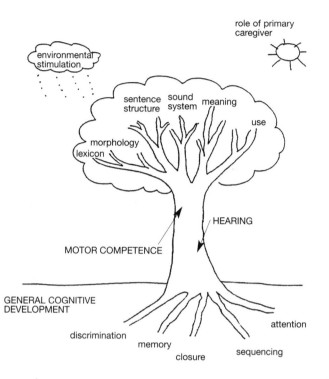

Figure 3.3 External and internal factors at work together.

Physical difficulties and speech development

It is worth mentioning here that while many young children have difficulties with the articulation of speech sounds, this is rarely due to physical
impairments; it is more commonly attributable to weak phonological
awareness, or maturational lag. Of course, a physical condition such as
cerebral palsy can affect the motor control of the organs of articulation; a
cleft palate affects their structure.

A 'tongue-tie' is another rare physical condition which can affect some
speech sounds. This is caused by a short phrenum, which is the mem-
brane attaching the underside of the tongue to the floor of the mouth. If
it is very short, vertically, or if it extends far along the length of the tongue,
so the tip is anchored to the floor of the mouth, it may be difficult for the
child to pronounce sounds that use the tip or blade of the tongue, such
as /t/, /d/, /s/ or /sh/. In the majority of individuals with a short phrenum,
speech is unaffected. In severe cases, the problem can be solved by a simple surgical procedure, but speech and language therapy may be
necessary afterwards to teach the new patterns of articulation. Motor patterns are laid down and become habituated at an early stage; they are

then reinforced through the articulatory loop, so therapy may need to include an element of phonological perception training.

The underlying skills

Returning to the tree, look next at the branches, the outcomes of the language acquisition process. These are the same as in Figure 3.2. The foliage is there to indicate the increasing complexity and richness of language as it develops beyond the early stages. The main change on this diagram is the labelling of the roots; each of these roots is a specific perceptual skill that is rooted in general cognitive development, but is not solely reliant on it. Some children with high underlying ability have difficulties with these skills. We will consider them from left to right, as they are arranged in no particular order on the diagram.

Discrimination

Discrimination is the ability to hear very fine differences between sounds. There is a great deal about speech sounds in the next three chapters, and about how fine the differences between sounds are; the ability to perceive these fine distinctions is crucial.

Memory

Memory for language is very important; we use information coming into short-term memory, which may then be organized and stored in long-term memory. If short-term auditory memory skills are weak, the organization and storage of information in the long-term memory store, and its subsequent retrieval, will be difficult. Obviously, all learning depends on a well-functioning memory; acquiring the mother tongue is a learning process, even though the underlying predisposition is already there.

Closure

Closure is the ability to interpret the whole from its parts, or from an incomplete part. When a great deal of information is coming into the brain, we often anticipate what is coming next, or interpret the message before it is finished. In Chapter 6 there is a discussion of how we accurately interpret a phrase such as 'fish 'n' chips'. The *'n'* is correctly interpreted as *and* although all the sounds of *and* are not actually said. This is how skilled users of the language process incoming speech, without being aware that they are doing so. Closure is a skill that has to be intact in order for a child to acquire language, because the sounds in the words they hear every day will vary according to context. Some sounds will be missed out, some will change, and the ability to perceive and interpret the contextual changes well enough to understand the language is vital.

Sequencing

Sequencing, the ability to perceive the order of incoming information, is clearly important to the development of phonological skills and grammar. It is also essential to the learning of vocabulary, especially longer, multi-syllable words. A child with an auditory sequencing difficulty often places the sounds or the syllables of a word in the wrong order:

'cue-be-bar' for 'barbecue'

'pollilop' for 'lollipop'

'par cark' for 'car park'

This is a normal developmental stage, but if it persists, it may indicate a difficulty in this area.

Attention

Clearly, if a child cannot pay selective attention to the spoken word he will not be getting the information and the benefits from the environmental stimulation that is around him. Attention to sound, and particularly to the spoken word, is crucial. Stop reading for a moment and listen to what you can hear in the environment; you may be able to hear traffic, birdsong or people talking, but you may have been able to block out those sounds in order to pay attention to reading. If someone were to speak to you, that would probably take precedence over the written word; you would probably be able at the same time to ignore background music, a passing aeroplane, or even a conversation going on in another part of the room. However, if the other conversation suddenly included a word or phrase full of meaning for you, such as your name, a place you have recently visited or something of special interest, you would be distracted from your own conversation and drawn towards the one in the background. This is known, for obvious reasons, as the 'Cocktail Party Phenomenon'. If you are shopping alone you are likely to be more aware of the background music than if you are with another person.

If you are listening to the car radio while driving, you can attend to what is being said while paying visual attention to the road, but the sound of a car horn or siren would demand – and receive – your greater attention instantly. If you have to negotiate a tricky junction in heavy traffic you can find afterwards that you have not heard the last few moments of the radio programme because you have selectively blotted it out. To some extent, paying selective attention is a learned skill; we can largely control what we hear.

If all sound had equal value to you, or equal claim upon your attention, you would find it very difficult to have a conversation. Some children are unable to pay attention to auditory information, or find it difficult to attend selectively to language against a background of other sounds. Such a child will fail to draw information from the environment and therefore the learning of the specific building blocks of the mother tongue will be impeded. Research has demonstrated that a noisy environment adversely affects the language development of children; there is a lack of contrast between the spoken word and the background noise. Children need some quiet as a background to acquiring language.

These perceptual skills are often impaired in children with literacy difficulties; it seems that the same perceptual skills that are important in the development of spoken language are also crucial to written language. This is suggestive of close links between spoken and written language.

A final thought: rules rule, OK

Fiona, at about 3 years old, said she knew it was raining when she woke up, without looking out of her window, because she could hear the cars 'swittering'. She had not only invented an excellent onomatopoeic word for the noise made by car tyres on wet road, 'to switter', but she had given it an appropriate verb ending.

Jane, a 10-year-old girl with dyslexia, was writing a sentence. She knew that the past tense of *bring* was not *bringed*, so she wrote *brang*, crossed it out, and finally settled on *brung*.

Summary

In this chapter we have looked at:

■ how language development happens

■ four theories of language acquisition:
 – behaviourist
 – language and cognition
 – process theory
 – biological capacity theories
 – how these theories interact

■ the sequence of language acquisition:
 – sounds in the first year of life
 – emerging words
 – early sentences
 – learning the rules
 – moving on in grammar and vocabulary

■ factors affecting language development:
 – cognitive ability
 – environmental factors
 – physical factors
 – underlying skills

CHAPTER 4

An introduction to phonology

Can you believe your ears?

The aim of this chapter is to convince you that you cannot really believe your ears. First, let us consider why it is important to study speech sounds. Are you aware of what sounds you make when you speak? Do you really make the sounds you write down as the letters in the word, or are they different in some way? Do the sounds change according to context? Why is it so easy to hold a conversation with a friend, or even a stranger, on the telephone, but very difficult to give or take a name and address precisely, or to take down a name correctly from a telephone message?

Task 4.1

Read this sentence aloud, at normal speed, preferably into a tape recorder (or you could get several other people to read it to you):

The girls and boys had cake for tea.

Listen to what you actually say. For example, what is the sound at the end of *girls*? The letter is s, but the sound is /z/.

How did you say *and*? Was it /and/; /an/; /n/; /und/; /un/; /nd/; /um/ or /m/? What about *had*? Did you really say /had/ or did the /d/ run into the next word, so it sounded rather like /hag-cake/? Was *for* more like /fuh/?
One version would be something like this:

The girlz mm boyz hag cake fuh tea.

I am a professional speaker, using what may be called BBC English and I assure you the sentence does not sound strange when I say it like this. I would not always use this way of saying these words, but what happens is that we automatically use the most efficient speech patterns consistent with intelligibility. This means that sounds change according to their context. There is nothing wrong with this; it is a normal phenomenon. Our ability to interpret is related to auditory closure, one of the perceptual skills described towards the end of Chapter 3.

This is covered in more detail in Chapter 6, but the example above serves to illustrate, I hope, that you cannot always believe your ears.

Meet the schwa

To read this chapter and the next two, you need only one piece of prior knowledge: the schwa. This is the name given to the vowel sound made by

er	in *mother*
our	in *colour*
ar	in *beggar*
a	in *again*

It is only ever found in an unstressed word or syllable, and there are at least 17 different ways of spelling it in English. Each speech sound, or phoneme, has its own symbol; you will find it easier to understand what follows if you know just one: the symbol for the schwa is /ə/.

Some useful definitions

Phonetics

Phonetics is a branch of linguistics; it is the scientific study of speech sounds, and is sometimes divided into 'pure phonetics' and phonology. Phonetics covers issues such as:

- the anatomy and physiology of speech sounds;
- the total range of speech sounds (not just English) it is possible to make;
- how sounds are made;
- classification of speech sounds;
- the physical attributes of speech sounds (articulatory phonetics);
- how sounds are transmitted through the air (acoustic phonetics);
- how sounds are heard (auditory phonetics).

Phonology

Phonology is sometimes considered as a subset of phonetics. It is the applied aspect of the subject. Phonology covers such issues as:

- the selection of sounds used in any language (44 in English);
- the function of phonemes as units that alter word meaning;
- the rules governing the use of sounds in a language;

- how sounds combine to make syllables and words;
- how sounds may not combine;
- the effect of sounds on each other in context;
- other features of speech apart from sounds (supra-segmental phonology).

Phoneme

A phoneme is an individual speech sound, the smallest linguistically significant unit, which means the smallest unit of sound capable of changing meaning. The vocal tract is capable of making very many sounds, from which each language has a fixed number to form the building blocks of syllables and words.

> **An important distinction:**
> Phonetics is concerned with the form of sounds.
> Phonology is concerned with the function of sounds.
> Phonics is a method of teaching reading.

About these chapters

What this chapter and the next two are chiefly concerned with is English phonology: the range of sounds used in English; the production of these sounds; their characteristics, and the rules operating to govern their combination. We will also consider how meaning is affected by the supra-segmental or prosodic features of language. These are the features of the pronunciation and use of speech sounds, over and above the characteristics of the individual sounds. Volume, stress, intonation, pitch and tone come under this heading.

You may find it helpful to go back to Chapter 1 and look again at Figure 1.2 (the diagram of the vocal tract) before we go on to consider where each of the sounds of English is made.

The classification of speech sounds: overview

When describing speech sounds, several attributes have to be considered. The first one is airstream mechanism, or how the energy to produce the sound is released. Next, individual sounds have to be divided into vowels and consonants, which have very different characteristics. Consonants are described in terms of three features: whether the sound has voice, where it is made and how it is made. These are known, respectively, as voice, place and manner. Vowels are all voiced, but the features used to distinguish them include the height of the tongue in the mouth, the part of the tongue raised and the shape taken by the lips (Figure 4.1).

Phonemes (44)	
Consonants (24)	**Vowels (20)**
Voice	Part of tongue raised
Place	Degree of tongue raising
Manner	Position of lips

Figure 4.1 Classification of English speech sounds: a summary.

Airstream mechanisms

Normal speech in most languages uses a pulmonic, egressive airstream, which is air from the lungs being breathed out. That is by no means the only way to make vocal sounds; there are other possibilities. In some languages, sounds can be made by air coming in; in some of the languages of southern Africa, Zulu for example, a number of clicks are used. English speakers can make some of these sounds easily because they are commonly used in non-verbal communication.

Exercise 4.1

Make a click at the side of your mouth, using the side of your tongue and your side teeth (molars), as if you were calling a horse over to you. It sounds slightly like 'clack'.

Make a click using your tongue and top teeth. This click is the sound we make when mildly annoyed, which is usually written as 'tut'.

Make a click with rounded lips; this sound, a bilabial click, does not, as far as I know, appear in any language. It is a kiss!

Clicks are made by forming a closure towards the back of the mouth, so air cannot get in or out, and forming a seal further forward using tongue, lips or teeth, or a combination, thus creating a partial vacuum. The front seal is released, so air rushes in, making the sound. If you decide to try the last example, choose your context carefully. A young man of my acquaintance tried 'Shall I demonstrate a bilabial oral click?' as a 'chat-up line' at parties!

To use clicks as part of a continuous string of speech, if they are not in your mother tongue, feels strange, because the direction of the airflow has to be reversed for each one. For this chapter, as it is concerned with

English phonology, we will be focusing on sounds made with a pulmonic egressive airstream.

Classification of consonants

Consonant sounds are described according to three criteria: voice, place and manner; any consonant phoneme, not just the ones used in English, can be identified by these three descriptors.

Voice

The first characteristic, voice, denotes whether the vocal folds are vibrating. If they are, the sound is said to be voiced; if they are at rest, the sound is unvoiced.

Exercise 4.2

You can demonstrate this difference on yourself:

Cup you hands over your ears and hum /mm/; you can feel the vibrations as /m/ is a voiced sound. Repeat with any vowel sound /ah/ or /ee/.

The same effect can be achieved by placing the hand on the front of the neck, but it is less dramatic.

To compare, repeat with some unvoiced sounds: /ss/, /shshsh/.

For an easy contrast, say /fff/ then /vvv/ and feel the difference on the lower lip. You can tell that /v/ is voiced, because you feel, on your lower lip, the vibrating air coming from the vocal folds.

Strong and weak sounds

A consequence of this voiced/unvoiced distinction is the difference in the strength of sounds; voiced sounds tend to be weak. If you hold your hand in front of your mouth and make two sounds (sounds, not letters, and make them continuous, without a schwa /ə/ sound after them) /s/ and /z/, you will feel a huge rush of air on /s/ and less air on /z/. This is because when /z/, the voiced sound, is made, quite a lot of energy goes into vibrating the vocal folds; when /s/ is made, the air is coming unimpeded from the lungs into the mouth, and emerges in a great rush. The technical terms are fortis (strong) to describe unvoiced consonant sounds, and lenis (weak) to describe voiced ones.

This fortis/lenis distinction has an important linguistic function as well; if we were to say unvoiced sounds weakly, it would be very difficult to hear them. Much of what is heard in an unvoiced sound is the rush of air coming past the articulators.

> **Exercise 4.3**
>
> Place a tiny scrap of paper (up to about a centimetre squared) on the back of your hand and hold your hand in front of your mouth. Say the sounds /p/ and /b/. Keep them as pure as possible and try not to say /pə/ and /bə/. The paper should blow off during /p/, but remain on your hand during /b/. This demonstrates the difference in the strength of the unvoiced /p/ and the voiced /b/.
>
> Then say /p/ very weakly, trying not to disturb the paper; you will find it is almost inaudible.

Place of articulation

The next classification is where the sound is being made, which is called the place of articulation. There are normally two organs of articulation, or articulators, involved, and the place label normally denotes both (labiodental: lip and teeth, for example). The exception to this is when one of the articulators is the tongue, in which case only the other articulator is named (dental: tongue and teeth, for example). Occasionally, only one articulator is involved, because it has two parts, such as the lips (bilabial: two lips).

You may find it helpful to keep a marker on Figure 1.2 at page 8, for the next section, in which we will consider all the places of articulation used in English.

Bilabial

Starting from the front of the vocal tract, the most anterior place for a sound to be made is the lips. If both lips are involved, this is called a bilabial sound. Examples include /p/ and /b/.

Labiodental

Moving back, the next place of articulation is labiodental, lips and teeth; /f/ is an example. The next few have only one label, because the tongue is one of the articulators. We could prefix these places of articulation with *linguo-*, as in *linguo-dental*, but the convention is to name only the other organ of articulation, *dental*. It is important to remember that the tongue is involved, although it does not appear in the label.

Dental

A dental sound is made with the tongue and front teeth, such as /th/.

Alveolar and blade-alveolar

The alveolar, or teeth ridge, is the hard, bony ridge behind the top teeth. If you explore with your tongue inside your mouth, you will be able to feel it. The alveolar ridge is very important in English phonology because it is the place of articulation for several phonemes, such as /t/ and /d/. Most alveolar sounds are made with the tip of the tongue against the alveolar ridge.

Two sounds, /s/ and /z/, are made with the blade of the tongue against the alveolar ridge; the blade is immediately behind the tip of the tongue. We will look at this in more detail in the next chapter.

Post-alveolar and retroflex

Just behind the alveolar ridge, where it begins to go up to become the hard palate, the roof of the mouth, is the place of articulation known as post-alveolar. English sounds made here are normally articulated with the front of the tongue, the wide part immediately behind the blade, and therefore a little way behind the tip.

A variation on the post-alveolar place is called retroflex. For this place, the tip of the tongue is curled back to articulate with the post-alveolar position on the roof of the mouth, as in /r/.

Palatal

Moving further back, the bony roof of the mouth is called the hard palate. It articulates with the front of the tongue to produce palatal sounds, such as /y/ in yes.

Velar

Next comes the velum, or soft palate, which is that part of the roof of the mouth behind the hard palate; it is formed by muscle and extends from where the bone ends to the uvula (see the diagram in Chapter 1). The main function of this muscle is to move up and back to seal off the nasal cavity during swallowing; a secondary function is to form this seal during the articulation of most speech sounds. The other organ of articulation is the back of the tongue; sounds made here, such as /k/ and /g/, are called velar sounds.

Glottal

There are several other places of articulation within the vocal tract, which are not discussed here, because they are not used in English sounds. The only other place of articulation used in an English phoneme is the glottis. The glottis is the space between the vocal folds, down in the larynx. A glottal sound is made by the articulation of the two vocal folds. There is one glottal sound in English, /h/, the sound at the beginning of *hat*.

Manner of articulation

The final classification criterion is manner of articulation, which is the way in which the sounds are made. There are five manners of articulation used in English.

Plosives

The first is the plosive, or stop sound. This is formed by the two articulators coming together to form a seal somewhere in the vocal tract, causing pressure to build up behind the closure. As the articulators are forced apart, the air comes rushing out. Plosive is an easy term to remember; it sounds quite like *explosive*.

A plosive sound has two phases; the stop phase, when the articulators are together, which is essentially a silent phase, and the release phase, when the air rushes out. The making of the sound is in the transition from stop to release. One example of a plosive is /p/. The stop phase is when the lips are together, and the release phase is after the lips have separated. The production of the sound is in the movement, the parting of the lips, and the air being released. This means it is not possible to prolong a plosive sound; it is essentially transient. There are six plosives in English, a voiced and an unvoiced pair in three different places of articulation. We will look at them in more detail in Chapter 5.

Fricatives

The next manner of articulation is the fricative sound. In order to make a fricative (the word has the same root as *friction*), the two articulators have to be placed close together, not close enough to form a seal, but close enough so that, when the air is forced between them, friction occurs, giving the phonemes their characteristic sound. An example of an English fricative is /f/; the top teeth are placed adjacent to the lower lip, and the airstream is forced between them, under some pressure, causing the sound. There are several voiced and unvoiced fricatives in English (see Chapter 5).

Affricates

An affricate is a hybrid sound, which starts with the articulators making a seal as if for a plosive. Instead of being fully released, which would produce a plosive sound, the organs of articulation move very slightly apart, just enough for the air to be forced out under pressure, causing friction. The sound begins with the stop phase of a plosive and it is released as a fricative, so it has characteristics of both these manners of articulation. There are two affricates in English, one of which is the sound /ch/, as in *church*. The articulators are placed together, as for /t/, then released slightly so that the fricative sound /sh/ follows. The sound /ch/ is a combination of /t/ and /sh/. Try saying the sound slowly, and you should be able to hear and feel the two parts.

Nasals

In order to make an oral sound, the velum, or soft palate, has to be moved up and back, creating a seal against the back wall of the pharynx, so that air cannot escape down the nose. To make a nasal sound, the velum stays down, a seal is made at some point in the mouth so that air cannot escape that way, and the air is released through the nose. An example of a nasal sound in English is /m/, which is made by the lips coming together to form a seal, the soft palate being lowered, and air being released through the nose. All nasal sounds in English are voiced.

Frictionless continuants

This last category is a sort of catch-all, into which the other English con-sonants can be collected. There are two subsets of frictionless continuants, each containing two phonemes, which will be explored in the next chapter. As the name suggests, these sounds are continuous, and the organs of articulation move into the characteristic shape required for the sound, which may include a seal somewhere, but without a stop and release phase and without the proximity that gives rise to friction. The air is released continuously, and in English all the frictionless continuants are voiced.

Other possibilities

There are, of course, other manners of articulation; clicks, as we have seen, would be an example. As they are not used in English, they are not described here. A general textbook on phonetics and phonology would be the best source of further information.

The glottal stop

There is a consonant-like sound that is not a phoneme of English, but increasingly occurs in speech, especially, but not exclusively, in Cockney and the regional variations in the south-east of England that are sometimes called 'Estuary English'. It is called the glottal stop, and it occurs mainly in the syllable-final position. It is the sound that comes in the middle of *water* in Estuary English 'wa'er'. The /t/ is omitted, but there is something between the two vowel sounds. This 'something' is a plosive sound; the vocal folds come together to form a seal, then they are released and a column of air rushes out. The mechanism is the same as for /p/ which we considered above, but the organ of articulation is the glottis. The glottal stop is an unvoiced glottal plosive. While most people outside its region would not use the glottal stop in this context, it is becoming increasingly common across the country, and in all areas of society, to omit the final plosive (/p/, /t/ or /k/) from a word. This usage by the Prime Minister at the time of writing, Tony Blair, has been pointed out by several commentators.

Commentators and journalists may take a view on this usage, but it is the role of the phonetician and linguist to observe and record, non-judgementally, the trends and changes in language use. We will return to this topic in Chapter 10.

Conclusion

Any consonant in English, or in any language, can be identified by listing its voice, place and manner. It is a useful labelling system because each consonant phoneme has a unique combination of these three characteristics.

Classification of vowels

Three different characteristics are used to classify vowel sounds. All vowel sounds are voiced frictionless continuants (the consonant frictionless continuants were touched on briefly above). The individual identity of a vowel lies in the shape formed by the mouth. The organs of articulation mainly involved in the articulation of vowels are the tongue and the lips. The three characteristics required to identify a vowel sound are: the degree of tongue raising, the part of the tongue that is raised, and the position of the lips.

Degree of tongue raising

If the tongue is fully raised, it is said to be in the **close** position, in which the jaw is almost closed, the mouth is almost closed and the tongue is very close to the roof of the mouth. When the jaw drops a little, the mouth is slightly open and the tongue is about one-third of the way from the roof of the mouth to its lowest possible position, we say it is in the **half-close** position. The half-open position is when the mouth is open, the jaw is a little lower, and the tongue is about two thirds of the way from its highest possible to its lowest possible position. **Open** is when the jaws are far apart, the tongue is in the floor of the mouth and the mouth is wide open.

Obviously, these descriptions are not precise; vowel sounds are concerned with approximations. The precise position will depend to some extent on the physical features of the speaker; individual differences in mouth shape, for example, contribute to the differences in people's voices that help us to recognize them.

The part of the tongue raised

The tongue is an immensely flexible organ, and it is possible to raise any part of it independently. It is necessary to establish whether the front, the middle or the back of the tongue is raised, relative to the rest. Vowels may be labelled as front, middle or back sounds, depending on which part is raised higher than the rest.

The position of the lips

The lip position is the third criterion to be considered in identifying a vowel sound. The lips may be:

rounded, as for /oo/ (spoon), /or/ (saw), /ah/ (calm)

spread, as for /ee/ (tree), /air/ (share), /ă/ (ant)

neutral, as for /ə/, (across), /ir/ (girl)

You may like to try these in front of a mirror. In English, lip position is always linked to the part of the tongue raised, so that back vowels always have lips spread and front sounds always have rounded lips. This is not a link that occurs in all languages.

A word about regional variations

In order to avoid confusion, it is important to remember that when describing a phoneme, and giving an example of it in a word, I am describing it as if that word was being spoken by a user of southern British English. This is also known as Received Pronunciation (RP), and which you may recognize as 'BBC English'. Regional differences in pronunciation, or accents, are not normally made by different ways of articulating phonemes; they are made by using different phonemes in a given word. The principal differences in accent are in the use of vowels, so let us take as an example the word *bath*:

In RP the vowel sound is /ah/, a back open vowel with rounded lips.

In the north the sound is /ă/, a front open vowel with spread lips.

In North America it is /air/, which is a vowel glide, or diphthong.

They are three different phonemes, three different vowel sounds, used in the same word. All are equally correct. This is not the same as individual vocal characteristics, which mean that there are slight differences in how two people may pronounce the same phoneme. There are some other regional variations, including the degree of nasalization of vowels (think of New York) and stress patterns (think of African English).

More about phonemes

A phoneme is an individual speech sound capable of changing meaning. Take a word such as *cat*; it has three phonemes. By changing the middle phoneme to /ŭ/, the meaning is changed from an animal to a wound, or possibly an action with scissors. If you then change the final phoneme to /p/ the meaning is changed again to a piece of tableware (or maybe a prize). By changing just one phoneme, we are dealing with a different word, a different part of speech perhaps, a different concept. This is a crucial element of the definition of a phoneme.

Within each phoneme there are different ways of pronunciation, depending on the phonetic context. As a student, I remember attending a two-hour lecture on the different realizations of the phoneme /t/ in the sentence:

> It's the eighth time the Bennett twins have travelled to Littlehampton.

The fact that I can still remember the sentence after 35 years suggests that the learning must have been effective! There are indeed many variations of /t/ in that sentence, but they are all recognizable as /t/ and the differences do not change the words into different ones, or alter the meaning. These very subtle differences in realization of a phoneme are called **allophones**. We use allophones automatically, influenced by the context, and the untrained ear does not recognize that there are differences (if I used them in the wrong context you would conclude that I had a strange accent, though you might find it difficult to pin it down).

Allophones are not a subject for this book, but interested people will find more information in any good introduction to phonetics and phonology (see Bibliography).

The importance of clues

If, as I suggested at the beginning of this chapter, you can't believe your ears, what can you believe? How do we get the essential information to understand precisely what is being said to us? Why is it easier to give your name face-to-face than on the telephone? The telephone, though much improved acoustically in recent years, is not as precise an instrument as the human ear.

It tends to distort high-frequency sounds, which includes all the consonant phonemes. In normal conversation, we do not need all the information we receive; the skill of auditory closure is used to make sense of partial information. For example, if I were talking about my pets, and began the word *dŏ-* you would assume I was going to say *dog*, rather than *doctor* or *documentary*. If the topic of conversation was my health, you may expect *dŏ-* to become *doctor*. If someone forgets a word in mid-sentence, you would sometimes be able to prompt. We use context, and high-level phonological skills, to complete. If, however, I am giving my name, there are no context clues to help the hearer. The phonological skills will suggest possibilities, but not always with a great deal of accuracy. It is easy to mistake an unfamiliar word for a familiar one; for example, when I give my surname, *Townend*, it is often fed back to me as the more familiar *Townsend*. If speaker and hearer are face to face, there are additional visual clues as to the sequence of phonemes, such as lip position, and there will be less distortion of the consonants, but on the telephone perception is much more difficult.

Conclusion

In English there are 44 phonemes, made up of 24 consonants and 20 vowels, of which 12 are single vowel sounds and 8 are diphthongs, or vowel glides. There are three characteristics that contribute to the classification of consonants and three different ones that contribute to the classification of vowels. The next chapter looks at each of the phonemes individually.

Summary

In this chapter we have looked at:

- the difference between speech and the perception of speech
- the unstressed English vowel, or schwa /ə/
- definitions of the terms used in phonetics and phonology
- airstream mechanisms
- the 44 phonemes, or speech sounds, of English
- 24 consonant sounds
- 20 vowel sounds, of which 12 are single vowel sounds and 8 are diphthongs, or vowel glides
- the three characteristics that contribute to the classification of consonants: voice, place of articulation and manner of articulation
- the three characteristics that contribute to the classification of vowels: lip position, degree of tongue raising and the part of the tongue raised
- regional variations
- the role of phonemes in changing meaning

CHAPTER 5

The sounds of English

Introduction

This chapter is concerned with the 44 phonemes, or individual speech sounds of English; the 24 consonants and 20 vowel sounds that go to make up the English language sound system. We have already established that all English sounds are produced by expelling air from the lungs. We will consider first the consonant sounds, and look at the voice, place and manner for each of them, then the lip and tongue positions for the 12 single vowels, and finally the positions and movements involved in making the eight diphthongs, or vowel glides.

A note about RP

What is it?

You will notice that Table 5.1 (see page 64) is headed 'English RP Consonants'. RP stands for **Received Pronunciation**, another term for which is southern British English. This is one kind of English, a regional variation. It is not 'best English', standard, proper English; it is not something to which people ought necessarily to aspire, though it is fine to aspire to it if you want to. RP is a descriptive term, describing the variation of English that has commonly been spoken in the south-east of England and to an extent in other areas, by some educated people. You would probably recognize it if I called it 'BBC English'. It cannot be overemphasized that this is a description, not a value judgement. It is the variation of English used by a relatively small, and probably diminishing, number of speakers.

How did it come about?

It was adopted as a benchmark because it was the kind of English spoken by the 'founding fathers' of phonetics, in the latter part of the nineteenth and early part of the twentieth centuries. In those days it was expected that educated people should speak in a certain way, and those who did not naturally do so would set about learning! Nowadays the variety of regional accents in English is valued and accepted. (For further discussion of how language changes over time, see Chapter 10.)

Why is it still useful?

The existence of one agreed benchmark for pronunciation makes it possible to write down sound. Clearly, writing down sounds by means of traditional orthography, or normal spelling, is virtually impossible. To return to the example used in the previous chapter, if I described a vowel sound as /a/, as in *bath*, a reader in the south-east would think I was writing about the sound /ah/, while someone in the north would think I meant /ă/, as in *cat*. In the south-west they would think the same, but the sound would be twice as long, and an American reader might think I was writing about /air/, because he would pronounce *bath* rather like *bairth*. (Of course this is an over-simplification; there are regional differences within the USA, and even within regions of the UK. For example, there are differences in vowel length between east and west Cornwall.)

The International Phonetic Alphabet

Each sound, therefore, needed its own symbol, which would stand for that phoneme, to enable phoneticians to record and communicate sounds on paper. The International Phonetic Alphabet (IPA) was devised at the end of the nineteenth century to enable scholars to communicate precise linguistic and phonetic information in a consistent and reliable manner. So while in traditional orthography we spell a given word in the same way regardless of how it is pronounced by different people, in a phonetic alphabet different symbols are used depending on the pronunciation. There is no direct connection with spelling, except that many of the symbols used are letters of the alphabet. In the example above, *bath* could be written in the IPA using four different vowel symbols to represent the four regional accents we considered.

There is a symbol for each phoneme it is possible to make, not just the RP ones, or even the English ones; it is truly international, and any sound the vocal tract can produce can therefore be written down. Anyone who can read and write IPA can therefore 'hear' sounds straight from the page. This has proved very valuable in recording languages that have only had an oral form, and is used in recording erroneous speech, such as that of a young child, or an individual with a language impairment.

It is customary to put phoneme symbols between slanting brackets. There are some extra symbols, and subscript or superscript markings, which are used to record additional information, such as the allophones, or variations within a phoneme. Such distinctions need not concern us here.

The use of RP in this book

It is not necessary to know the phonetic symbols to be able to understand the fundamentals of the sound system of English, but an awareness of their existence helps to separate sound from spelling, which is an important distinction. Where possible, the words used as examples have been selected because either their pronunciation is fairly consistent throughout the English-speaking world, or the 'BBC English' pronunciation would be easily recognizable. The consonants are relatively straightforward because they are less subject to variation than the vowels. Regional variations are carried substantially by the vowel sounds, though stress patterns also contribute. Regional variations in consonants are mainly restricted to a few sounds, called the frictionless continuants (/r/, /l/, /y/). (This topic is covered in more detail in Chapter 10.)

The English consonants

Table 5.1

MANNER OF ARTICULATION	V+ / V-	PLACE: BILABIAL	DENTAL	LABIO-DENTAL	ALVEOLAR	POST-ALVEOLAR	PALATAL	VELAR	GLOTTAL
PLOSIVE	V-	/p/ pen			/t/ ten			/k/ car	
	V+	/b/ ball			/d/ dog			/g/ gate	
FRICATIVE	V-		/f/ fire	/θ/ think	/s/ sock	/ʃ/ shoe			/h/ hat
	V+		/v/ van	/ð/ this	/z/ zoo	/ʒ/ gigolo			
AFFRICATE	V-					/tʃ/ church			
	V+					/dʒ/ judge			
NASAL	all V+	/m/ map			/n/ nest			/ŋ/ ring	
FRICTIONLESS CONTINUANT	all V+	/w/ wet			(lateral) /l/ lame	(retroflex) /r/ red	/j/ yellow		

Look at Table 5.1. It may be helpful for you to refer to Figure 1.2 (p. 8) to check the anatomical position of each place of articulation. A mirror would also be useful, and you are strongly urged to join in and make the sounds as they are described. Across the top of Table 5.1, from left to right, are the places of articulation, with the front of the vocal tract at the left of the chart and the back at the right-hand end. This line can be mapped on to the vocal tract diagram, in which the lips are on the left and the throat on the right.

Down the left side of the chart are the five categories of manner of articulation used in English. Within each box (representing a place and manner) there may be two sounds, one voiced and one unvoiced. Against each manner of articulation there are two symbols: V– at the top denoting the unvoiced sound and V+ below denoting the voiced sound. It is thus possible to plot each pair of phonemes in its box on the grid, according to place and manner of articulation, and where there are two sounds in a box, the top one will be the unvoiced one and underneath will be its voiced counterpart. You will see that in one box there is no voiced sound, and some manners of articulation produce only voiced sounds, so there are not two sounds in every box.

Only the places and manners of articulation used in English have been included, and some boxes are empty. This is because there is no English phoneme made in this manner in this place. It would be possible to draw on other languages and fill all the boxes, and many more, but that is for a different book!

Start at the top left-hand corner of the chart, in the first box that has sound symbols and word examples in it. It can be seen by tracking vertically that the sounds are bilabial and by tracking horizontally that they are plosives. There are two bilabial plosives in the box and the V– and V+ symbols indicate that /p/ is unvoiced and /b/ is voiced.

The English plosives

The bilabial plosives

Let us consider first the two bilabial plosives /p/ and /b/. They are made in the same manner, by placing the lips together, making a seal, then air is expelled as the lips part. If you hold your hand in front of your mouth and make the two sounds, you will find that for /p/ there is a strong puff of air, while /b/ produces much less air on your hand. In Chapter 4 it was stated that voiced sounds are *lenis*, or weak, while unvoiced sounds are *fortis*, or strong. The unvoiced sounds are strong because the air rushes out, unimpeded, whereas the voiced sounds are weak because much of the energy in that column of air coming up from the lungs is used to set the vocal folds vibrating, to produce voice. That is the physical, phonetic explanation. The phonological aspect of this difference is that if a voiceless sound was weak, it would not be possible to hear it.

The alveolar plosives

Moving back in the mouth the next pair of plosives are those made on the alveolar ridge: /t/ as in *ten* and /d/ as in *dog*. Try making them: you will feel that the tongue tip is in contact with the hard bony ridge behind the upper teeth, and as the sound is made the tongue tip breaks contact and air rushes between. For /d/, exactly the same happens, but with the addition of the vibration of the vocal folds to give voice. You can experience the strong nature of the unvoiced /t/ and the weak nature of its voiced counterpart, /d/, by holding your hand in front of your mouth and feeling the strong push of air being expelled on /t/ and its relative absence during /d/.

A note on English places of articulation

Looking at the chart as a whole, you will notice that if a line were drawn vertically at the end of the post-alveolar column, that line would be about two-thirds of the way across the chart, from left to right. However, we are still examining sounds made towards the front of the mouth, on the alveolar ridge. Behind this imaginary line there are only five symbols; only five English phonemes are made further back in the vocal tract than the back of the alveolar ridge. This illustrates the preponderance of front consonants in English. Most English consonant sounds are made on or around the alveolar ridge, or with the teeth and lips, and involve the forward parts of the tongue. There are very few English phonemes made using the posterior parts of the vocal tract; there are none that use the uvula or the pharynx, and only a small number involving the hard and soft palate. A language such as Russian has far more sounds made in the back part of the vocal tract.

The velar plosives

The two plosives made towards the back of the mouth are the velar sounds /k/ and /g/. Before looking at them in detail, please make these two sounds and note which parts of the vocal tract you can feel moving, and whether you think the two sounds are being made in the same place.

/k/ is the unvoiced velar plosive and /g/ is the voiced velar plosive. People often say it feels as if these sounds are being made far back in the throat. In fact, they are made at the back of the mouth, with the back of the tongue rising to make contact with the soft palate, or velum, the posterior half of the roof of the mouth. These sounds are made in the mouth, not further back. As the back of the tongue rises, the velum itself also rises to make a seal against the back wall of the pharynx, to prevent any air from escaping down the nose. The air builds up behind the closure; then, as the closure is broken, the air rushes between the soft palate and the tongue and out through the mouth.

Many people perceive that /g/ is being made further back than /k/. In fact, they are made in exactly the same place, but there is a good reason why it feels as if they are not. From the diagram of the vocal tract, in Chapter 1, it can be seen that all the activity for /k/ is at the back of the mouth; there is no movement further back. For /g/, the vocal folds are vibrating, so there is movement at the back of the mouth and down in the larynx. Because we are not accustomed to paying attention to where sounds are made, and which muscles are moving, kinaesthetic feedback from this area is not well developed. This means that we do not distinguish well between the feedback from different parts of the back of the vocal tract. The perception of place for /k/ is straightforward, because the movement is in one place, but for /g/ we receive feedback from two places and perceive it as coming from somewhere between the two. Thus it feels as if /g/ is coming from further back. It is possible to train oneself to become more aware of what is happening.

One way to improve feedback from the front parts of the vocal tract is to sensitize the lips, tongue or alveolar ridge by rubbing gently with a finger or toothbrush, or applying an ice cube wrapped in a handkerchief. After this, the area treated will be more sensitive to movement and touch, making it easier to feel where a sound is being made.

The English fricatives

The labiodental fricatives

There are no bilabial fricatives in English (though there are in Spanish, for example), so the first place of articulation to be considered is lips and teeth. There are two labiodental fricatives, /f/ and /v/, made by placing the top teeth and lower lip close together, but not making a seal. Air is forced between the articulators, making the characteristic sound of friction that gives these sounds their name. Normally the inside of the lower lip is used, but some speakers do place the upper front teeth over the lower lip and articulate with the outer part of the lip. This does take longer, because it is a more extreme movement, and in continuous speech most speakers automatically use the smallest possible movement distance between sounds. Variations in the place of articulation are normally brought about by individual anatomical differences, such as the relative position of the upper and lower jaw.

When saying a sound in isolation in the teaching situation, it is important to try to make it in the same way as you do in continuous speech, and avoid over-articulation. Look at yourself in a mirror as you say *fire* and if you make /f/ on the inside of your lower lip, try to say a continuous /f/ (without any vowel sound after it, so /f/ not /fə/) with your teeth in the same position on your lip.

A note about detecting vocal fold activity

It is very easy to perceive the difference between a voiced and an unvoiced phoneme using this pair of sounds. Make /f/ and then /v/ as strongly as you can, and you should be able to feel the vibrations on your lip when you say /v/.

There are two other easy ways of detecting voice or lack of voice. One is to place the fingertips of one hand in a line down the middle of the front of your neck. You will need to bend your fingers to make the tips line up. Say a fairly long 'aaah', and move your fingertips round until you can feel the vibrations during this sound. This is easier for men, who have a larger and more prominent larynx than women. The protrusion known as the 'Adam's apple' in men is the larger larynx that is necessary to accommodate the longer vocal folds, which are the reason for the lower pitched voice. Now make the sounds /f/ and /v/; you should be able to detect vibrations during /v/ but none during /f/.

The other way to perceive voice is to cup the hands over the ears. Placing the hands flat over the ears will not give the same effect. With cupped hands covering both ears, say /f/ then /v/, or any other voiced/unvoiced pair. During the voiced sound you will be able to hear and feel a buzzing sound inside your ear, which is caused by the vibration of the vocal folds. This is probably the easiest method of the three.

The dental fricatives

The two dental fricatives, voiced and unvoiced, are both spelled /th/. They are made by the tip of the tongue articulating with the upper front teeth, but not close enough to make a seal, so the air is forced out, making friction. Normally, the tongue tip is placed close to the back of the upper front teeth, but in some people the tongue protrudes between the teeth. The voiced dental fricative is the /th/ sound as in *them*; the unvoiced is the /th/ sound as in *thumb*.

Although these sounds are English phonemes, many people never use them, substituting /f/ for the unvoiced /th/ and /v/ for the voiced one. It can be seen from Table 5.1 how this cross-over between phonemes can happen. The two sounds spelled as *th* are fricatives, and so are /f/ and /v/. /th/ as in *thumb*, and /f/ are both unvoiced, whereas /th/ as in *then* and /v/ are voiced. So each of these pairs, /th/ and /f/ or /th/ and /v/ has two of the three characteristics in common. We can also see that they have neighbouring places of articulation, so the third characteristic is similar. These pairs of sounds are closely linked phonetically; only the smallest physical adjustment needs to be made to slip from one to the other.

The /th/ sound is particularly difficult for a young child to make. With maturity, if that sound is not in the environment as she grows up, because those around her substitute /f/ and /v/, she will not develop the adult form. This is increasingly common now, and although it used to be associated with a regional variation of English used in and around London (Cockney, and 'Estuary English' are examples) many younger people from all over the United Kingdom habitually use /f/ and /v/ where *th* appears in the spelling. It is not the place of the phonetician or even the teacher to make value judgements about pronunciation; if it is part of the regional or cultural identity of an individual's language, it has to be accepted.

When I was a young speech and language therapist, many years ago, an enthusiastic school doctor sent along a small boy from a new housing estate just outside London, with the usual label 'speech indistinct'. It turned out that he was fine except for the substitution of /f/ and /v/ for /th/. When I asked his mother what she thought about his speech she replied, "'E can't say 'is tee haitches, and 'is brover was just ve same'. We agreed to leave him be; it would not have been appropriate for him to be the only child in his block of flats who did use /th/!

Both the /th/ sounds are made by the tip of the tongue articulating with the top front teeth, usually the back of those teeth, or the gap between the top and bottom teeth. The difference between them is that /th/ in *thin* is unvoiced and /th/ in *this* is voiced. They are both dental fricatives, so the other characteristics are common to both. Unusually in English, both these phonemes are spelled in the same way.

The alveolar fricatives

Next come the two alveolar fricatives /s/ and /z/. These are not straightforward alveolar fricatives, because the tongue tip does not go up to the alveolar ridge to create friction in the usual way. For these two sounds, the tongue tip is actually free.

Exercise 5.1

Try saying both now, and try to work out where the tip of your tongue actually is. If you find this difficult, rub your tongue tip with a fingertip, and this will sensitize it and make it easier for you to feel where it is in your mouth. Make the sound /s/ while consciously trying to push your tongue tip upwards, then again, while trying to push it down behind your lower front teeth. You will probably find that it does not make any difference to your ability to make the /s/ sound. This is because the tongue tip is not playing a part in the articulation of the sound, but is free.

In all the sounds we have considered up to now, the tongue involvement has been by the tongue tip, but for these two sounds the blade of the tongue is involved. This is the part immediately behind the tip, and in front of the flat, wide part of the tongue known as the front. The blade of the tongue articulates with the alveolar ridge, but there is another complication. For /s/ and /z/ the tongue contracts in the middle, so a groove is formed running down the centre of the blade of the tongue from front to back.

The influence of airstream strength

Exercise 5.2

Now hold your hand in front of your mouth and make two sounds, /s/ and /sh/. When you have done that, try to work out what is the difference you can feel on your hand between the two sounds.

The differences you should have felt were that for /s/ the column of air landing on your hand was very narrow, and for /sh/ it was much broader. You may also have felt that /s/ made your hand cold, while /sh/ felt warmer. If you did not feel those differences, try again now.

Why does this happen? The reason for this narrow, strong stream of air for /s/ is that the air is being pushed out along the groove described above, so through a very small space. On the other hand, /sh/ comes out over a wide flat tongue. The perceived difference in the temperature of the air is strange, because the air for both sounds is coming from the same place: your lungs. The reason may be described as the 'wind chill factor'! In /s/ the same amount of air as for /sh/ is being forced through a smaller space, taking the same time, so it has to be travelling faster. We all know that the stronger the wind, the colder it feels, while the air temperature remains constant.

Have you ever thought about the strange phenomenon of cooling your tea? If your cup of tea or coffee is too hot, you may round your lips and blow on it. Blow on your hand now; does it feel cool? If you have cold hands you may try to warm them by blowing on them in a different way, by opening your mouth and making a sort of /h/ sound. Try it now, making sure you whisper /h/. It probably feels warm. The air has come from the same place, so it should feel the same temperature. It is the same wind chill effect as I have described above. In the first, you blow through a small space between your lips and the air is forced to travel fast to get out. In the second, your mouth is wide and the air escapes more gently, thus feeling warmer.

Returning to the two sounds /s/ and /z/, their full title is grooved blade-alveolar fricatives, grooved because of the central groove, and blade to indicate which part of the tongue is involved in the articulation. /s/ is of course unvoiced; /z/ is its voiced counterpart.

The post-alveolar fricatives

In the post-alveolar position there are two fricatives, /sh/ and /dʒ/, made by the wide, flat front of the tongue, articulating with the part of the hard palate just behind the alveolar ridge. /sh/ is the sound at the beginning of *sheep* and *champagne*, but /dʒ/ is more difficult to identify. It is the sound at the end of *garage* if that is not pronounced like the last sound in *bridge*. It is not used at the beginning of a syllable in English, except in a very small number of words borrowed from other languages, such as *gigolo*. It most commonly occurs between vowel sounds, as in the middle of words such as *treasure*, *measure* and *pleasure*. The /sh/ sound is unvoiced, and the /dʒ/ sound is made in exactly the same place and manner, but with the addition of the vibration of the vocal folds, making it voiced.

The glottal fricative

The last phoneme in this group is the glottal fricative /h/. This sound only occurs in the syllable-initial position in English; it may occur in the middle of a word, such as behind, where it is the first sound in the second syllable. It is unvoiced, and has no voiced counterpart. It is made by the two vocal folds coming so close to each other that when air passes between them it creates friction, making the characteristic sound.

The English affricates

There are only two affricates in English, a pair, made in the post-alveolar place of articulation. They are the unvoiced /ch/ and the voiced /j/. The tongue tip moves to the alveolar ridge as if to make /t/, then slides back slightly and parts from the roof of the mouth slightly, creating friction, so the sound is released as the fricative /sh/. The phoneme /ch/ is a hybrid between /t/ and /sh/. The voiced alveolar affricate /j/ starts with the tongue tip being placed on the alveolar ridge as if for /d/, then the tongue slides back slightly and the sound is released as the fricative /dʒ/, as in treasure. So /j/ is a hybrid between the voiced alveolar plosive /d/ and the voiced post-alveolar fricative /dʒ/. This can best be perceived by saying the sounds aloud slowly several times and trying to feel the movement and to hear the two parts to the affricate sound. The unvoiced post-alveolar affricate /ch/ may be spelled ch, as in *child* or tch as in *match*; the voiced post-alveolar fricative /j/ has many spellings: *j* as in *jam*; *g* as in *giant*; *ge* as in *cage*, and *dge* as in *badge*. Despite the many spelling choices, it is one single phoneme or speech sound.

The English nasals

There are three nasal sounds in English, and they are all voiced. The first is the bilabial nasal sound /m/, which is made by the lips being placed together to create a seal in the mouth, the soft palate or velum is lowered and the vibrating column of air from the larynx escapes down the nose. This is the phoneme spelled *m*, as in *mop*.

The next is the alveolar nasal, /n/, in which the tongue tip forms a seal with the alveolar ridge. In order to complete the seal in the mouth, the sides of the tongue have to be in contact with the upper side teeth, and the lowered velum allows the air to exit through the nose. This is the phoneme spelled n, as in *nose*.

The third nasal sound is the velar nasal, /ng/, made by the back of the tongue forming a seal with the velum, as in /k/. This time the velum is not raised, so air can escape through the nose. This phoneme does not occur in the syllable initial position in English, though it does in Zulu and Swahili. It is the first sound in the South African national anthem *Nkosi sikelel iAfrica*. In English it is confined to the end of the syllable, and is spelled *ng*, and in a blend with /k/, when it is spelled *nk*. Although we spell /ng/ with two letters, it is one phoneme. You can demonstrate this by saying it to yourself; the /n/ sound does not form any part of it. Because there are only 26 letters to cover 44 phonemes, some doubling up has to take place, hence for example the use of *sh* for one phoneme, *ng* for another and *th* for two more.

It can be seen from the chart that there is a nasal sound for each place of articulation where there are plosives. There are two plosive sounds and a nasal sound in the bilabial, alveolar and velar positions.

The English frictionless continuants

The last set of consonant sounds is the group called frictionless continuants; they are also called approximants. They are all voiced.

The phoneme /l/

The first to be considered are the two in the middle of the bottom line of the chart, the alveolar and post-alveolar sounds. The phoneme /l/, spelled with the letter *l* or with *ll*, is made by placing the tongue tip against the alveolar ridge, as if for /t/ or /d/. The difference is that the sides of the tongue are lowered. Instead of making a seal all the way round the edges of the tongue and the upper side teeth, which would be necessary for the plosive sounds /t/ and /d/, there is a gap between the top teeth and the sides of the tongue. The air escapes over the sides of the tongue, which gives rise to the label lateral. Make the sound now; if you are not sure what is happening in your mouth, rub the sides of your tongue with your fingertip or your toothbrush, which will sensitise it and make it easy for you to track the movements. Make the sounds /t/ /l/ /t/ /l/, and you should be able to feel the sides of your tongue moving towards and away from your upper side teeth as well as your tongue tip moving up and down as it makes and releases contact with the alveolar ridge. We describe /l/ as an alveolar sound, because of the position of the tongue tip, and as lateral because of how the air escapes from the mouth. There is no friction, as you can hear when you make the sound, but it is continuous and voiced. The full title is a voiced alveolar lateral frictionless continuant.

The phoneme /r/

Let us look next at /r/, which is closely related to /l/. This is made in the post-alveolar position. You will probably find it helpful to sensitize the tip of your tongue by rubbing it before making this sound, which is spelled with the letter *r*. Make the sound and try to identify the position of your tongue. This phoneme is known as retroflex, because the tip of the tongue is curled back to make contact with the post-alveolar position on the roof of the mouth. This phoneme is a voiced retroflex post-alveolar frictionless continuant.

Many people find this a difficult sound to make, and it is in fact the last sound to be acquired by the young child. Some individuals fail to develop the ability to make the sound in the way described above, and use an approximation made by the top teeth and the inside of the lower lip. This would be described as a voiced labiodental frictionless continuant, and it is used by a number of people with varying degrees of close approximation to the correct model. A person using a poor approximation would be recognized as someone who 'can't say his Rs'.

The phonemes /w/ and /y/

The two remaining frictionless continuants are /w/ and /y/. You are now going to try an exercise to demonstrate the unusual qualities of these two phonemes.

Exercise 5.3

Round your lips as if to say /w/, the sound spelled *w* in the syllable initial position, such as in *win*. Now start to say the sound, but extend it, not by adding /ə/, the unstressed schwa sound, but try to carry on saying /w/ without moving the position of your lips. You should find yourself saying something that sounds like /oo/.

Do the same with /y/, the sound spelled *y* in the syllable initial position, such as in *yes*. Spread your lips to say the sound, then try to extend the pure sound, without moving your lips, so without adding a schwa. You should find yourself making a sound like /ee/. You should be able to feel the front of your tongue, spread flat, near the hard palate.

We call these two phonemes semi-vowels. All vowels are frictionless continuants, and these two consonant phonemes are called semi-vowels
because they have many of the phonetic properties of a vowel, although
they behave in the language as consonants.

A word of warning! Please try to ignore the fact that the letter y can
sometimes be a vowel, as in words such as *cry* or *baby*, and that both
these letters often appear in vowel digraphs such as *oy* and *ow*. In phonetics and phonology we are considering speech sounds, and spelling is
referred to only to help you to know which sound is being described.
Each phoneme is considered as a unit of speech sound *no matter how it
is spelled*. The vowel sounds mentioned in this paragraph will be examined later in this chapter, and have no connection to the fact that the
consonant sounds /w/ and /y/ are, phonetically speaking, semi-vowels.

Let us look first at /w/. We have established that phonetically (the way
it is made, physically) it is closer to a vowel, but phonologically (in the
language) it is a consonant. The lips are close and rounded, so it is
described as a bilabial sound; as a frictionless continuant it has to be
voiced, and you can hear or feel the voicing if you extend the sound as in
the exercise. Its label is a voiced bilabial frictionless continuant or a
voiced bilabial semi-vowel.

Now we will consider /y/. This phoneme is also phonetically closer to a
vowel, but phonologically, in function, it is a consonant. It is made by
placing the front of the tongue near the hard palate, the bony roof of the
mouth, and the lips are slightly spread. This lip spreading is part of the
phoneme's vowel characteristics, because in English any vowel which has
the front of the tongue raised has associated lip spreading. Because of the
proximity of tongue and hard palate its label is a voiced palatal frictionless continuant, or voiced palatal semi-vowel.

The glottal stop

The glottal stop is not a phoneme of English, so it does not appear in the
table, but if it were, it would be placed in the empty square in the top
right-hand corner. A stop is another word for a plosive, and it is made in
the glottis, by the two vocal folds coming together to form a seal, then the
air rushing out as they part. It is an unvoiced glottal plosive.

The English vowels

What is the difference between a vowel and a consonant?

This is a question that has interested linguists for some time. As we have
seen, physically there are major differences in how they are said, except

for the two semi-vowels that are made like vowels but behave like consonants. It is more helpful to consider the differences in terms of function, the role each plays in the language.

The vowels have syllabic value; every syllable must have a vowel sound in it, and some syllables consist of just a vowel sound: the word *a* or the sound /o/ in *open* for example. The vowel sounds contribute length to the syllable.

Consonants cannot stand alone as syllables. (There are one or two exceptions to this rule, which will not be explored here, but will be covered in any general textbook on phonetics and phonology.) Consonant sounds are found at the edges of syllables: at the beginning and end as in *cat*, *ship*, *bring*, *wife*, *just*; at the end, as in *it*, *ash*, *off*, *ants*; or just at the beginning, as in *go*, *she*, *bacon*, *student*. In *wife*, although the last letter is a vowel, the last phoneme, the last sound, is a consonant /f/. It is important, but difficult, not to let spelling get in the way of listening.

The single vowel sounds

There are three characteristics to be considered when looking at each vowel sound: the part of the tongue raised, the degree of tongue raising and the lip position. Voicing is not an issue because all vowels are voiced. You will find it helpful to refer to Figure 1.2 (p. 8) as each vowel phoneme is discussed.

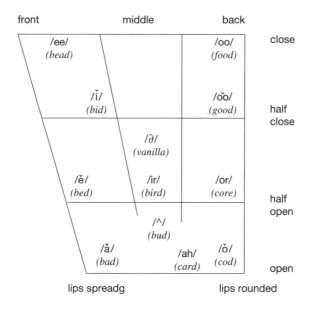

Figure 5.1 English RP vowels: single vowels.

Reading the vowel chart

Look at the figure entitled English RP vowels: single vowels (Figure 5.1) above. The part of the tongue raised, the front, middle or back, is plotted across the top of the chart. This is a diagrammatic representation of tongue positions, with all the vowel sounds plotted on it. The phonemes that are close to each other on the chart are made close to each other in the mouth, and are therefore phonetically similar.

The horizontal lines are showing the degree of tongue raising:

- The top line of the figure represents the close position, with the tongue near the roof of the mouth.
- The line one third of the way down is the half-close position.
- Two-thirds of the way down is the half-open position.
- The bottom line of the grid represents the open position, when the jaws are wide apart and the tongue is low in the floor of the mouth.

The characteristic which is not plotted on the grid is the position of the lips: rounded, spread or neutral. You will see that at the bottom of the figure, underneath the front of the tongue, it says 'lips spread' and underneath the back of the tongue it says 'lips rounded'. In English, front vowels always have spread lips, back vowels always have rounded lips and middle vowels always have neutral lips. This is not the case in all languages.

Exercise 5.4

Look at the top left-hand corner of the vowel figure, at the symbol /ee/ and the word *bead*. This represents the sound /ee/. You will feel that your lips are spread wide as you say it. Say the sound, then keeping your tongue in the same position, round your lips and say the sound again. The second time you should produce the French phoneme /u/, as in the word *tu*, meaning *you*, in the second person singular.

The second phoneme you made was a close front vowel with lips rounded; it does not occur in English. The connection between front vowels and lips spread, and back vowels and lips rounded, is particular to English; it is not a phonetic rule, but a phonological rule of the language. However, it is a convenient one for the student of English because it removes the need to identify the three independent characteristics.

The four front vowels

First we will consider the four front vowels; you are advised to say these vowels in a list, with a mirror in front of you.

You should have felt that your mouth was quite closed when you started, and gradually opened as you said each successive sound. You were saying the close sound, the half-close sound, the half-open sound and the last one was nearly open. You kept your lips spread, and the front of your tongue was always relatively the highest part, but you were changing the height of your tongue by gradually lowering your jaw.

The sound /ee/ is a very close front vowel, with the front of the tongue very near the roof of the mouth. Lowering the jaw slightly gives /ĭ/, which is slightly above half-close, still using the front of the tongue. We tend to think of these two sounds as completely different because they are spelled differently, but they are in fact made in a similar way physically. It is possible for some children to have difficulty in discriminating between these two sounds, which would not be immediately obvious to a teacher because of the different letters we associate them with. This is another example of how important it is when considering phonetics and phonology to put all ideas of spelling away and concentrate on the sounds.

The half-open front vowel /ĕ/ (as in net) is a very front sound. You can see on the chart that the symbol is very near the front edge, which marks the front of the tongue. The lips are still spread. As the jaw lowers, the lips become very widely spread for the sound /ă/ (as in *cat*), which is almost in the fully open position, and the part of the tongue fairly near the front is the highest.

The five back vowels

There are five vowels made using the back of the tongue. Say them from the list below, starting from the most open, and try to feel your jaw raising your tongue closer to the hard palate. Use the mirror to demonstrate what is happening to your lips. If you say these sounds fairly forcefully you will probably be able to feel that it is the back of your tongue that is involved.

The lips are wide and rounded for /ah/, and closely rounded for /oo/. The circle made by your lips gets smaller as the vowel sounds become increasingly close. The open back vowel, /ah/, is a very open vowel; the symbol is on the line. The back part of the tongue is used, but not as far back as for the back half-open vowel, /ŏ/ (as in *orange*), which is made right at the back of the tongue.

Moving up to above the half-open position, and not so far back, is the sound /or/, as in *caught, door, jaw*. This is a back vowel, between half-close and half-open. The next sound uses the anterior part of the back of the tongue, so it is near to being classified as a middle vowel, and getting closer to the hard palate. It is /u/ as in *put, good, bull*. It is not a sound we often say in isolation, so it may be difficult, but it is important to be able to isolate a phoneme, so please persevere.

The last back vowel is very close and fairly far back. It is /oo/ (as in *boot*). If you say it forcefully you can feel the back of the tongue. A look in the mirror will reveal that the circle made by your lips is now very small, denoting the close position. So /oo/ is a back close vowel.

The three middle vowels

There remain the three middle vowels, those that have the middle of the tongue as the highest part. The most open one is /ŭ/ as in *cup*. This RP sound does not occur in the sound system of many regional variations of English, including the south-west, the whole of the north of England, and parts of the south-east. In the north, the sound would normally be replaced by either the fairly close back vowel /u/, as in *good* or *put*, or the neutral schwa, /ə/. In the south-west the vowel sound used would be nearer to the middle half-close /ir/ sound, as in *bird*, *her*, *fur*. In London and the south-east it would be more like the front open /ă/ (*cat*) sound.

This phoneme is probably used by a minority of people, but has to be included as we are describing RP sounds. The best way to hear it if you do not use it yourself is to listen to a television or radio announcer or newsreader who does not have a regional accent. It is the sound he or she will use in the middle of *cup*, *gun* or *stuff*. It is a middle vowel, between open and half-open. The mouth is fairly wide open and lips are neither rounded nor spread, but neutral, as for all middle vowels.

We now move into the central box on the chart. There are two vowels in this box, the two most neutral vowels in English. They are similarly positioned, with the middle of the tongue between half-open and half-close, though the tongue is nearer half-close for /ir/. In both cases the lips are neutral. The main difference between them to the hearer is in the length, because /ir/ is always stressed in a word, and therefore longer in duration, while the schwa is always unstressed, and is therefore very brief. (Long and short in this context are to be taken literally; in literacy, the terms **long vowel** and **short vowel** have a specific meaning which is not being used here.)

Say these two middle sounds now, in front of a mirror: /ir/ as in *her* and /ə/ as in *vanilla*. You will notice that your lips are in a totally neutral position; these sounds seem to require little effort. The middle of the tongue is neither open nor close, the lips are neither rounded nor spread, and the middle part of the tongue is the highest, so they are appropriately placed in the middle of the chart.

The neutral quality of the /ə/ shows why it is used so often in English as the vowel in the unstressed syllable, because it is not necessary to move the organs of articulation very far in any direction to make the sound.

The diphthongs

These are set out on the second vowel chart headed English RP vowels: diphthongs (Figure 5.2). A diphthong is a vowel glide; it is made by gliding from one vowel position to another. A mirror is essential for this section.

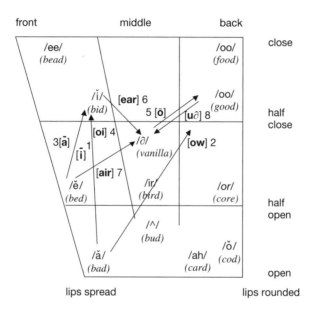

Figure 5.2 English RP vowels: diphthongs.

Each of these vowel glides has a start position and a finishing position, which are shown by the beginning and end of the arrows on the chart. The sound is made as the organs of articulation move from the start position to the finishing position. Each sound is no longer in duration than a single vowel, but is made during the movement of the lips and tongue. On the chart, the diphthongs are numbered; they are described here in numerical order.

The movements for glides tend to be as far as possible towards the middle. It is easier and quicker to move from /ă/ to /ĭ/ than from /ă/ to /ee/. The two sounds that start with /ă/ have the greatest movement. We will consider them first because they are the easiest to perceive for the beginner.

1. The first sound to be examined is /ī/, as in *ivy* or *eye*. Say it slowly in front of a mirror. Think about the position of the mouth at the beginning

of the sound; it starts in the open position for /ă/ and it glides towards the position for /ĭ/. You will be able to observe the spreading of the lips during the articulation of the sound, while you are actually saying it. If you say it slowly you may think you are gliding from /ă/ to /ee/, but, as we established in the last paragraph, in speech the glide only goes as far as /ĭ/, which is not so close, or so near the front. This is the only diphthong that moves from a front position all the way to a back position.

2. The other vowel glide starting at /ă/ and moving a long way is /ow/, as in *cow*, *out* or *bough*. Again, using the mirror, place your mouth as if to start saying /ow/; your organs of articulation will be in place for /ă/, as in *at*. Now watch as you slowly make the /ow/ sound, and observe the change in lip position, from open spread, to close rounded. You have glided to the sound /oo/, as in *book*. It may feel as if you have moved to /oo/ as in *boot*, but in continuous speech this would take too long and the organs of articulation make the more energy-efficient movement only as far as the /oo/ in *book*, which is less back and less close. As the movement for this diphthong is relatively extreme, you may be able to detect the movement of your tongue; the back of the tongue replaces the front as the highest part during the articulation of the sound.

3. The next diphthong is /ā/, the long vowel sound as in *bacon*, *cake* and *alien*. First, put your mouth ready to start the sound, and make a sound in that position without moving anything. You should be making the sound /ĕ/, as in *egg*. This demonstrates that the articulation of this phoneme starts at the front, above the half-open position. The sound is made in the movement towards the /ĭ/ sound, as in *it*, which is still towards the front, but closer. This is relatively difficult to perceive because the movement is not very far. Try saying /ā/, several times, more and more slowly, and you should be able to feel what is happening. You should be able to see your spread lips closing during this sound.

4. An easier diphthong to feel and see is /oi/, which you can probably work out for yourself with the aid of a mirror. When placing your articulators for this sound, you should recognize that you are ready to make the sound /or/, made with the back of the tongue nearly in the half-open position. As you say /oi/ very slowly you should be able to see the lips spreading and the jaw closing, as you finish in the position for /ĭ/, a front sound, just above half-close. This is the only diphthong to move all the way from back to front.

5. The other four diphthongs involve middle positions, so the movements are small. The sound /ō/, as in *open*, *bone*, *toe*, starts in the neutral, schwa position /ə/, and moves up and back to /oo/, as in *book*. Even

when said slowly it is not easy to feel the movement. People who speak with a regional accent such as Scottish, Irish or Caribbean will use a single vowel, not a diphthong for this sound. Please be forbearing, and remember that what is being described here is the English received pronunciation sound system.

6. The remaining three diphthongs all end at /ə/. The vowel sound /ear/ as in *theory* (without the /r/ sound), or *pianist*, starts at /ĭ/ as in *it*, and moves slightly forward and slightly down to the neutral middle position /ə/. You should be able to see and feel your lips moving from spread to neutral as you say it.

7. The next phoneme to consider is the sound /air/, as in *stare, fair* or *heir*. This is another problematic sound for speakers of regional variations of English, many of whom will use something nearer to the previous vowel, /ĭə/ (ear) sound for these words. In received pronunciation this sound starts at /ĕ/, as in *bed*, a front sound just above half-open, and moves to /ə/, the neutral, unstressed schwa sound. This movement is visible in the mirror and can be felt as a closing of the mouth and a movement towards a neutral lip position.

8. The last diphthong is /uə/, the vowel sound in *dour*, in *sewer* if said quickly, and for some RP speakers, in *sure*, though many people would use /or/, and pronounce *sure* in exactly the same way as *shore*. This diphthong is made by starting with the articulators placed as if for /oo/, as in *good*, and the tongue moving forward and down to /ə/.

A final word about received pronunciation

The authors (who were born one on either side of the Pennines) feel strongly that readers should understand that RP is just *one* kind of English pronunciation, no better and no worse than any other regional variation. In describing RP phonemes we are not making a case for the standardization of English pronunciation. This chapter is descriptive, not prescriptive.

If you are still unsure about the difference between a single vowel and a diphthong, this story, told to me many years ago by an infant school teacher, may help.

One Monday morning, her class of 6 year olds was writing 'news', and one little boy arrived at her desk for help with spelling a word; the word he wanted was 'pissed'. She decided, of course, that this would not do, so she suggested that he try to think of a different word to use instead. Nothing she said could persuade the boy to change his mind, and he insisted that this was the only word that would fit. She sent him to fetch his book, so they could think of an alternative together. As you can imagine, all sorts of possibilities were running through her mind! When the child returned and put his book in front of her, she read what he had written:

On Saturday we went to town and my Mummy had her ears ...

Summary

In this chapter we have looked at:

- received pronunciation ('RP')
- the International Phonetic Alphabet
- the English consonant sounds:
  - plosives
  - fricatives
  - affricates
  - nasals
  - frictionless continuants
- the English vowel sounds
  - single vowels
  - diphthongs (vowel glides)

CHAPTER 6

Putting sounds together: the phonological rules

Introduction

Having looked at the phonemes of English individually in some detail, we now come to consider what happens when we put them together. A word is not just a lot of phonemes, one after the other, and connected speech is very different, phonologically, from the single-word utterance. Sounds vary according to the phonetic context, the speed, the intonation and the circumstances in which the speech is taking place. First we will consider some examples of the constraints placed on the sound system of a language. We will look next at stress, and intonation patterns, then move on to two phenomena called assimilation and elision, and also discover what happens when assimilation and elision occur together. Finally, blend theory will be considered, which is what happens when two or three consonants occur next to each other to form a blend. Consonant blends are also known in some contexts as consonant clusters.

What is possible and what is acceptable

How many phonemes?

In any language, a selection of phonemes is used; in English there are 44, all of which we examined in the previous chapter. Some languages have as few as 18 phonemes, while others use over 60. One of the complications of our spelling system is that we have only 26 letters to represent 44 sounds, so a straightforward sound–symbol correspondence is impossible to achieve. Of course, that is not the only difficulty. It does not explain why several spelling patterns can represent one sound (*e*, *ee*, *ea*, *ey*, or *j*, *g*, *ge*, *dge*, for example). Nor does it explain why the same spelling pattern can represent several sounds (*ough* is a good example: think about *tough*, *cough*, *bough*, *though*, *bought*, *through*, or homographs such as *wind*, *bow*, *sow* with their two pronunciations apiece).

Possible and impossible sound combinations in English

Apart from the number of phonemes in a language, there is the question of how they can be put together. In English, as we shall see in detail below, some consonant blends are possible (*sp*, *str*, *pl*, *dr*), but not others (*sr*, *sdl*, *dl*). This is not to say that they are phonetically impossible, but they do not occur in English. Other languages have consonant blends that we do not; bw is a blend in Swahili, in a word such as *bwana*. So is *ms*, as in *msungu* (a white person). Look out for the plural form *wasungu* in Chapter 7.

English vowels, we have discovered, if they are made with the front of the tongue, have spread lips, if with the back of the tongue have rounded lips, and if with the middle of the tongue have neutral lips. However, in other languages it is possible to use other combinations, such as the French /u/, as in tu, which is a front vowel with rounded lips.

The position of sounds within words and syllables

Another phonological variation between languages is the possible position of certain phonemes within the syllable. In English, for example, the velar nasal sound /ng/ and the *nk* blend always occur at the end of the syllable. This is not because it is impossible to say them in the syllable-initial position; indeed they occur here in many African languages. The first words of the South African National Anthem are *'Nkosi sikelel' iAfrica'*, which is 'God bless Africa' in Zulu. In English, /h/ always occurs at the beginning of the syllable, as do all the consonant blends with /r/, but many other blends, such as /sp/, /st/ and /sk/ can occur at either end of the syllable.

Prosody

Supra-segmental phonology, or prosody, is the group of features of speech above and beyond speech sounds; it includes stress, intonation, pitch, tone, volume and speed.

Stress in single words

Stress is the label given to the pattern of stronger and weaker syllables in a word, or in a string of words. The strong syllable is said to be the stressed syllable. For example, in a word such as *garden* (say it) the stress is on the first syllable, *gar-*, while in *forget*, the stress is on the second syllable, *get*. Some people find this challenging, so there is an exercise to practise on.

Task 6.1

Which is the stressed syllable in these words?

rather	bargain	again	butterfly	commit
comet	entertain	politics	political	politician

You will find this exercise much easier if you say each word aloud, several times if necessary. If you still find it difficult, try saying each one with the stress on a different syllable each time, and see which one sounds right. For example, is it **because**, or be**cause**?

A

Cover the answers until you are ready to check.

rather	**bar**gain	a**gain**	**butter**fly	com**mit**
comet	enter**tain**	**pol**itics	po**lit**ical	poli**ti**cian

The effect of stress patterns

Changes in stress can alter sounds. Take the word *contract*. Write it down. What does it mean? Now underline the stressed syllable. Now write down another meaning, and underline the stressed syllable. *'Contract* is a noun, meaning a legal agreement, such as a contract of employment, while *con'tract*, a verb, means to become smaller, such as when a company reduces its size due to lack of orders. The stress in the former is on the first syllable, while in the latter it is on the second syllable.

However, the stress pattern is not the only thing that has changed. In *'contract*, the first vowel sound is /ŏ/ and the second is /ă/; in *con'tract*, the second vowel is still /a/, but the first has changed (try saying the two words again) and is now /ə/, the schwa. We established in the last chapter that the schwa occurs as the unstressed vowel in a word, and here it is doing so. In a word, the unstressed syllable is given less emphasis and less length, and typically the vowel letter is not pronounced as its spelling suggests, but is replaced by the schwa sound. If you have another look at Task 6.1, you will discover that several of the unstressed syllables in the words have a schwa as the vowel sound.

Another interesting example is the word *politic*. Go back to the task, and look at the last three words on the second line. Your answers should look like this:

politics	a three- syllable word with the stress on the first syllable *pol*
political	a four-syllable word, with the stress shifted to the second syllable *it*
politician	another 4 syllable word, with the stress now on the third syllable *ish*

All three words come from the same root, *politic*, but the stress pattern varies according to the length and structure of the word, and the part of speech.

Stress in connected speech

Unstressed whole words in connected speech often take what is called the weak form. There was an example of this in Chapter 4, when you were asked to write the sentence:

The girls and boys had cake for tea.

The word *m* for *and* is a weak form. Other weak forms of *and* are *un*, *und*, *'n*, *'nd*, *ăn*. Many of these have the sound /ə/, not the sound /ă/. A weak form is an unstressed version of a word.

Another example of a common weak form is /əv/. Out of context it is impossible to tell if this is a weak form of *of*, as in 'a pair of shoes', or a weak form of *have*, as in 'You could have (could've) let me know'. So the same weak form is used for *of* and *have*. This explains how the erroneous phrase 'should of' has crept into the language, because in the weak form, how is a child to know whether the fully extended word is *have* or *of*?

Exercise 6.1

Consider (aloud) these two examples:

It was good *of* her to come.

He should *have* heard by now.

The chunk in the middle (the italicized bit) sounds, in continuous speech, almost identical in the two sentences.

English stress patterns

A typical pattern in English connected speech is to have stress on alternate syllables, or to have perhaps one strongly stressed syllable in a word of three or four syllables. The words which normally carry the major stress are the content words: the nouns, the verbs, the adjectives. The words which often take the weak form are the little grammatical words, the words that would be difficult to define or to visualize as a concept. Obviously, this can create problems for learners, because the words that are longer or more important are the ones that are stressed, and often the ones that are unstressed in continuous speech take the weak form. This means that many of the small, unstressed words have the same vowel sound, the schwa sound /ə/ in continuous speech. So the learner has no auditory clues at all about how to spell the word.

Unusual stress patterns

There are some circumstances in which small grammatical words are stressed. Returning to *and*, what would you conclude if a child told you he had had 'jelly *and* ice cream for pudding'? You would conclude that this was something unusual, and that one or the other would be more normal. The stress on a word that is normally weak contributes significantly to the implied meaning.

Intonation patterns: the music of speech

Intonation and meaning

Another way to use intonation patterns to change meaning is by turning them into a question. You may say 'Coffee' to remind yourself that you were about to make some when the phone rang. It is a statement, but would have a falling intonation. Try saying it; the pitch goes down at the end. However, 'Coffee?' (say it) has a rising intonation pattern, which is instantly recognizable as a question. Before they can manage to change word order to form a question, young children use intonation to turn a statement into a question:

Daddy gone.

Daddy gone?

These two sentences use the same words, but convey different meanings simply by altering the pitch-change pattern on the final syllable.

Similarly, taking the word *careful*, it can be said with the stress on the first syllable '<u>careful</u>', fairly gently, maybe when handing someone a fragile item. However, spoken loudly, with stress on both syllables '<u>CAREFUL</u>!' it carries urgency, danger, a warning. Here, stress and volume change the meaning of the utterance.

Take the phrase 'That's very nice': said at a fairly high pitch, rising on *nice*, it is suggestive of surprise at the niceness. On the other hand, said at a lower pitch, falling on *nice*, it is more gentle, more affirming, as if the speaker is pleased, but not really surprised. However, by placing exaggerated stress on each word, particularly on *very*, especially accompanied by some harshness of tone, the speaker can make the same words into a sarcastic or ironic utterance, and all the pleasantness of the words disappears.

Consider what changes in meaning can be made by changing the stress from one word to another, in a simple imperative sentence such as 'Look out there':

Look out *<u>there</u>*   (admire the sunset)

Look <u>*out*</u> there   (mind that car)

You would probably respond to the first, but maybe not immediately; you would certainly respond to the second.

Pitch, volume, tone and speed

Pitch and volume are particularly susceptible to the influence of emotion; we all recognize the high pitch of a frightened or excited speaker, for example, and recognize a voice raised in anger. Tone is also infinitely variable, but more subtle and difficult to analyse. A voice can be whining, persuasive, mellow and affectionate, light, or harsh and aggressive, depending on the relationship between the speakers and the nature of the messages being exchanged. Sometimes people will use a gentle, conciliatory tone, with some musicality in the voice, particularly if the message being conveyed is likely to be unpleasant or unwelcome to the hearer. It is as if the message will be softened if it is delivered disguised as good news. When listening to a skilled newsreader, you may notice that an item of bad news will be flagged up by a slight reduction in speed, maybe a lower pitch and falling intonation, which prepares the hearers for something sad. An amusing news item may be flagged up by increasing speed, variations in intonation, a lightness of tone and a briskness to the delivery.

Assimilation

Assimilation is what occurs when the place of articulation of a phoneme changes according to the following sound. It becomes similar to the adjacent sound; this is to simplify the movements involved in articulation. For example, take the phrases

good dog

good girl

good boy

In the first one, the /d/ in *good* may be fully articulated before the following /d/ begins, or the stop phase of the first /d/ may be followed by the release phase of the second. In this case, what is heard is a slightly prolonged single /d:/ sound, indicating that there are in fact two /d/ sounds. They are already similar; no assimilation is necessary.

In the second phrase, the /d/ at the end of *good* may be released before the /g/ of *girl* begins, or the two may be run together, as in 'good_dog'. In this case what would be articulated is 'goog_girl', where the /d/ at the end of *good* becomes assimilated to the following /g/. Similarly, the /d/ at the end of *good* in the third phrase may become assimilated to the following

/b/, making 'goob boy'. Alveolar sounds, of which /d/ is one, are particularly susceptible to assimilation, moving back or forward to assimilate to a neighbouring bilabial sound, /b/, or velar sound, /g/.

Some people do not use assimilations such as these, and complete the sound at the end of a word before beginning the initial sound of the next. I have heard people become quite outspoken on the subject, describing the patterns above as 'sloppy speech'. However, we all use assimilation within words, albeit unconsciously. Try the following short exercise:

Exercise 6.2

Say *ban* then say /k/.

Now say *bank*.

What you are actually saying in *bank* is *bang+k*, not *ban+k*.

If you are sceptical, repeat the exercise in front of a mirror and you will see that your tongue tip does not go up to your alveolar ridge, which it has to for /n/. Instead, the back of your tongue goes up after the vowel, and stays there, making the velar nasal /ng/ followed by the velar plosive /k/. This is not sloppy speech, but efficiency of movement.

The alveolar /n/ assimilates to the following velar sound.

There is a story told about a special needs teacher who was teaching a dyslexic boy, now about 13 years old. When he was much younger he had tended to reverse *b* and *d* in writing, but had now overcome this. At the time of the story he was learning in history about Lord Nelson, and he brought a piece of work to show his special needs teacher, in which he had spelled *Admiral* as 'Abmiral'. The teacher was disappointed because she thought he had grown out of b/d confusion. In fact it was a case of assimilation; the boy was assimilating the /d/ to the neighbouring /m/, and saying 'Abmiral', then simply spelling what he heard.

I once taught a boy who spelled *bank* 'bangk', which indicated that he was hearing the phonemes in the word very clearly. It was an understandable error, and he was pleased to be told that it was made because he was a particularly good listener to sounds!

Elision

Elision is what happens when sounds disappear from words. Some elisions are historical, such as in *Christmas*. No one pronounces the /t/, which was originally *Christ-mass*. It is still there in the spelling but it has disappeared from speech. Similarly, sounds have been elided from *Wednesday*, *shepherd* and *mortgage*. Wednesday comes from *Woden's Day*, and shepherd from *sheep-herd*, in both of which all the now missing sounds are present.

Sounds can also be elided in continuous speech, for example in weak forms, where *and* can become *an'* and the /d/ is dropped, or *have* becomes /əv/, eliding the /h/. It can happen in content words too; *handbag* can become 'hanbag'. Now that the /d/ has been elided, of course the alveolar /n/ is next to a bilabial sound, /b/, so we may have assimilation as well, and the word may be pronounced 'hambag'! You may like to hold up a handbag among a group of friends and ask them to name it. When I do this with groups of students (before teaching the point above) there are usually roughly equal numbers of 'handbags', 'hanbags' and 'hambags'. What problems this can cause for the poor speller!

Consonant blends

Immature speakers often simplify blends, which are among the last sounds to develop in young children. So you may hear *wing* for *swing*, *swirrel* for *squirrel*, *crips* or *quips* for *crisps*. These immaturities can continue into spelling, and blends are notoriously difficult for the literacy struggler to hear, segment, read and especially spell.

Blend theory: the effect of /s/

Consonant sounds can change when combined in blends. For example, when /s/ is put with a voiceless plosive, making the blends /sp/, /st/ and /sk/, something strange happens. Try this exercise:

Exercise 6.3

Hold your hand in front of your mouth and say the sounds /p/, /t/, /k/. They should be single sounds, coming out as a whisper, and without any vowel sound after them. So you are saying /p/, not /pə/ (which sounds like /puh/). They are all voiceless plosives, and therefore strong, or fortis sounds; you should be able to feel the air on your hand as they are released.

Now say them at the beginning of words: *pan, tan, can*. You should still be able to feel a strong puff of air on your hand on the first phoneme of each word. The voiceless plosives are said to be heavily aspirated.

Exercise 6.3
continued
> Now add /s/ at the beginning: *span*, *Stan*, *scan*. This time, while you feel the air on the /s/ sound, you do not feel such a strong puff on the plosives.

The reason is that when /s/ is placed before a voiceless plosive, that plosive becomes weaker. Much of the force goes into the /s/, as you have felt. The voiceless plosives lose their aspiration. The phonological effect is that in an /s/ blend, these voiceless plosives sound a bit like their voiced counterparts. So /sp/ sounds a bit like /sb/, /st/ sounds a bit like /sd/, and /sk/ sounds a bit like /sg/. Happily, there is a 100 per cent reliable spelling rule to be applied here: in English there are no such blends as /sb/, /sd/ or /sg/. Of course the sounds can occur next to each other in words, such as *husband*, but here the /s/ is at the end of the first syllable and the /b/ at the beginning of the second, so they are not a consonant blend.

Blend theory: other relationship effects

The frictionless continuant phonemes, especially /r/ and /l/, crop up in several consonant blends. In blends with voiceless plosives, the nature of /r/ and /l/ undergoes changes.

The blends to be considered are: /pr/, /tr/, /cr/, /pl/, /cl/, and all of those when preceded by /s/, such as /spr/.

Exercise 6.4
> Hold one hand in front of your mouth, place the fingertips of your other hand against your larynx and say (slowly) *ram*. Listen and feel; you should be able to hear and feel the voicing start at the beginning of /r/ and continue throughout the word, as all the phonemes are voiced. There is not a strong puff of air on your hand.
>
> Now, with your fingers still in place, slowly say *pram*. This time you should feel air on your hand during /pr/ but the voicing does not begin until the vowel sound. The /r/ has become unvoiced, and fricative; this is due to the influence of the preceding voiceless plosive.

You can feel the same effect by comparing the following pairs of words:

rise	>	prize	rip	>	trip
rum	>	crumb	late	>	plate
lame	>	claim	ring	>	spring
rap	>	strap	ripped	>	script
lash	>	splash			

In each case, in the blend, the voiced frictionless continuant has become a voiceless fricative. It also happens with the other frictionless continuants, /w/ and /y/; this is exemplified in the difference between *wins* and *twins*, where the /w/ is replaced by a voiceless fricative in the /tw/ blend, and in the difference between you and cue, where the same thing happens to /y/. (*Cue* is made up of three phonemes /k-y-oo/.)

This is not of purely theoretical interest; it can get in the way of spelling. Let us consider the words *chain* and *train*. You can see that for spelling one begins with *ch* and the other with *tr*, so at first glance, apart from rhyming, they appear to have nothing in common.

If we listen more closely to the phoneme /ch/, which you may remember is an affricate, we will hear that it is a hybrid of /t/ and /sh/. /sh/ is an unvoiced fricative made by the blade of the tongue in the post-alveolar position. Now listen to /tr/. It, too, starts with /t/, but then the frictionless continuant /r/ becomes, in the blend, an **unvoiced fricative**, made by curling the tip of the tongue back to the post-alveolar position. So it is very like the /sh/ sound. A diagram will demonstrate how similar these two sounds, /ch/ and /tr/ are:

ch	starts with t	+ released as sh (voiceless post-alveolar fricative)	= voiceless post-alveolar affricate
tr	starts with t	+ released as (r) (voiceless post-alveolar retroflex fricative)	= voiceless post-alveolar retroflex affricate

If you say a few pairs, quite slowly and deliberately, listening out for the characteristic friction in the second half of that initial sound, you should be able to feel and hear the similarity. It is necessary in this case to dismiss from your mind all thoughts of spelling, which influences strongly how literate people perceive words as different or similar, and focus on the sounds and the physical feedback. The difference in my mouth between /tr/ and /ch/ is about 4 mm:

train   chain
true   chew
trip   chip

Conclusion

To sum up, sounds change according to their phonological context, influenced by adjacent sounds. They also change according to stress and intonation patterns, which may be affected by the meaning of the utterance. It is important for those who can spell to set their letter knowledge aside in order to hear and feel some of these phonological effects.

Summary

In this chapter we have looked at:

- how sounds change according to their phonological context
- the influence of adjacent sounds
- possible and impossible sound combinations in English
- how sounds change according to prosodic features such as stress and intonation patterns
- English stress patterns
- the links between prosody and the meaning of the utterance
- assimilation
- elision
- consonant blends and blend theory

CHAPTER 7
Words

Introduction

We have spent some time exploring the sounds of English, how they go together and how they behave in relationship to each other. This chapter looks closely at what may traditionally be thought of as the building block of language: words.

What is a word?

Task 7.1

Write down your definition of a word. Are you happy with your definition? Does it work in all circumstances? Take a bit of time to think about it – it may not be as straightforward as you think. When you have examined your definition carefully, make any necessary changes, and then we will look at some other peoples' attempts.

What a word is not

I have yet to find a definition of a word that I am really satisfied with! Let us consider some of the possibilities:

* **A word is a unit of meaning.**
  Is it? *Sent* (s-e-n-t) is a single word, but two units of meaning, *send* and the past tense. Is *seaside* one word or two? *Boa constrictor* is two words, but represents one thing. As far as I know the two are inseparable; you cannot have a *boa-anything else* or some other sort of *constrictor* (but I am ready to be corrected!)

* **A word is a minimum free form, that is the smallest unit that can stand alone.**
  Do *the* or *its* ever stand alone? No, but they are definitely words. Of course, they stand alone in written language, in the sense that they are

separated from other words, but they would never constitute an acceptable utterance in spoken language.

- **A word is the smallest unit of grammar that can stand alone as a complete utterance, separated by spaces in written language and potentially by pauses in speech.**
  This has several problems. A word like *sheep* can stand alone, but it is no use as a piece of communication if we don't know whether it means one sheep or two, or a whole flock. Similarly, *drive* can stand alone, but is it a noun or a verb? It needs some contextual clues.

We already have established that some words never stand alone, such as *its* or *the*. The issue of word boundaries is a difficult one; in spoken language, we do not make spaces between spoken words. The rhythm of speech is dependent on syllables, not on individual words. Of course, the spaces between words in written language are essential to intelligibility, but we manage very well without them in spoken language.

You will remember the difficulty small children have with word boundaries (an example in Chapter 3 was the infant single word *allgone*), but how these children show evidence of being able to isolate words as concept labels in primitive grammar. This is how we get a range of open-class words being substituted to form new sentences ('Allgone milk'; 'Allgone Daddy').

This definition also breaks down if we look beyond English; I once wrote, with the help of a German friend, to the 'Oberammergau Passion Play Ticket Office', which translates into German as one huge long word. It is a word, but it is not the smallest unit that can stand alone, as each of the components was also a word in its own right. We can see this in English with compound words: *cowboy*, *sunshine*, *pancake*, and so on.

Other ideas on the characteristics of a word

Jean Aitchison, in her clear and straightforward book *Teach Yourself Linguistics* (1987a), says that the definition of the word depends on what kind of word you are talking about, and suggests three possibilities:

- **The lexical item, or dictionary definition.**
  If this is the sort of word we are referring to, then, for example, *drive* is two words: the tarmac or gravel leading up to the house, a noun, and the verb whose most usual meaning is to control a vehicle as it goes along.

- **The syntactic item (that is to say, to do with grammar).**
  Should *drive*, the verb and *drives*, the third person singular, be considered one word or two, and what about *drive* (leading up to the

house) or *drives* (more than one)? If we add all the syntactic forms to each meaning, we get a larger number of words than we might have thought. You can see how complicated it is to establish how many words an individual has in his or her vocabulary!

- **The phonological item.**
  You will remember, from Chapter 6, that the sounds in the spoken word change in context, so should variations of *and* such as /and/, /ən/ and /n/ be considered one word, or three?

In English, these differences are removed in the written form, but in some languages, Welsh for example, the contextual variations may remain in the written form. People who go to remote places to study hitherto unknown languages are courageous indeed, for little can be assumed! (I do not, of course, include Wales!)

One identifying characteristic?

We have not gone very far into linguistics before we have encountered fundamental difficulties in standing back from concepts that are all too familiar and trying to unpack them. One guideline for identifying words is that they are generally indivisible. Words are not usually inserted into the middle of other words, so it is possible to discover word boundaries by studying how they move around and re-group.

For example:

red house
blue house
red dress

These phrases suggest that *red* is a separate word from *house* because each of them can be paired up with different words. You can still come unstuck, of course, with *greenhouse*! In the written form, the distinction is obvious because of the absence of a word boundary in *greenhouse*. There is an old joke, which only works orally:

If a red house is made of red bricks and a blue house is made of blue bricks, what's a green house made of? (Answer: glass.)

There is always an exception

This is a good time to reiterate the point that the study of language is not confined to neat, well-constructed sentences, written or spoken, but with every kind of linguistic output. Newspaper headlines, exclamations, slang and even swearing have to be capable of being examined and subjected to linguistic analysis. This is why linguistics is light years away from traditional grammar, as used to be taught in school grammar lessons. The statement above, that words are not *usually* inserted into the middle of other words, was not a vague generalization. It can happen in an utterance such as 'Angry? I was incan – flipping – descant!' David Crystal, in *The Cambridge Encyclopaedia of Language* (1985b), quotes another example: 'abso – blooming - lutely'. You can probably add your own examples.

Word origins and word relationships

In English we get our words from a variety of roots. (It may be interesting to reflect on my thought processes as I wrote this sentence: I knew that I needed the word *roots* but as I wrote it down I hesitated between *roots* and *routes*. I opted for the former, though you can see how a case could be made for the latter.)

Returning to the point – this variety of roots means that, in English, words that are closely related in meaning may have no similarity in structure as they may do in another language. For example, the word *sailor* derives from the Old English word *seglian* (to sail) while *nautical* comes from the Greek word for sailor, *nautes*. Had we gained our word for *sailor* from the Greek too, then it is likely those two words would have had some structural similarities.

Conversely, words that appear to be unrelated in meaning or context may have a common origin. One example of this is the Latin word *navis* (a ship), which gives us *Navy* (as in the Royal Navy, and therefore of course, navy blue), *navigate* (so far the connection is obvious), but also *nave*, the long, narrow body of a church, where the congregation sits. Apparently, the barrel shape of the roof timbers resembles the upturned hull of a wooden ship.

Homonyms and polysemes

Let us move on to words which look and sound the same, but have different meanings: some have obvious relationships, such as *fly* (noun) and *fly* (verb), or the one we have already considered, *drive*, with both its meanings. These identical pairs of words, with a common origin, are called polysemes.

There are more problems with homonyms, which are also identical, but totally unrelated, such as *nap* (a short sleep) and *nap* (the pile on a cloth, such as velvet, or on carpet). My dictionary gives a third meaning, a card game, in which case *nap* is short for Napoleon, which was a 20-franc coin named, of course, after the Emperor Napoleon. Nap (the little sleep) comes from the Old English noun *hnappian* (with a silent *h* at the beginning) which is related to the Old High German word for slumber. The pile-on-the-velvet nap comes from a word in Middle Low German and Middle Dutch, *noppe*, from *noppen*, to trim. The two original words were quite different, as different as, say, *cat* and *cot*, but found their way to an identical arrangement of phonemes in English.

Task 7.2

Think about the following words; write down all the meanings that you know, including all the different word categories (parts of speech) to which they can belong. Do you think they all come from the same origin? Check in a dictionary.

Cover the answers until you are ready to check.

plump   press   date   hold   trifle   stern

plump

A

rounded (adj.); to become rounded (v) *[Middle English plompe/Middle Dutch plomp]*
drop or plunge (v) *[Middle English/Middle Low German plumpen]*
company, cluster (n) *[Middle English unknown orig.]*

press

crowd (n); urgency (as in pressing) (n); juice extractor (n); printing machine (n); publishing house (n); newspapers, etc. (coll. n); exert steady force (v); be urgent (n); squeeze, flatten (v); oppress or bear down upon (v); force gift, etc. upon (v); urge, persuade (v); hurry (v); force into use usually in emergency (v); force into military service (v) *[all from Latin pressare > Old French presse > Middle English]*

date

calendar time (n); to establish a time period in history (v); to write the calendar date on a document (v) go out with (colloq. v) *[Medieval Latin data > Old French> Middle English]*
fruit of palm tree (n) *[Greek daktulos (finger) > Latin > Old French> Middle English]* (also look up palm)

hold

contain, grasp, withhold, cease, restrain, keep, retain, be in possession of + others (all v) *[Old English healdan/haldan]*
container on ship (n) *[? Old English hol (hollow)]*

Task 7.2
continued

A

trifle
of only slight value (n); to deal frivolously (v); slightly (adj); pudding of cake, fruit, custard, etc. (n) *[Old French truffe (deceit) > Middle English]*

stern
grim, rigid (adj) *[West Germanic sternja > Old English styrne]*
back part of ship (n) *[Old Norse stjórn > Middle English]*

Changes in the meaning of words over time

Language is constantly changing. Many words have changed their meaning over the centuries; for example, the word *indifferent*, which now means uncaring, used to mean impartial, making no difference between. So, 'indifferently to administer justice' (*Book of Common Prayer*, 1662) was a virtuous practice in the seventeenth century, whereas today it would be considered careless rather than conscientious.

Glad used to mean shining or bright in Anglo-Saxon England; this may be the origin of the term 'glad rags', meaning special or fancy clothes. There are many words in the Book of Common Prayer, the King James Bible, the works of Shakespeare and his contemporaries that no longer mean to us what they did at the time of writing. As recently as the nineteenth century, words were used in ways we now find strange and unfamiliar. No doubt young readers still snigger at Charlotte Brontë's Jane Eyre saying, 'I had intercourse with Mr Lloyd this morning'. What word or phrase would we use in that context? Discourse, a conversation, a talk, a word, or a chat, maybe.

Even in our lifetime, words seem to have changed meaning before our eyes. *Gay*, which meant cheerful when I was a child, has become a synonym for homosexual and is now rarely used in any other context. The grandmothers of teenagers probably scratch their heads over oxymorons such as 'This hot weather's really cool' or 'I love this – it's wicked', or become puzzled when they hear the young people refer to their parents enjoying themselves as 'sad'. If it's fun, it isn't sad, is it? And while we are on the subject, what has *political correctness*, that enemy of linguistic richness, got to do with politics? The origin of that term is indeed a puzzle.

New words are entering our vocabulary all the time, seeming strange at first, but becoming very familiar very soon. It is difficult to believe that a few years ago no one had heard of the Internet, email or e-anything else. Many of the new words are derivatives or compounds of existing words (*miniskirt, mobile phone* for example, or *cling film*) or even polysemes, such as *mouse*. I know that the plural of the little grey rodent is *mice*, but what about the plural of the mouse attached to a computer?

Task 7.3

Make a list of any words you can think of that have changed their meaning or acquired a new meaning. You can use any time-scale you like, so include Shakespearean words that mean different things now, or words from your own earlier years whose meanings have changed or developed. Cover the lists below until you have finished.

Not really answers, but a few suggestions:

indifferent:	impartial	>	careless
meat:	food	>	animal carcass food
wife:	woman	>	married woman
naughty:	wicked, sinful	>	childish misbehaviour
intercourse:	conversation	>	sex act
gay:	bright, cheerful	+	homosexual
net:	to catch fish	+	the worldwide web
mouse:	small rodent	+	cursor control on computer
merry:	happy, content	>	slightly inebriated
semantics:	language meaning	+	verbal sophistry
charity:	love (not physical)	>	good cause / donation to such
foil:	sword	+	thin, flexible metal sheet
fleece:	sheepskin	+	light, warm jacket

Task 7.4

Make a list of words that have come into being in your lifetime, either new or derived, or compound words. (This is one of the few times when those of us on the far side of 50 have an advantage!) Make another list of words no longer in common use. Cover the lists below until you have finished.

Not really answers, but a few suggestions:

New words since 1950	Words no longer in use
Internet	drawers (underwear)
cling film	farthingale
supersonic	Brougham
computer (not sure of date)	cutlass
telecommunications	blunderbuss
antibiotic (probably just pre-1950)	doublet
aerosol	victuals
supermarket	tun (wine barrel)
AIDS	cooper (barrel-maker)
dyslexia (not sure of date)	swineherd
ultrasound	shriven (absolved)
environmental (prob. recent derivation)	saith
tights	wast
e-anything	art (are)
mini-anything	thee
jeans	thou

How many words do you need?

Next we are going to think about subtlety and fine distinctions in meaning.

I once went on a walking holiday in the Pyrenees – the sort where they give you maps, instructions and a packed lunch, and your luggage is waiting for you when you stagger into the next hotel at the end of the day. After a couple of days, the instructions became known among our party as the 'obstructions'. It took us a little time to work out why we were having such problems. They had been written by local walking experts, mainly in French. They were, I think, well written, but had then been translated into English. The word *la route* had been translated literally as *the road*. It may have been better translated as *the way* or even *the route*; *road* suggests something substantial, with a surface, probably navigable by cars and maybe even covered with tarmac. The route to be followed, as it turned out, while sometimes going on roads, also went up tracks, footpaths, bridleways, lanes and on bearings with no path discernible underfoot, but following a line of cairns, or a stream bed. The instruction, 'walk' meant anything from 'walk' through 'pick your way' to 'ascend (or descend) using both hands, while exercising extreme caution'! We did learn the meaning of a new word: *vertiginous*. (You can probably discern the meaning from the context.) What the instructions lacked was the subtlety of nuances of meaning that can be introduced by careful choice of precise vocabulary. 'La route' and 'walk' needed to be translated as several different words.

It is said that the Inuit (Eskimo) people have many different words for snow, depending on what sort of snow it is. In English there are many different words for rain, and for other kinds of weather too.

Task 7.5

Make some lists of weather words, illustrating the range of fine differences in meaning that can be accessed, and notice how your choice of words can demonstrate how you feel about different sorts of weather. Divide the words into three lists: good weather, bad weather (other than wet) and wet weather. When you have finished, and maybe had contributions from other people if you like, compare your list with mine.

Cover the list overleaf until you have finished.

Task 7.5   Not really answers, but a few suggestions:
continued

A

Good weather	Bad weather	Wet weather
fine	cold	damp
warm	chilly	thick mist
sunny	freezing	sea fog
glorious	foggy	Scotch mist
hot	misty	drizzle
dry	pea-souper	raining
fresh	nasty	spitting in the wind
clear	dreadful	a few spots
promising	muggy	a downpour
breezy	mucky	pouring down
sea breeze	cloudy	raining hard
broken cloud	frosty	hailing
gorgeous	hazardous	sleet
lovely light	stormy	blizzard
lovely	rough	thunder
cool	gale	storm
blowy	hurricane	shower
bracing	humid	wet
blue sky	sticky	tipping down
windy		miserable

We will be revisiting words and meaning when we look at the semantic aspects of language in Chapter 9.

Morphology

It is very difficult to discuss aspects of language in isolation; we have already seen how discussion of vocabulary is closely bound up with meaning. We are now going to focus on two topics under the 'words' umbrella, but which have close links to syntax, or grammar, which is the subject of the next chapter.

The first is morphology. Morphology is the study of morphemes. A morpheme is a unit of meaning. At the beginning of this chapter, we considered whether a word can be defined as a unit of meaning, and I rejected it as a definition. One reason why it is inadequate is that the *morpheme* is a unit of meaning, and fits the definition perfectly. A morpheme may be a word, or it may be part of a word.

Free morphemes and bound morphemes

There are two kinds of morphemes: **free morphemes** and **bound morphemes**. A free morpheme can stand alone; in other words, it is a word. A bound morpheme cannot stand alone; it has to be attached to a free morpheme:

Help is a word. It is also a morpheme – it is a unit of meaning.

Because *help* is a word that can stand alone it is a free morpheme.

Helpful is a word, but it has two units of meaning: two morphemes.

Help is a free morpheme; -ful (with one l) is a morpheme because it has meaning – it means 'having the characteristics or properties of', but it cannot stand alone as a word; it has to be attached to a free morpheme or whole word. It is therefore a bound morpheme.

Take the word *unhelpfulness*. It has four morphemes – the free morpheme *help* (meaning aid, support, succour) and three bound morphemes: the prefix *un-* (a negation), the suffixes *-ful* (having the characteristics or properties of) and *-ness* (a state of). All the bound morphemes need the free morpheme to be anchored to for their meaning to be applied. If we change the free morpheme we can build a similar word – *unkindness* (we cannot fit in *-ful* this time, because the free morpheme *kind* is already an adjective).

A compound word, such as *helpmate, sunshine, cowboy* or *pancake*, is made up of two free morphemes.

Task 7.6

Make a list of compound words, spending just a few minutes. Remember that a compound word is one word, not hyphenated, made up of two free morphemes. The meaning does not necessarily derive obviously from the two parts; ladybird would be an example of this. Cover the lists below until you have finished.

Just a few suggestions:

A

cowboy	redcurrant
sunshine	grapefruit
pancake	peardrop
handbag	teardrop
butterfly	snowball
supermarket	snowflake
gooseberry	lampshade
strawberry	footprint
wallpaper	tablecloth
goldfish	waterproof
undercoat	barmaid

In written English, bound morphemes are normally represented by prefixes, such as *un-*, *re-* or *dis-*, and suffixes such as *-less*, *-ness*, or *-ing*. There are, of course, spelling rules for the attachment of these affixes and these are covered in the Written Language section of the book (Part 2).

Morpheme forms

Allomorphs

By now you will not be surprised to learn that it is not as simple as that! There is another kind of morphological structure that does not consist of two or more part-words joined to each other in a sequence. In order to understand this we need to explore the variants, or different forms of a morpheme, which are called allomorphs.

Some bound morphemes have only one form: *-less* and *-ness* are examples. Other bound morphemes have several forms. Consider, for example, the morpheme that means 'more than one' – the plural morpheme. It seems easy: it is *-s*. Or is it? Certainly, it is sometimes so.

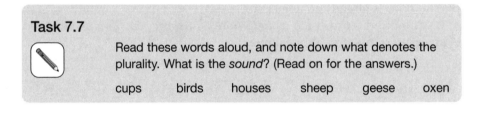

Task 7.7

Read these words aloud, and note down what denotes the plurality. What is the *sound*? (Read on for the answers.)

cups   birds   houses   sheep   geese   oxen

In cups the plural morpheme is the sound /s/, in birds it is /z/, in houses it is /iz/. These are called phonologically conditioned allomorphs; the form is influenced by the neighbouring sound.

/s/ occurs after a voiceless sound as in *cups*

/z/ occurs after a voiced sound, as in *birds*

/iz/ occurs after /s/, /z/ or /sh/, as in *houses*

Another example would be the *-ed* past tense morpheme, which may be pronounced

/t/ after a voiceless sound (*picked*)

/d/ after a voiced sound (*banged*) or

/ïd/ after /t/ or /d/ (*planted*).

The other three plurals in the list in Task 7.7 are different words, containing plurality, but it is impossible to identify any rule-governed plural markers. These are the irregular words that we all have to learn as small children, and which lead to errors in the very young, such as 'sheeps' and 'gooses'. Interestingly, I learned in the summer of 2003 (from Test Match Special, on BBC Radio 4!) that 'gooses' is an acceptable plural form in the West Indies – because the mongoose is more common than the goose, and the plural of *mongoose* is *mongooses*! I do not know if gooses would be acceptable in written West Indian English, but it offers an interesting insight into the cultural and environmental influences on language.

Inflectional and derivational morphemes

There is another distinction among bound morphemes. There are two main categories: inflectional morphemes and derivational morphemes. An inflectional morpheme adds to the existing word, so, for example, *-s* may make the word plural, as we have seen above, it may denote the third person singular in a verb (you talk; he talks), or it may make the word possessive, such as *John's*. The part of speech is unchanged; the noun is still a noun or the verb remains a verb.

Derivational morphemes

A derivational morpheme, *-ful* or *-ment* for example, when added to a free morpheme creates a new word, often a different part of speech from the free morpheme. For example, *help* is a noun, or possibly a verb, but *helpful* is an adjective; *punish* is a verb, but *punishment* is a noun. The new word does a different job in the sentence from the job done by the free morpheme from which it is derived.

Inflectional morphemes

Inflectional morphemes can be added on to derivational morphemes, but not the other way round. So we build the word *punishments* as *punish+ment+s*, not *punish+es+ment*. This may be a rather difficult concept, so there are now two tasks to help you to check if you have understood. Morphology is also revisited in the next chapter, which is about grammar.

Task 7.8

Make two lists of bound morphemes – prefixes and suffixes.

Cover the answers (overleaf) until you are ready to check.

Task 7.8
continued

A

Not an exhaustive list

Prefixes	suffixes
pre-	-ed
un-	-s
dis-	-es
bi-	-ing
de-	-er
re-	-est
in-	-ment
tri-	-less
multi-	-ness
	-ish
	-ful
	-en
	-ous
	-y
	-ly

The prefixes over- and under- are not included because they are free morphemes.

Task 7.9

Now divide the bound morphemes in my list above into inflectional morphemes (grammatical) and derivational morphemes (changing meaning and/or word category). Cover the answers until you are ready to check.

A

Inflectional	Derivational	
-ed	all prefixes	
-s	-er	-en
-es	-est	-ous
-ing	-ment	-y
	-less	-ly
	-ness	
	-ish	
	-ful	

A problem with morphemes!

In our family there is a number of 'words' that have been coined over the years by various members, based on the same device, namely to unpick the apparent morphological structure. This began when one of the children asked if there was a word 'molish' (rhymes with pŏlish, not Pōlish). We asked what it meant, and were told it was something to do with building or putting up – in fact, the opposite of *demolish*. This has given rise to *underwhelming* (meaning not very impressive – in common parlance, I think), *gruntled* (meaning pleased) and others, including my personal favourite, *one mump* (mumps, but with the swelling on only one side). Many such apparent free morphemes were, in former times, whole words, but have been lost in the linguistic changes of the centuries. It is interesting to notice that even when you can remove the prefix, the meaning is not what might be expected (consider *disgraceful* and *graceful*, for example).

Word categories

Word categories are what used to be called 'parts of speech' in grammar books. Please do not groan! Word categories are covered in more detail in Part 2, so in this chapter we will look briefly at some of the models used to categorize words according to function.

In traditional grammar books, English is said to have eight parts of speech. This is derived from old Latin grammars, themselves derived from old Greek grammars, which described eight parts of speech. There is an element of 'trimming the facts to fit the formula' about this classification. A number of models has been suggested by linguists, who prefer the term 'word categories' and that is the one we will use in Part 1 of the book.

A simple model is as follows:

- nouns, including pronouns
- verbs
- adjectives
- prepositions
- determiners (a, this, etc.)

In this there are five categories (four main ones plus determiners): nouns (which includes pronouns because they do the same job in a sentence), verbs, adjectives, prepositions and determiners (such as a, the, this, etc.). This model does not allow for adverbs. Some linguists describe the label 'adverb' as a sort of dustbin category, into which are dumped all the words that do not fit comfortably anywhere else. Nor does this system have a place for expressions such as 'Bother!' 'Hello' or 'Goodbye', but it does claim four *main* categories, so maybe there is room for the rest along the edges!

A more traditional model, but with more complexity and more possibilities for fine-tuning is as follows:

- nouns
- pronouns

- verbs
- adjectives
- adverbs
- prepositions
- conjunctions
- interjections

However, this one probably lends itself more to written language than to spoken. We have already seen how difficult classification of words can be. Some of the additional material that might be added to this model, to increase the depth of analysis, is:

- participles (*smiling*)
- articles (*the, a*)
- auxillaries (*do, be, have* and derivatives), as part of verb tense
- particles (infinitive marker *to, not*) – a dustbin class

Some complications of word categories

Word categories are not really as clear-cut as we would like. Some words behave as if they belong to another class – for example, *railway* or *bus* would normally be classified as nouns, but are used adjectivally in the phrases 'railway station' or 'bus station'. In 'Blessed are the merciful', a phrase from the Sermon on the Mount in the New Testament (St Matthew's Gospel), the word *merciful*, which on its own we would classify as an adjective, is behaving like a noun, following *the* and not apparently describing or modifying anything. However, we may say that it is modifying the implied noun *people* and that what Jesus meant was 'Blessed are the merciful people'. The film title *The Good, the Bad and the Ugly* presents the same problem.

If, by now, you need something secure to cling to, it has been suggested that the word categories noun and verb may be universal; in other words, they may appear in all languages. This is particularly interesting if you think back to the infantile grammar system we looked at in Chapter 3. The two 'words' that were put together had the function of a verb followed by a noun: 'Allgone milk', 'Allgone Daddy'.

We will look further at how the forms of words change to signify grammatical structures in the next chapter. Much of what we have said about word categories, and about morphology, leads us into a consideration of how English sentences are constructed; we call that grammar. There is more about word classes in Part 2.

Summary

In this chapter we have looked at:

- the definitions of a word
- the characteristics of words
- word origins and word relationships
- homonyms and polysemes
- how words can change in meaning over time
- the size of an individual's vocabulary
- morphology: bound and free morphemes
- word categories

CHAPTER 8

Grammatical issues

The differences between spoken and written language

This chapter is concerned with the grammar, or syntax, of spoken language, and some of the problems of describing grammatical structures in speech. In Part 2 you will learn about some of the rules that govern *written* English. Spoken language is far less rigid. We do not always speak in full sentences; in fact, we probably use fewer 'sentences' that would translate unchanged into correct written English than ones that would not! There are huge differences in style and form between written and spoken English. This book is based on a series of lectures, and in the oral version I said, 'As you listen to these talks, I wonder if you can tell which ones were recorded from notes and which were read from a script. It is quite a challenge making the jokes sound spontaneous if they have been scripted.'

Task 8.1

An interesting exercise you may like to try is to have a tape recorder running while you are having a conversation with a friend or a member of your family or describing an event to them. Then transcribe on to paper faithfully – and I mean really faithfully – what was said. Would it make good written prose? Don't forget to include all the 'erms', repetitions, and so on. You may find it difficult to transcribe accurately; most people attempting this task need to play the tape many times to achieve accuracy.

On one occasion, when my son was about two years old, he went to find his grandmother in another room, saying as he left, 'Better see ... Bromma's up to'. Grandfather, who overheard this, repeated it later to Grandmother as 'I'd better see what Grandma's up to'. Certainly, this was the sense of the utterance, but it was much more grammatically and phonologically sophisticated than what Richard actually said.

Even the most fluent and accomplished speaker does not speak in written English. Think how many of our utterances are single words or phrases. How would you analyse grammatically such exchanges as:

'Tea?'

'Please – two sugars.'

'Right.'

Is 'Morning' a sentence? In the right context we could consider it to be an abbreviated form of 'I hope you have a good morning', which can be analysed formally as a written sentence, but that is not how we speak to each other, and that is not what was said in this example.

Linguistics: descriptive, not prescriptive

Linguistics is the study of language, and it is descriptive, not prescriptive. This means that we can observe, describe, analyse and explain utterances, but the student or even the professor of linguistics does not make rules for speaking English. So a one-word utterance, or an abbreviated form, is no less valid or correct than the full, extended version. Such rules and conventions as govern spoken language serve the very important purpose of enabling communication to take place. As we have already seen, there are overlaps between aspects of language, and we will encounter the interdependence of words and sentences, of grammar and meaning, and all of them with language use. Language meaning and use are discussed in the next chapter.

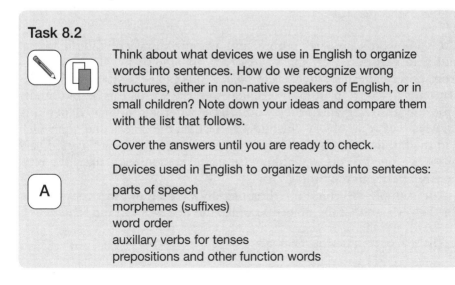

Task 8.2

Think about what devices we use in English to organize words into sentences. How do we recognize wrong structures, either in non-native speakers of English, or in small children? Note down your ideas and compare them with the list that follows.

Cover the answers until you are ready to check.

Devices used in English to organize words into sentences:

A

parts of speech
morphemes (suffixes)
word order
auxillary verbs for tenses
prepositions and other function words

The analysis of utterances

Introduction

In order to consider grammar, we will need to revisit word categories and morphology, and their role in sentence structure. Word order is particularly important in English, as is the use of function words, such as *by* and *of*. English also makes quite a lot of use of auxiliary verbs such as *to have*: 'I have been', or 'He will have done it', for example.

When we have considered word order and word structure, we will look briefly at one method of analysing sentences, to show the differences in meaning between superficially similar constructions, and to explore how to deal with complexities. Many linguists make a distinction between morphology (word structure) and syntax (word arrangement), considering the two together to be the main ingredients of English grammar. This can be quite a helpful distinction, and one you will meet again in Part 2.

Syntax

First, let us start with syntax, which for this purpose may be defined as word arrangement, or word order. This is a very important ingredient in English grammar, because English does not have case endings to indicate the function of a word in a sentence. For example, compare these two sentences:

The snake bit the dog.

The dog bit the snake.

The same words are used in both, and we only know who did the biting, and who was bitten, by the word order. In English the most common word order pattern is *subject verb object*. This can be written as an abbreviation: s → v → o. In Latin, by comparison, the words can be put in any order because *dog* and *snake* would have different endings, depending on which was the subject (the biter) and which the object (the one which had the biting done to it). If we want to depart from *subject verb object* order, we need to do something else to the sentence, to show the relationship between the protagonists.

For example, we could use the function word *by* and the passive voice for the verb, so that the object becomes the first word in the sentence.

The snake was bitten by the dog.

The dog was bitten by the snake.

In these examples, the use of the object at the beginning of the sentence brings about a subtle change in the meaning, suggesting an emphasis on the object, such as in answer to a question:

How was the snake killed?

What's happened to the dog?

Even in other constructions, the *subject verb object* pattern remains in place. Examples include:

the interrogative (question) form	*Did the dog bite the snake?*
the negative form	*The dog did not bite the snake.*
changes of tense	*The dog was going to bite the snake.*
	The dog had bitten the snake.

In most situations, the interrogative is denoted by placing the auxiliary verb at the beginning, as in the example above, but in some situations, where there is no auxiliary verb, for example, it is denoted by bringing the main verb to the beginning:

He *is* busy.

Is he busy?

Notice that another situation in which this reversal takes place is after the phrase 'not only':

Not only *is he* busy today, but he's busy all week.

This *subject verb object* pattern is the dominant pattern in about 75 per cent of known languages, and *object-first* patterns are quite unusual. Some languages have *subject object verb*, or are order free, so that the words can come in almost any order and there are markers such as case endings to identify the function of each word in the utterance. A very small number of languages has neither case endings nor rigid order rules, and the function of each word depends upon context and common sense.

Word boundaries

Of course, one of the difficulties surrounding word order is the problem we may have in identifying word boundaries. Please read the sentence below aloud; could you really tell, if you didn't understand the words, where one ended and the next began? One important difference between spoken and written language is that in spoken language there are no word boundaries, whereas in written language it is customary to leave a space between words.

Abrieflookatthissentenceillustratestheimportanceofthisconventionindecodingprint.

Because you can read English fluently, you probably had little difficulty in deciphering the last sentence, but if you could not do so, it would be a challenging sentence indeed!

Readers may remember the comedians Ronnie Barker and Ronnie Corbett's brilliant sketch, set in a hardware store, in which the humour was based on word boundaries; it began with a confusion between 'four candles' and 'fork 'andles' (handles).

Task 8.3

Look at these sentences in Swahili. How many words do they have?

Cover the answers until you are ready to check

Mimeainasitawi.
Mkateunapoa.
Wazunguwanapandamlima.

A

For interest, the sentences translate as:

Mimea inasitawi. (2 words)	'The crops are flourishing'.
Mkate unapoa. (2 words)	'The bread is cooling'.
Wazungu wanapanda mlima. (3 words)	'The Europeans (white people) are climbing the mountain'.

Word boundaries are blurred in spoken language, but essential to grammar, because word order is so important. We probably learn to perceive word boundaries by the clues we get from grammatical rules, which make words move around in the sentence and acquire morpheme endings:

The dog *chased* the cat.

The cat might *chase* the dog.

The cat was *chasing* the dog.

Did the dog *chase* the cat?

The young child learns by experience that a 'word' is a chunk that can be picked up and moved around in the utterance; the concept of 'wordness' comes long before we begin to learn literacy and discover that in written language we leave a space between words.

Morphemes

Inflectional morphemes

We need to look again at morphology and, in particular, the role of inflectional morphemes in the English grammatical system. It is the inflectional morphemes that are important to grammar – the endings that denote the plural or past tense for instance. (Remember the *derivational* morphemes change the word to a new one, usually a different part of speech, such as the noun, *happiness* from the adjective, *happy*.) Inflectional morphemes allow the word to keep its identity, but conform to grammatical constraints.

Case endings in Latin

There are many inflectional morphemes in Latin, far fewer in English. In Latin they are used to denote case, such as subject and object, as in the example

Corinna Deliam amat.	(Corinna loves Delia.)
Corinnam Delia amat.	(Delia loves Corinna.)

(Jones, 1997)

You can see how the word order in Latin remains the same and the identity of the lover and the beloved are denoted by the inflectional endings, whereas in the English translation, the words remain the same but their function in the sentence is denoted by the word order.

Case markers in English

We have a few case-related distinctions in English among the pronouns, such as those in the table below. Confusion of these, as in 'Him did it' is a common developmental error. There are also a number of regional dialectal variations, as in "I said to 'e."

SUBJECT	OBJECT
I	me
she	her
he	him
they	them

Of course, in the second person singular and the second person plural, we use the same word *you* for the subject and the object.

Phonological conditioning

Inflectional morphemes can be phonologically conditioned, that is to say they are influenced by the surrounding sounds, the phonological context. Examples include:

- adding -s to denote plural; -s may be pronounced /z/ after a voiced sound (compare cats and cars)
- adding -ed (pronounced /id/, /d/, or /t/) to denote past tense

Different endings are possible, depending on the word category; some words come in several categories, so the ending may give a clue as to the word category being used. It does not always work, however:

- *sound* (noun) may have -s added for plural (the sounds of English);
- but *sound* (verb) may also have -s added for third person singular (the bell sounds loudly);
- but *sounded* could only be a verb, because *-ed* is a verb ending.

Gradience (or how much of an adjective are you?)

Words do not always follow the rules, so the class boundaries are fuzzy. **Gradience** is the term used to describe the degree of adherence a word may have to a particular class. A word may fulfil some, but not all of the criteria of a word class. Examples include words such as *train* and *bus*, which are nouns, but are used adjectivally in a phrase like *train station* or *bus station*. In this context, the words train and bus fulfil only a few of the criteria for adjectives:

- They cannot have *-ly* added to form adverbs.
- They cannot be preceded by modifiers such as *very*.
- They do not have comparative or superlative forms, as many adjectives do.

Word	Capable of -ly ending?	Capable of modifier (very)?	Comparative/ superlative
bus	no	no	no
train	no	no	no
anxious	anxiously	very anxious	more/most
big	no	very big	bigger/biggest

The identification of word class

Some words can belong to several classes, and need the context (meaning) to help to identify the class they belong to in this situation. Sometimes an inflectional morpheme helps, as in the example *sounded* that we had above. A further aid in identifying which class a word belongs to is its position in the sentence. For example, adjectives usually come before nouns ('a green carpet', not 'a carpet green'). Adverbs more commonly come after verbs ('to run quickly' is more usual than 'to quickly run'). Word order helps to identify a part of speech because parts of speech have their own places in the sentence.

Agreement

Word order is critical because we do not use agreement, for example, between an adjective and the noun it is modifying. In many languages, the adjective would take a feminine or a plural ending for a feminine or a plural noun. For example, in French:

un chien noir	*a black dog* (masculine singular noun)
une vache noire	*a black cow* (feminine singular noun)
les chiens noirs	*the black dogs* (masculine plural noun)
les vaches noires	*the black cows* (feminine plural noun)

Notice how the French adjective *noir* is different in each sentence, while the English adjective, *black*, remains the same.

In English, agreement is necessary particularly in pronouns and in verb endings 'He sit', for example, would be recognized as not agreeing, and therefore wrong.

The awkward squad

We can run into difficulties when language seems to be failing to obey the morphological rules. Let us consider a few examples.

- Rule: We use *s* to denote plural.
  But what about *scissors* and *trousers*? Can we talk about one scissor, or one trouser? When my son was very small he had mumps, but with the swelling on only one side. When someone commiserated with him, 'I hear you have mumps', he replied, 'Oh no, only one mump!'
  Compare the words *oats* and *barley*. They are both crops, and have similar uses. But is *oats* plural? Can it be singularized? It seems it can, in compound words such as *oatmeal* and *oatcake*, and in a phrase such as *oat biscuits*.

- Rule: We sometimes use Latin plurals for words of Latin origin.
  The word *media* is the plural form of the word *medium*, and a medium of communication may be email, the telephone, and so on. When we use the word *media* now, we usually mean the mass media: radio, television and the newspapers. We often use the word as if it were singular: 'the media is' rather than 'the media are' and I have heard someone refer to 'all the medias'. Language is constantly changing, and I suspect that it is only a matter of time before *media* becomes a grammatically singular collective noun in English, like *furniture* or *fruit*.

- Rule: We use the past tense for things that have happened in the past. But do we? What about headlines?
  We find phrases such as 'Actress marries boy next door', or 'Plane crashes in sea', quite acceptable in newspapers.
  People often relate personal anecdotes in the present tense: 'So there I am, up to my knees in mud, when along comes Henry...'.

Morphology and acronyms

One interesting aspect of morphology is the way we treat acronyms. Let us take two examples: Ofsted (The Office for Standards in Education) and SPAD (a signal passed at danger, a term heard in the context of railway accidents). If we were referring to the contribution Ofsted has made, we would say 'Ofsted's contribution', placing the apostrophe at the end. If we were to extend it, we would say 'The Office for Standards in Education's contribution', with the apostrophe at the end, not as we might expect, 'The Office's for Standards in Education contribution'. We would however, say 'The Office's contribution'.

If an acronym is pluralized, the plural morpheme goes on the end, as in 'The number of SPADs has been reduced by 35 per cent in the last six months', but if the acronym were extended, the plural would go on to the noun: 'The number of signals passed at danger...', which is unlike the apostrophe example above.

We treat acronyms as if they were real words, and give them morphological structures, so they fit neatly into sentences. However, how we treat them when we expand them to use all the words depends on the morphological structure being applied. This is another illustration of how difficult it is to apply the rules universally.

Other grammatical features

Syntax, or word arrangement, and morphology, or word structure, are the main features of English grammar. Let us now move on to consider some of the other ingredients, and along the way think about some of the anomalies.

Gender

The first feature to consider is gender, and how we represent gender differences in language.

Gender is not necessarily linked to sex. Obviously, when we use he for a man, she for a woman, he for a bull and she for a cow, we are relating gender labels directly to the gender of the person or animal being referred to. However, we sometimes hear ships, and even cars, being referred to as *she* by their affectionate owners.

In German, there are three gender labels, masculine (*der*), feminine (*die*) and neuter (*das*). A man would be '*der* Herr', a woman would be '*die* Frau', but a girl is '*das* Mädchen'. Not only in English are gender labels not strictly related to the gender of the subject.

In English we do not use gender markers in the definite and indefinite article, as happens in many languages: *a*, *an* and *the* apply to all.

Mood

Mood is sometimes referred to in grammar books, especially older books. In particular, those of us who learned French many years ago learned the subjunctive, and learned to dread it on the examination paper! In my (1930) copy of *Fowler's English Usage* the subjunctive mood is described as 'virtually extinct'. I think that, 75 years on, we may safely forget about it. The only common usage is the phrase 'If I were', which indicates some meaning difference from the indicative (usual) form, 'I was'. We do not normally use 'I were' in any other circumstances. A well-known example is a verse from the Christmas carol 'In the bleak mid-winter':

> What can I bring him
> Poor as I am?
> If I were a shepherd,
> I would bring a lamb.
> If I were a wise man,
> I would do my part...'

The phrase 'if I were' indicates that the writer is not in fact a shepherd or a wise man.

Person

Personal pronouns – *I*, *me*, *you* – vary according to case, as we have established above. There has been an interesting change over time in the use of the second person singular, from *thee* and *thou*, to *you*. In the past the verb 'to be', in the present tense, would have been:

I am	we are
thou art	you (plural or formal) are
he/she/it is	they are

This form remains in some very traditional liturgy, which may be why many believe it, erroneously, to be formal! Referring to the Almighty as 'Thou' was an expression of familiarity or personal closeness. 'You' was reserved for formal address, and for the plural, when addressing more than one person. This distinction remains in French, with the use of 'tu' for family, close friends and the Godhead, and 'vous' for others as well as for the plural form. There was nothing respectful or formal about 'Thou art a knave!'. A modern translation would be 'You're an idiot!'

We normally use the pronoun 'we' to refer to a group of people in which we are included. However, in another departure from the rules, a mother may pick up her crying baby and say 'We're a bit grumpy this morning, aren't we?'. Remember that this part of the book is about spoken language – about what real people actually say, so we should not be surprised that so much of it defies our attempts to tidy it up into neat grammatical analysis.

Agreement

In English, there is not much agreement between words in sentences, though in some languages it is very common. For example, in French, adjectives have to agree with the nouns they modify. In English, adjectives normally precede nouns, so there is a word order link, making it relatively easy to understand which noun is being modified.

There is some agreement in verbs, depending on person and number, such as the inflectional morpheme -*s* in the third person singular:

I walk

you walk

he walks

Even in verbs, there is very little difference compared with many languages. This can lead to some ambiguity; consider the following example:

The dress came in a box. It was brown.

We are left not knowing whether the dress or the box was brown.

Function words

These are the small, grammatical words that indicate relationships between parts of the sentence. They make syntactic links, for example, between phrases and clauses. Words such as *by*, *of*, *that*, *who* and *for* come into this category. Consider the difference in meaning between these two:

A basket *of* clothes

A basket *for* clothes

Auxiliary verbs

These are a very important feature of the English tense system. In particular, we use the verbs *to be* and *to have*, in association with the present or past participle.

Think how infrequently we use the simple present tense. Take the example of the verb *to clean*:

I clean the bathroom (means *on Tuesdays*, or *if I have to*, and denotes a habitual activity)

I am cleaning the bathroom (means *I am doing it as I speak*, and denotes present activity)

I am cleaning the bathroom *when I've finished making the bed* (means I will do it in future).

Similarly,

I'm phoning her at eight (uses the present continuous tense to denote future activity)

I'm going out later (is an apparent contradiction for the same reason)

I'm retiring in two years' time (can be used even for activity in the quite distant future).

The simple present tense is used only in the first example; in the others the verb *to be* is used as an auxiliary, with the present participle, which normally ends in -ing. Other examples include:

I am going to clean (future)

I was going to clean (but now I'm not)

I have been cleaning (past, continuous, or is it still going on?)

I was cleaning (when she arrived)

I had cleaned (by the time she got home).

Complex tense structures are used to add levels of meaning to utterances about activity. There are layers of information in this construction:

I *have been meaning to clean* (indicates intention, continuous and ongoing)

A new verb in the language?

Anyone who spends time with older children or young adults will recognize this one! There is a trend to replace the verb *to say* with the verb *to be like*. Sceptics have only to listen in on a conversation at the bus stop, which may go something like this:

'He was like "What are you doing this evening?" and I was like "Staying in and washing my hair", and he was like "Don't do that – why don't you come down to the pub?" and I was like "Well, I don't know – I'll see".'

You can see that in each case, 'said' has been replaced with 'was like'. Yes, it really happens. It will be interesting to see whether this construction survives the test of time and passes into the language, or whether it will turn out to have been a passing phase.

Task 8.4

Choose a verb and make a list of sentences, illustrating as many different tense variations as you can. Don't worry about the names of the tenses; the object of the exercise is to get a feel for the range of possibilities. You may use the auxiliary verbs *to be*, *to do*, *to go* and *to have*. There are 20 variations on the verb *to cook* below; this is not an exhaustive list.

Cover the answers until you are ready to check.

A

I cook	I will have cooked
I am cooking	I am going to have cooked
I am going to have been cooking	I will cook
I will be cooking	I was going to cook
I am going to cook	I was going to be cooking
I was going to have cooked	I cooked
I was going to have been cooking	I have cooked
I will have been cooking	I had cooked
I have been going to cook	I did cook
I have been cooking	I had been cooking

How to set about analysing utterances

What is a sentence?

Task 8.5

At this point, stop and try to define a sentence. Never mind about capital letters and full stops; think about a spoken sentence. Cover the paragraph below until you have finished.

David Crystal (1994: 94) defines a sentence as follows: 'a sentence is ... the largest unit to which syntactic rules apply'. He quotes Bloomfield (1933), who says that

> a sentence is 'an independent linguistic form, not included by virtue of any grammatical construction in any larger linguistic form'.

The key word is *larger*. The problem in defining sentences is not how big it has to be but how small. The important question is 'When does one sentence become two?' The answer is, when the two parts could stand alone, and each could form a complete syntactic unit, or sentence. A syntactic unit is a group of words that goes together, and is capable of syntactic analysis. The biggest group of words that can stand alone and be analysed as a sentence, is a sentence; anything over and above that has to be another sentence.

It is possible to have one-word sentences or sentence-type utterances. In identifying a sentence in spoken language, we have to take into account the fact that some utterances are incomplete because it is unnecessary to repeat what has gone before, immediately or maybe in the past. For example, 'Tea?' means, and is understood to mean 'Would you like some tea?'

Consider the question and answer:

'What are you doing?'

'Sewing.'

The answer stands for the complete sentence 'I am sewing', which has been made unnecessary by the form of the question. This kind of utterance is called an elliptical sentence.

Two ways of analysing utterances

We will look briefly at two different ways of analysing sentences: constituent analysis, and generative, or transformational, grammar.

A morpheme is the smallest syntactic unit; constituent analysis breaks down a sentence into its morphemes. We start by looking for large units: groups of words, such as clauses or phrases. The clauses, or phrases, are broken down into individual words, which are in turn broken down into morphemes.

It is possible to have a sentence with two or more sentence-like structures within it; these are called clauses. A clause is like a sentence, in that it has a main verb, but it cannot usually stand alone ('which came yesterday'). A phrase is a group of words, such an adjectival phrase ('green apples'), or a noun phrase ('the door'), that does not have the characteristics of a sentence.

It is possible to combine an infinite number of clauses into one large sentence by the use of conjunctions; these are called complex sentences, and we will return to them below.

Generative grammar (Chomsky, 1957) is an approach to linguistic analysis that seeks to produce a set of 'rules' (descriptors) that can generate any sentence in the language. It is a more complex, but more creative way of looking at structure.

Constituent analysis

Constituent analysis means analysing the constituent parts of a sentence until they cannot be further reduced. Take, for example, 'The cat sat on the mat':

- *The* and *cat* go together; it is a noun phrase, which stands for a noun, and could be replaced by a noun, *Felix*, for example, or a pronoun, *he*.
- *Sat on the mat* is a verb phrase, because it has a verb at its head. Again, it could be replaced by one verb, such as *slept*, so the function of the verb phrase is the same as that of a verb.
- We can further break down *sat on the mat* into the verb, *sat* and an adverbial phrase, *on the mat*, qualifying *sat*. It could be replaced by a single adverb, such as *quietly*.

Once a sentence has been analysed to the level of the morpheme, it can be represented by a tree diagram, which shows the analysis of each part.

For example, here is the constituent analysis of the sentence 'The dog bit the snake':

1. Divide the sentence into two phrases
(The dog   bit the snake)

2. Subdivide the second (verb) phrase
(bit   the snake)
Keep dividing, e.g. bit
(bite   -ed)

3. Divide the noun phrase (the noun and its article)
(The   dog)

4. Divide the other noun and its article
(the   snake)

Now all the parts are analysed and you can show it as a tree diagram (see Figure 8.1).

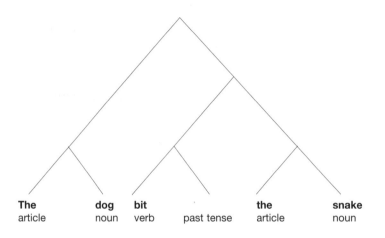

The   **dog** **bit**   **the**   **snake**
article   noun verb   past tense   article   noun

Figure 8.1 Tree diagram representing the analysis of 'The dog bit the snake'.

Generative grammar

Generative grammar has gone through several changes since Chomsky's early work, but it is based on the model that a sentence has a surface structure and a deep structure. It is possible to say the same thing in different ways, by changing the surface structure. This is achieved by a series of 'transformations', which are the rules that show the changes that would have to take place to transform one sentence to another, with the same meaning. The change from active to passive would be a good example:

The dog chased the cat.

The cat was chased by the dog.

Transformational grammar also enables us to take a pattern 'rule' and generate other sentences from it; therefore sentences can be generated with the same surface structure but different deep structure. For example,

The fast train was very late.

The green apples are slightly sour.

Our cricket team played quite brilliantly.

It can help us with ambiguity, such as in the sentence:

> Rolling stones can cause accidents.

We can access the two deep structures that are being represented by a single surface structure:

> You may cause an accident if you roll stones.
> Stones that are rolling can cause accidents.

The way that generative grammar represents the 'rules' for generating grammatical sentences is by a series of symbols, which look rather like mathematical or scientific formulae. There are many excellent and accessible introductions to Chomsky's work available. The internet website obtained by typing 'Chomsky' into a search engine is especially useful.

Complex sentences

So far we have considered mainly simple sentences. There are two kinds of complex sentences: conjoined, or co-ordinated, and embedded, or subordinate. Both can exist on their own, together, or in multiple forms, so it is possible to use the same construction over and over again to form a huge sentence. This repetition is called recursion. A good example of this is the children's poem, 'I know an old lady who swallowed a fly'; there is a line something like this: 'She swallowed the dog to catch the cat; she swallowed the cat to catch the bird; she swallowed the bird to catch the spider ... she swallowed the spider to catch the fly ...'. And it goes on for several more verses, until she swallows a horse ('She's dead, of course'). The children's story, *The House that Jack Built*, is similar, in ending with an enormously long sentence. Somewhere in the middle comes 'This is the cat that ate the rat that ate the mouse that lived in the house that Jack built'. It would be possible to go on adding *and* or *that* so that a sentence could go on indefinitely. The logical outcome of this is that it is possible to generate an infinite number of sentences.

Conjoined sentences

Conjoined sentences are those which are joined in sequence by a conjunction, such as *and*, *but*, *because* or *if*.

> The children came in.   It was raining.
> The children came in *because* it was raining.

They may be conjoined by a semicolon:

> He turned on the lamp.   The room filled with light.
> He turned on the lamp; the room filled with light.

The conjunction may be replaced by a phrase:

I am giving you a light sentence.   You co-operated with the police.

I am giving you a light sentence *in view of the fact that* you co-operated with the police.

Various sequences are possible:

In view of the fact that you co-operated with the police, I am giving you a light sentence.

A common error in written language is to attempt to conjoin two sentences with a comma; this is incorrect punctuation. An example would be to rewrite the earlier sentence with a comma where I have placed the semicolon (see p. 126).

Embedded sentences

In this construction, one sentence or clause is embedded inside the other. For example:

The train is going to Reading.   The train is running late.

The train, *which is going to Reading*, is running late.

Two sentences are joined into one, but one is buried within the other, not following on at the end. They are normally marked by the use of *that*, *which*, *who*, or by a conjunction and the absence of a pronoun.

Let us look at an example which demonstrates how, not only can multiple conjoined or embedded sentences occur, but they can both occur in the same sentence:

The plumber came yesterday. (simple sentence)

The plumber mended the tap. (simple sentence)

The plumber came yesterday and mended the tap. (conjoined sentence)

The plumber who lives in Mullion came yesterday. (embedded sentence)

The plumber who lives in Mullion came yesterday and mended the tap. (both)

The plumber who lives in Mullion and drives a white BMW came yesterday and mended the tap because it wouldn't turn off. (both x 2)

Let's look at it another way. Each clause is in a different typeface. *The original sentence is in bold italic*:

Original sentence

Embedded clause 1

Embedded clause 2

CONJOINED CLAUSE 1

Conjoined clause 2

The plumber who lives in Mullion *and drives a white BMW* ***came yesterday*** AND MENDED THE TAP because it wouldn't turn off.

Summary

In this chapter we have looked at:

- the difference between spoken and written language
- syntax (word order)
- the boundaries between words
- inflectional morphemes
- case endings
- putting words in the right class
- agreement
- exceptions ('the awkward squad')
- the morphology of acronyms
- other grammatical issues: mood, person, agreement, auxiliary verbs
- analysing utterances by constituent analysis
- analysing utterances by transformational grammar
- complex sentences

CHAPTER 9

Language meaning and use

Introduction

In this chapter, we tackle some of the less tangible and structured aspects of language. When we looked at phonology there were patterns, and things were predictable, if rather complicated. Vocabulary, too, was reasonably governed by logic, though when we got to grammar it began to hang together rather loosely and we saw how difficult it could be to fit things into neat categories with clearly defined boundaries. This chapter is about **semantics** and **pragmatics**; semantics is the study of the meaning of language, and pragmatics is the study of language use.

Jean Walker once commented to me that making sense of a complex and multifaceted topic was 'like knitting fog'. I hope this will not be your experience! There are many examples provided to illustrate the points.

Semantics

Semantics has come to have pejorative overtones; we sometimes use it to mean verbal sophistry, or quibbling, or playing with words, usually to win an argument. For example, a politician who is trying to avoid giving a straightforward answer to a question in an interview may be told by the interviewer 'That's just semantics'. It may be that the interviewee is using a form of words that implies either 'yes' or 'no', but avoids having to say it.

Semantics in the sense we are using it here has no such emphasis; it is the study of meaning in words and sentences. We have already referred to meaning when talking about words, and again when looking at grammar, but we are now more concerned with meaning at the level of the whole utterance, and meaning above and beyond the simple and superficial.

The lexeme

There is a useful term to learn in this context: the **lexeme** or **lexical item**. A lexeme is a unit of meaning. It is not the same as a word because, for example, *eat*, *eats*, *ate*, *eating*, *eaten* are five words, but having the same root, *eat*, and are variations made only for grammatical purposes. They constitute one single lexeme. When we use several words to mean one thing, such as *boa constrictor*, or *orang-utan*, which are inseparable units of meaning, they are two-word lexemes. Similarly, *to fall asleep*, means a single activity (if you can call falling asleep an activity); it is one verb, but two words, therefore one unit of meaning, or lexeme. You could say that in my example in the previous chapter, *to be like* in that context is one lexeme synonymous with *to say*.

Semantic fields

Some linguists have tried, with variable success, to classify lexemes into categories called **semantic fields**. For example, lexemes are put into groups under headings such as clothes, furniture, parts of the body, and so on. It is very easy for some things, but for others, impossible. For instance, does watercolour painting come in hobbies, art forms, professions, or another category?

Semantic fields were used by Peter Roget to devise his Thesaurus of 1852, still widely used today. You can see how it is of limited value, because it fails to deal with subtleties of meaning. Do you remember my story of walking in the Pyrenees and missing the nuances that would have told us what sort of path, road or whatever we were looking for? That leads us on neatly to synonyms.

Synonyms

Synonyms have to be considered under the heading of semantics. There are many words that we may, on first consideration, call synonyms, such as road, street and avenue or sea and ocean, but on closer inspection we realize that there are overtones to each that would lead us to select one in preference to the other in a given context. There are remarkably few perfect synonyms; German measles and Rubella, or cancer and carcinoma would fit the criteria, being popular and technical names for the same illness.

Task 9.1

Spend a few minutes making a list of synonyms. First, list any true synonyms you can think of, then a list of near-synonyms. There is a list of some examples below; you may like to decide which are true synonyms and which only approximations. Cover the following list until you are ready to check.

Task 9.1
continued

A

Rubella	German measles
cancer	carcinoma
melody	tune
stream	brook
hurry	hasten
rapidly	quickly
old	ancient
engine	locomotive
help	assist
help	aid
walk	perambulate
trip	stumble
raincoat	Mackintosh
raincoat	waterproof
pants	knickers

Synonyms and context

Let us next consider synonyms in context. Suppose we take a sentence such as

John broke the stick.

Compare it with

John snapped the stick.

We appear to treat *broke* and *snapped* as synonyms. If we say

John broke into the house.

We cannot use the same synonym to make the statement

John snapped into the house.

What about these two sentences?

John took his camera and snapped the children playing.

John took his camera and broke the children playing.

Synonymity depends substantially upon context.

The problem of word definitions

Linguists have struggled continually to find fixed ways of defining and classifying words. For example, what is a sofa? It is something you sit on. Yes, but you can also sit on a grassy bank. Is a grassy bank a sofa?

Let us try saying a sofa is a piece of furniture you sit on. This is limited again; I often sit on the edge of the table when I'm giving a lecture, or on the edge of the bed to do up my shoes. Is a sofa, then, a piece of furniture designed for sitting on? That is getting closer, but what about a stool or a chair?

The next problem concerns words that look and sound the same; are they the same word with different meanings, or different words with the same shape? Dictionaries are based on the assumption that they can be either.

Homonyms

Homonyms are said to be different words with the same shape; in other words, the meaning and derivation are totally unrelated. An example would be *bank*, which can be a place where money is deposited, as in 'the high street banks', or the land at the edge of the river, 'the banks of the Nile'. Another example would be *nap*, a word we looked at in the vocabulary topic, where the progression from two different sources has resulted in the same string of phonemes in English. We consider these to be two different words.

Polysemes

Polysemes are said to exist where one lexeme (remember a lexeme is a unit of meaning) has several meanings in English, or that common origins have led to one word doing service several times over. *Chip* is a good example: 'a chip (of potato)', 'a chip (of wood)' and 'a microchip' clearly have the same antecedents. We consider them to be the same word with different meanings.

It may be a little easier to understand if we use the analogy of people's surnames. Not everyone called Cooper is related, though many will be if we look far enough back. However, one set of related Coopers (no matter how distantly) descends from a maker of barrels (a cooper). Another set of Coopers got their name from the Norman French arrival called Coupe, which became Anglicized. The two sets of Coopers are not related, even distantly, despite having the same name.

This has happened much more recently, when European refugees from Nazi persecution settled in England and Anglicized their names. I knew a family called Freeman, whose parents were German, with the family name Friedmann, but they changed to what happens to be a very old English name, easily traceable to serfs and freed men.

Homophones and homographs

There are words that are part-homonyms, called **homophones**, such as *see* and *sea*, which sound the same but are spelled differently and

homographs, that are spelled the same but pronounced differently, such as *wind* and *sow*. We have no difficulty in treating both as different and separate words, despite their common features.

A memory tip
One way to remember it is that the homo- group of labels (homonyms, homophones, homographs) are different words, with different origins, but with one or both features in common. Polysemes are the same word with different meanings, but they are in some way related.

Task 9.2

Spend a few minutes making a list of homophones and homo-graphs. (There are more homophones than homographs.) Look at the words below; are they homonyms or polysemes? You can look them up in a dictionary to discover their origin.

Cover the answers (overleaf) until you are ready to check.

fly	insect	(noun)
fly	go by air	(verb)
drive	operate a car	(verb)
drive	wide tarmac path	(noun)
nap	short sleep	(noun)
nap	pile on velvet	(noun)
page	boy in procession	(noun)
page	sheet of paper	(noun)
well	water-hole	(noun)
well	healthy	(adjective)
course	programme of study	(noun)
course	route of a river	(noun)

Here are some examples:

HOMOPHONES	HOMOGRAPHS
sea/see	wind
carve/calve	sow
rain/reign	contract
sow/sew/so	collect
doe/dough	puss
bear/bare	Polish
beer/bier	
pane/pain	
brows/browse	
male/mail	

Task 9.2	fly	insect	(noun)	polysemes
continued	fly	go by air	(verb)	
	drive	operate a car	(verb)	polysemes
A	drive	wide tarmac path	(noun)	
	nap	short sleep	(noun)	homonyms
	nap	pile on velvet	(noun)	
	page	boy in procession	(noun)	homonyms
	page	sheet of paper	(noun)	
	well	water-hole	(noun)	homonyms
	well	healthy	(adjective)	
	course	programme of study	(noun)	polysemes
	course	route of a river	(noun)	

The meaning of sentences

Now we move away from single words and on to what is, I think, the easier part of semantics: the meaning of sentences. It is certainly much funnier, as you will soon see. Remember that we are using the word 'sentences' rather loosely, to mean a string of words, an utterance; it may even be a very short string of one word! Bear in mind that we are in the area of spoken language, so we have no punctuation to help us, though we do have the prosodic features of language such as stress, intonation, volume, pitch and tone.

Let us consider a simple sentence with three meanings.

That's nice.   (statement of fact)

That's nice?   (is it? – question)

That's nice.   (sarcastic – it isn't)

The difference lies in the intonation patterns: there is a rise at the end of *nice* ↗ in the question, and undue emphasis on the words plus the fall on *nice* ↘ in the third example, to denote irony or sarcasm.

One way in which we recognize sentences as not acceptable, sensible, or meaningful is by spotting contradictions, or mutually exclusive lexemes. Returning to lexemes for a moment, many of them can be said to contain several elements of meaning. Take, for example:

- man: encompasses the characteristics male, adult, human
- bull: encompasses male, adult, cattle
- actress: encompasses female, adult, member of acting profession
- boy: encompasses male, young, human.

Each of these words has at least the three elements, which are clear and identifiable, until you get to the boundaries of the definition: is Neanderthal man a man, being adult and male (but is he yet human?). Is a 16-year-old youth a boy or a man?

'The man is an actress' does not work as a meaningful utterance because, although it is perfectly constructed in terms of sounds, words and grammar, *man* (essentially male) contradicts *actress*, which is essentially female.

Another example might be 'The parcel arrived tomorrow', where the lexical elements in *arrived* include past time and those in *tomorrow* include future time. It does not make sense.

In some cases the utterance causes difficulties of interpretation because it is genuinely ambiguous. Take the sentence:

Helping children can be tiresome.

More information is needed to ascertain whether the children are helping or being helped.

Interpretation of meaning

Interpretation of meaning is a learned skill; adults can, in normal circumstances, deal with very sophisticated layers of meaning in utterances. For example, you can easily tell that these two sentences mean essentially the same thing:

You are not permitted to deposit your refuse in this garbage receptacle.

You can't put your muck in our dustbin.

Task 9.3

Here is a version of a well-known song, taken and adapted from Jean Aitchison's book *Teach Yourself Linguistics* (1987a). Can you recognize it?

Scintillate, scintillate, globule lucific,
Fain would I fathom thy nature specific,
Elevated excessively beyond that planet, from the solar source
    the third,
Resembling in the firmament a colourless crystal of carbon,
    excessively hard.

Cover the answer until you have finished.

A   Twinkle twinkle little star,
    How I wonder what you are,
    Up above the world so high,
    Like a diamond in the sky.

Deep and surface structure, and meaning

The example above can be explained in the language of Chomsky's Transformational Grammar as two utterances in which the surface structures are different, but the deep structure is the same. We are indebted to Chomsky for demonstrating that sentences with perfectly formed structure (sounds, words, morphology and syntax), can collapse at the level of meaning. One of his examples is the sentence 'Colourless green ideas sleep furiously', which fulfils all the criteria for an acceptable English sentence, except meaning.

Task 9.4

You will need a dictionary for this activity, in which you will generate a random sentence, by inserting randomly chosen words into a given framework.

1st word	select *a* or *the*
2nd word	open the dictionary at random in the first half and select the first adjective on that page
3rd word	select the last noun on that page
4th word	open the dictionary at random in the second half and select the first verb on that page; use the third person singular, present tense
5th word	select the first adverb on that page; if no adverb, select the first adjective to which you can add *-ly*
6th word	select a preposition (*in*, *on*, *over*, *between*, etc.)
7th word	use *a* or *the*, whichever you did not select as the first word
8th word	let the dictionary fall open near the middle and select the first adjective on the page
9th word	look up, and write the name of the first thing (noun) your eyes fall on

Now read your sentence; it should be grammatically correct, but probably does not make sense.

This surface structure could generate such diverse sentences as:

A small boy stood timidly beside the open door.

A thick fog hung persistently over the old town.

The beautiful woman dressed elegantly in a black gown.

We use our knowledge of the semantic properties of words to make big pictures out of small utterances, and to deduce a great deal of information from a few words.

For example, suppose I were to say, 'On holiday I watched a lion kill a zebra'. You will be able to put together a story from your knowledge and experience of the world:

- I spent my holiday in Africa (or in a badly managed safari park perhaps!)
- I went on safari in the bush.
- I saw a powerful, carnivorous, large cat ending the life of a black and white striped horse-like mammal, probably a member of a herd, probably at the end of a chase, and that the lion would doubtless eat the carcass.
- You will also surmise that the lion's motive was hunger, not anger or self-defence, and you are unlikely to be shocked, because you know that this is part of everyday events in these parts.
- You will also surmise that unless I am very foolish or very brave, I probably witnessed the spectacle from some distance, or from the safety of a vehicle.

All that information comes from nine words! If you have been in the African bush, or seen such things on a television programme, you will probably have a fairly clear and accurate picture in your mind of the situation I told you about, although I did not include any description.

Consider, on the other hand, the difference in your response if the sentence had been, 'On holiday I saw a dog kill a sheep'. Your mental picture is more likely to be of a British landscape, irresponsible dog-owner and angry farmer; your feelings are probably closer to shock or outrage at something that should not have happened. The surface structure of the sentences is identical, and so is most of the vocabulary. Spoken language is a very efficient way of communicating information and generating thoughts and emotions.

Task 9.5

How much information can you deduce from this sentence? Some of it will be certain, and some probable:

My Granny is picking Jack up from school and taking him to the beach, so John can close the shop early and come with me for my 32-week scan.

Cover the answer (overleaf) until you have finished.

Task 9.5 This is the most obvious information to be inferred from the
continued   sentence; there is probably more:

A

It is a woman speaking. She is likely to be fairly young, as her grandmother is still alive, and fit to care for a small child. She is married, or
in a long-term relationship with John, and has a son, Jack, who is at
least 3 or 4 years old, as he goes to school. She is likely to be
between early 20s and early 30s, and 32 weeks' pregnant. It is likely
to be spring or summer (or not in the UK) and during term-time. If it
is in England, the new baby will have a summer or autumn birthday.
The woman has a supportive partner, and some family living or
staying nearby. They live on or near the coast, and own (probably) a
small shop. The hospital appointment is in the afternoon. It is a
contemporary or fairly recent account.

Funny, silly or absurd

We use our knowledge of semantic properties to reject nonsensical utterances such as those we considered a few minutes ago. The same skill
comes into action when we make puns, make or understand jokes and all
sorts of verbal humour, intentional and unintentional. This is a real conversation I heard only this week:

'She phoned me while I was mowing the lawn, and then complained
because I didn't answer the phone – she didn't seem to understand.'

'Doesn't she mow her lawn?'

'No, she's got shingles.'

'Oh, and they don't need mowing I suppose.'

'Don't be silly dear, they're on her upper body.'

Many jokes are based on synonyms. I married into a family of literalists,
who insist on interpreting messages literally, or in what seems to them the
most obvious meaning; this has provided a rich source of examples in
semantics.

Notices containing instructions, such as road signs, being necessarily
brief, are often ambiguous, though the meaning is perfectly obvious in
context:

'Use both lanes', or 'Use all three lanes' (at the same time?)

'Look out for cyclists on roundabout' (what should I do if I find one?)

Descending the several hundred steps down to the Blue John Cavern in
Derbyshire I heard a soft 'moo' beside me. I turned a raised eyebrow

towards my husband, who innocently pointed to a notice on the roof that read 'Low occasionally'. It will not be necessary, I am sure, to spell out what mental pictures were conjured up by the following:

> A radio news item during the Falklands war that began 'Prince Andrew has been flying round the clock in the South Atlantic'.

> There was a headline in The Sun newspaper, at about the same time, which read 'The Sun says knickers to Argentina!'

> During the Olympics, a radio sports journalist told listeners 'Today there's expected to be a nail-biting contest between...'

Some genuinely misleading statements can arise from grammatical or other errors. My children collected these two on South West Trains in their student days:

> 'We apologise for the late running of this service. This is due to a man being taken off the train which was taken poorly at Taunton.'

> 'For the benefit of passengers travelling on into Cornwall, the buffet will close at Plymouth.'

We think it was probably the man who was taken poorly, but we are still trying to decide if closing the buffet car before Cornwall, was not, after all, a benefit!

Figurative and idiomatic language

Small children have difficulty with figurative and idiomatic language such as 'pull your socks up' or 'it's raining cats and dogs'. Quite often, we do not actually say what we mean. This brings us to the area of pragmatics, the study of language use.

Pragmatics

The overlap with meaning

First we will consider some of the overlap between semantics and pragmatics and then go on to look at some of the other aspects of language use.

The implied imperative

Consider these three statements:

> It's rather chilly in here.
> I wonder if you'd mind if we closed the window.
> For goodness' sake shut that window.

All are designed to achieve the same end: to get the window closed. 'Please close the window' would be the most economical way of getting the message across, but would be perceived by native English speakers as rather abrupt in most contexts. The first is a very formal coded message, the second an implied imperative, disguised as an indirect question, the third is direct, and would be likely to be used with intimates, where the convolutions of polite society can, to an extent, be dispensed with.

Decoding the first message through to an action requires several logic leaps to be made; the window is not even mentioned:

> She's cold → the window is open → she'd like the window shut → she isn't going to shut it herself → do it.

The second is less convoluted, having 'closing the window' in the question. The hearer needs to work through the extraneous information to reach the essential message:

> (*I wonder*) (*if you'd mind*) clos(*ing*) the window → do it.

In the third one, there is very little extra language to discard:

> (*For goodness' sake*) shut the window → do it.

Of course, our processing of language is fast and efficient, and we are well used to such procedures, so we work through the code with no difficulty. It is more difficult for non-native speakers.

Teachers often use coded messages, such as 'Would you like to clean the board?' To this the most obvious response ought to be 'no thank you', but most children correctly interpret the implied imperative in the question, jump up and clean the board, whether they'd like to or not. You may have had a similar experience when the dentist's assistant says 'Would you like to come through now?'

Redundancy

One of the difficulties in language meaning and use is that of redundancy. We have already considered how much information can be gleaned from a brief utterance, and we use this to cut down our utterances to a minimum. One instruction, for example, can subsume several others. People with semantic-pragmatic disorder, which is a difficulty in language meaning and use, and those on the autistic spectrum can have particular problems in this area.

A young man with autism described recently some of his difficulties at school, including this one: if the teacher said 'Sit down', he did just that, wherever he happened to be. He often found himself sitting on the floor while everyone else was on a chair or at a desk. He was not told to sit on his chair, at his desk, so he did not realize that these instructions were subsumed, by convention, into the one that was given.

Words and messages

A young boy with semantic-pragmatic disorder was hovering round in the kitchen, getting in the way, while his mother was trying to cook a meal. She told him, not unkindly, to go away. He was later found in his room, distraught. On questioning, they discovered that he thought his mother was sending him away *for ever*, and that he was being banished from the family home.

Anyone who is, or has ever been, the parent of a teenager will recognize this exchange:

'It's Emma's party on Sunday and I really, really want to go.'

'Do you think that's a good idea, with school the next morning?'

'You never let me do *anything*!'

The parent has opened up the discussion, and has not, up to now, banned the young person from going to the party. The perception, however, is that a ban has already been issued. The question is not answered, and the response is to something which has not been said, or at least not yet. This illustrates how the actual words spoken can be relatively unimportant to the communication act. Consider how often we use questions such as:

What's that supposed to mean?

What are you trying to say?

What do you mean by that?

Sometimes, words are not enough; sometimes they are too much! On that cryptic note, we will move on to look at some other elements of language use.

Kinship labels

Kinship labels are the different labels we use for the same person: Mum, Grandma, Auntie Dorothy, Dorothy, and maybe nicknames and terms of affection, such as 'Dot' or 'darling' can all belong to one woman. She will also be known formally as Mrs Jones, and her birth certificate will say Dorothy Clare Williams. Any one of us may be a daughter, a sister, a niece, a wife, an aunt, a cousin, a mother, a grandmother, a stepmother and a mother-in-law. We are still one person. These distinctions are relatively difficult to understand, especially for children, and particularly those who have semantic or pragmatic difficulties.

Consider how quickly we can adapt from one to another, at a family gathering, for example, when talking to one member of the family about another. It is customary to use the term of address used by the more junior person in the conversation. For example, parents usually refer to their spouse as 'Mum' or 'Dad' when talking to their children, even when those children are grown up, but refer to them by their given name to someone in the same generation, almost in the same breath. It does not happen the other way round; children do not usually refer to a parent by their given name, even when speaking to someone who calls them by that name.

I was once in conversation with a teenage boy with semantic-pragmatic disorder, who was telling me something about another of his teachers. Knowing that the teacher in question was related to me, he referred to him by his given name, although he would always address him as Mr X. This sounded inappropriate and over-familiar, but was in fact an example of the difficulty the boy had in this area. I think he was mirroring me; I was referring to the teacher as Mr X, not my usual name for him, for the boy's benefit, and the boy was doing the same for me.

Even in this area, customs are changing. It was common, thirty years ago, for married people to address their parents-in-law in the same way as their spouse did, as 'Mum' and 'Dad', perhaps. It is now more common to address parents-in-law by their given names. As a new mother-in-law, when speaking to the couple together, I am never sure whether to refer to my husband by his name or as 'Dad'.

Kinship labels are linguistically and culturally determined. In Swahili, for example, many female relatives are known by the same label, a 'young mother', so an individual will have many 'young mothers' as well as his real mother. This reflects the importance of the extended family in African culture.

Language as a co-operative tool

Much of current thinking about pragmatics, which is a relatively new area of linguistics, stems from the work of an American philosopher called Paul Grice (1975). He looked at the use of language as a co-operative tool.

This is quite easy to appreciate if we take an example: if you ask the way, you assume the person who directs you is telling the truth, in so far as she knows it, and that she wishes to be helpful rather than obstructive.

In general, we understand that a question requires a reply, or some kind of response, an implied or direct imperative requires action, and a statement requires a related statement. One sometimes hears small children in conversation, each following his or her own agenda, but not engaging with the agenda of the other:

Child A: My Granny's coming today.
Child B: My cat isn't very well.

An adult would tend to respond to the former with a follow-up comment or a question such as 'That's nice' or 'Is she staying long?'

Appropriateness

Appropriateness in language is at the heart of pragmatics. It encompasses appropriate time and place, an appropriate amount of information, and choosing an appropriate form of language for the situation.

Time and place

There is a convention (not always followed in some institutions, such as the House of Commons) that we take turns to speak and do not interrupt. In some situations (a lecture, or a church service, for example) we do not engage in conversation with our neighbours or with the speaker. A small pupil of mine was once very indignant because his headteacher had refused to listen to him when he tried to tell him some very important news. This sounds like a serious lapse on the part of the headteacher until we learn that the little boy initiated this conversation in the middle of school assembly! Clearly it was an inappropriate time.

Judging how much information is enough

In exchanges, we are normally able to judge how much is enough. If someone asks 'What's your new boss like?' we can reply appropriately, depending on the situation. We may say, 'Seems very nice', or we may go into a bit more detail. We are less likely to say, 'Dark curly hair, brown eyes, 5 foot 10, about eleven stone, mole on the left cheek', because we know that is not the information asked for. However, if the new boss had some unusual characteristic (the first woman in the post, or possessing strikingly good looks, for example), we would probably choose to include that, although it probably was not in the mind of the questioner. The jury is still out on *how* we know what is required, especially as the question, 'What's someone-or-other like?' may be a quest for a different kind, or a different amount of information in a different context.

A good example of this is in the exchange:

'Hello, how are you?'

'Fine, thanks, how are you?'

'Fine'.

This often takes place without either party slowing his step. The content is unlikely to change even if one party is very far from fine. There will be other situations in which the same question will elicit a very different response, in the counselling room or doctor's surgery, for example. As skilled speakers, we are able to discern which is which. During the 1940s there was a BBC radio comedy programme in which one character, when introduced to someone, in response to 'How do you do?' would say 'We do very nicely, thank you'. Today we might call that 'too much information'. In some cultures, the greeting procedure is lengthy and formalized. In East Africa, the greeting begins as someone comes into view along the road (or at least into earshot) and continues until they have passed. The content of the greetings depends on the context, and reflects the culture, so it may include phrases which translate as 'I am sorry for your journey' or 'I am sorry for your burden.'

Tact and diplomacy

This is another aspect of appropriateness in language use. Some people earn a well-deserved reputation for being tactless, or 'putting their foot in it'. Such people fail to use language (or fail to restrain from using it) appropriately, and can cause offence or distress.

You may have had the experience of being asked what you think of a dress, and, being too tactful to tell the whole truth, have wriggled out by saying 'It's a lovely colour', only to have your friend reply, 'I can feel a "but" coming'. Deciding to be economical with the truth is exercising control over language use.

Political correctness

We have become much more aware of appropriateness since the arrival of 'political correctness' and we are growing accustomed to engaging in circumlocutions to avoid reference to age, race or gender. In at least one case, grammatical correctness has been sacrificed to political correctness; let me give an example. Consider the statement, 'Any student needs the support of his parents if he is to succeed.' This may be considered unacceptable, because a student may be female. 'His or her parents' is rather awkward, so people are beginning to use the following construction: 'Any student needs the support of their parents if they are to succeed'. Strictly speaking, this is not right, because *their* and *they* refer to more than one, and the subject of the sentence, *the student*, is singular. This construction has recently been listed as acceptable in a guide to English usage published at the end of the twentieth century. An alternative construction would be:

'*All* students need the support of their parents if *they* are to succeed.'

Political correctness with regard to gender can be carried to ludicrous extremes, as in the statement, 'Any teacher who becomes pregnant must inform the headteacher of their condition'. Surely no one would object to the use of '*her* condition' in that context.

Prosodic features and language use

Prosodic features of language are those over and above the sounds, words and sentences; they include stress, intonation, pitch, volume and tone. They constitute 'how' we say what we say. Prosodic features of language are used to deal with different communication needs. Compare, for example, these two utterances:

'Look out.'

'Look out!'

The first may be accompanied by a gesture towards a window opening on to a wonderful view, while the second may prevent someone stepping off the pavement in front of a car. In either of these situations, of course, it would be quite acceptable to issue an order without the convolutions of 'I wonder if you'd like to...', as the first is obviously an invitation and the urgency of the second excuses its abruptness.

There are other situations where we break the rules. Take, for example, this very common exchange:

'Hello, is supper ready?'

'Nearly. Had a good day?'

Compare it with:

'Hello, is supper ready?'

'Richard phoned.'

What this apparently unrelated response suggests is that the fact that Richard phoned, or whatever he phoned about, is so important or urgent that it takes precedence over supper. The first speaker would normally respond by asking about the phone call, not repeating his question about supper.

Speech acts

A speech act is an utterance that is, of itself, an action, so that the very act of saying it makes happen that which has been declared to happen. For example, the act of saying 'I now pronounce you man and wife' makes people married. The act of saying 'I therefore declare that a state of war exists between our countries' makes that state of war exist. The act of saying 'I resign' moves the speaker from being an employee to an about-to-be-ex-employee. The verbal exchange

'Will you marry me?'
'Yes.'

makes two people engaged to be married. This last one is slightly con-
tentious, because young couples sometimes say 'We're getting engaged at
Christmas', which, presumably, means 'officially engaged' as my mother
would have said.

Less dramatic examples include:

'Welcome to the party.'

'I apologise.'

'I forgive you.'

'Thank you.'

Many speech acts are, by their nature, difficult to retract. These are examples of the power of language.

Another form of speech act is the use of speech as a substitute for
action. It is sometimes suggested that statements made by politicians can
fall into this category. It could be said that a verbal expression of anger
may be a substitute for violence. Praise could be considered a speech act,
because it is perceived by the recipient as a reward, and contributes in a
real way to his or her well-being.

Idioms, clichés and metaphors

The last aspect of language use that we will look at is that of idioms and
clichés.

I referred earlier to someone who, every time he opens his mouth,
'puts his foot in it'. I once heard said, of an extreme case: 'She only opens
her mouth to change feet!' In this utterance, the idiom has been literal-
ized and developed. It is clearly nonsense, but we readily understand
what is meant, from our knowledge of the original.

A recent, and very funny 'slip of the tongue' from a politician in a radio
interview resulted in the phrase 'joined-up government' coming out as
'stitched-up government'! (A pedant would point out that *joined* and
stitched have commonalities, but what a wonderful way to exploit them!)

Clichés are meant to be treated as units. Once they are broken apart and
interfered with, as well as funny results like the one I have just described,
pieces of nonsense come about. You may remember, some years ago, the
Prime Minister, John Major, declared that he would 'rule nothing out and
rule nothing in'. The original phrase was 'to rule something out', which
came from the practice, in the days of writing in longhand, of placing a
ruler against a word or phrase to be deleted, so that the line crossing it out
was straight. It meant, 'to cross something out'. The phrase 'to cross something in' sounds absurd, but that is what 'to rule something in' means. This
has not prevented it from entering the language.

'Diametrically opposed' has become a well-worn phrase, used to refer to a pair of opposite views or objectives. It means, literally, at opposite sides of a circle. An interviewee was recently heard to use the phrase 'diametrically disproportionate'. I imagine he began to say 'diametrically opposed', decided in mid-sentence that it was too strong, and attempted to modify it, resulting in a phrase that made no sense at all.

Occasionally, a metaphor, which is a way of describing something by likening it to something else, comes 'full circle'. The term 'to get something back on track' is a metaphor drawn from railways and means, 'to restore something to a proper working state'. It was therefore rather surprising to hear it actually used about railways! A spokesman said the following: 'We will do all we can to get the train service back on track'. I suppose we should be reassured!

I shall let the poet Ogden Nash, have the last word on metaphor. In his poem 'Very Like a Whale', he says:

> And they always say things like that the snow is a white blanket after a winter storm.
>
> Oh, it is, is it, all right then, you sleep under a six-inch blanket of snow and I'll sleep under a half-inch blanket of unpoetical blanket material and we'll see which one keeps warm.
>
> (included in an anthology compiled by Smith and Wilkins, 1959)

Summary

In this chapter we have looked at:

- lexemes (units of meaning)
- synonyms, homonyms, polysemes, homophones and homographs
- the meaning of sentences
- deep structure, surface structure and meaning
- language sense and nonsense
- figurative language and idioms
- pragmatics and meaning
- redundancy in language; the relationship between what is said and what is meant
- kinship labels as a pragmatics issue
- language as a co-operative tool
- using language appropriately: when, where and how much
- the relationship between prosody and pragmatics
- speech acts: speech at its most powerful
- idioms, clichés and metaphors

CHAPTER 10

Language variation and theory

Overview

In this chapter we will look at how language changes over time, variations in language such as dialect, accent and the use of pidgin, and consider whether there are any social or gender differences in language use. Finally, we will look very briefly at one or two of the main themes in contemporary linguistics.

Language change

When did English become recognizable?

We all know that language changes, though we believe it happens relatively slowly. Think about how impossible it is to understand *Beowulf*, or the Anglo-Saxon Chronicles; the original is like a foreign language. Chaucer has many recognizable features, but is still very unfamiliar, maybe like a related foreign language.

Two centuries later come Shakespeare, then the King James' Bible, and the Book of Common Prayer in 1662. By this time, although we would not use some of the constructions or vocabulary in the same way now, we can understand almost everything on the page. Consider a story from the Authorised (King James) version of the Bible, Luke, Chapter 19, which tells us that 'Zacchaeus ... sought to see Jesus ... and could not, for the press, because he was little of stature'. What image does the word *press* conjure up for us today? In this context, it means *the crowd*.

Moving on two more centuries, Jane Austen is totally intelligible, though we will find some of the direct speech (which is, of course, the nearest thing we have to the spoken language of the time) rather laboured – charming, but convoluted perhaps (unless you learned to hate Jane Austen so much when you were 15 that you've never got over it, in which case omit 'charming').

The evolution of English

1000 years	*Beowulf* like a foreign language
800 years	Chaucer some recognizable vocabulary and grammar
450 years	Shakespeare mainly intelligible, some vocabulary, grammar and semantic differences
200 years	Jane Austen totally intelligible, some stylistic variations, a few unfamiliar words and some semantic differences

The development of speech and accent

What we do not have, unfortunately, is the speech of any of those times preserved, though scholars believe they can give us an accurate rendition of each of them. Spelling gives us some clues about historic pronunciation: *debt*, for example, in which the /b/ used to be pronounced.

As late as the early nineteenth century, even middle-class educated people would probably have had a measure of regional accent. When we see Jane Austen's characters in TV or film versions of her novels, they speak in received pronunciation (except the servants). In fact, if they lived, as Miss Austen did, in Hampshire, they would very likely have pronounced that final /r/, still considered characteristic of the south-west of England.

Think about the accent of the USA (there are, of course, different regional accents in the US, but just taking their commonalities, such as the final /r/,) there are marked similarities with the accent of the south-west. Could this have anything to do with the fact that the Pilgrim Fathers sailed from Plymouth in Devon? Many early settlers in the US departed from the south-west. Similarly, think about the similarities between Cockney or what we may now call 'Estuary English' and Australian, particularly in the vowels. I wonder how many of the people on convict ships in the nineteenth century sailed from London and the south-east, where that was the regional accent. There are isolated communities in the US that still use the language of the early settlers. We would consider it to be quaint and anachronistic, but without external influences, change has occurred very slowly, if at all.

Do we need a lingua franca?

It may be that language change is happening more rapidly now, in the environment of global communications that enables speech and writing to be transmitted worldwide in seconds. One effect of this is to make it increasingly important to employ a lingua franca, a universal language. In the last (twentieth!) century, Esperanto was devised to fulfil this function, but, as you know, it did not gain popularity. This may be because *everyone* would have had to learn it, so there was small motivation, and of course it is an artificial language, not one that has developed and evolved in a society. English is rapidly taking on the role of a lingua franca in politics, business and technology, and most students on the continent of Europe find it essential to have a good English in order to get a good job. This is a major language change that is taking place (at least for everyone else in the world!) in our lifetime.

How does language change happen?

When pronunciation changes, typically it starts small, starts locally and starts slowly. A few people pick it up and imitate, and at some point it seems that a critical mass is reached, the adaptation of the new pattern accelerates, and it rapidly takes the place of the previous pronunciation. The concept of *local* becomes difficult to define now, due to the influence of radio, and in particular, television.

It is easier to see this happening with something like a new cliché. A cliché takes hold slowly, with a few people using it, and before we realize, it is becoming widespread. Consider the two phrases 'went pear-shaped', and 'being economical with the truth'. The latter is usually attributed to Lord Armstrong, the former cabinet secretary, giving evidence at a judicial hearing in Australia, though apparently he did not invent it. However, from the first time the quotation was broadcast around the world, it was but a short time before journalists and broadcasters, and then the rest us, started to adopt it. It has now, a few years on, passed into the language.

Some phrases and clichés enter the language, while others have a very short shelf-life and pass mercifully into oblivion in a year or two. It is fashionable among educated people to look down on certain clichés and avoid using them, while others are taken into the personal linguistic store and used with impunity.

Historic changes in word meaning

Changes in vocabulary meaning over time are interesting. *Indifferent* used to mean impartial, whereas now it means careless, or without due consideration. *Naughty* is now a rather gentle form of misbehaviour, often used to refer to children. I remember having a conversation about the importance of teaching young children the difference between *naughtiness* and *badness*, in other words, between relatively harmless mischief such as leaving toys all over the floor or not putting your socks in the laundry basket, and real crime, such as thumping or biting another child, or deliberately breaking his toy. It is, in that context, a useful distinction, but a contemporary one: in the seventeenth century *naughtiness* meant real wickedness or sin.

Some words take on a more specific meaning over time, such as *meat*, which used to mean food in general and now means dead animal to eat (unless we are talking about the mixture of dried fruit that we put into mince pies, that is called, confusingly, *mincemeat*). By the way, compare that with meat that has been minced, which we just call *mince*. *'Meat* as *food* remains in some poetic contexts: "tis meat and drink to me', for example. And how quickly we have stopped talking about the *wireless* and the *motor*, replacing them with *radio* and *car*. That took only a few decades.

Historic changes in grammar

Some grammatical changes can be easily identified. For example, in British English we have dropped the use of the *-en* inflectional morpheme at the end of *gotten*, though it remains occasionally in words such as *bidden*, which is itself becoming anachronistic. One occasionally still hears 'we are bidden' meaning 'we have been invited', and we can find *holpen* for *helped* in seventeenth-century writing. *Gotten*, however, is still used in the United States, though, I am told, only in spoken English; it would not be considered good written American English.

Language change in the individual

Individuals may change their language – pronunciation, vocabulary, grammar, use of idiom and cliché – either consciously or subconsciously. We elect to imitate those we admire: school friends, peer group, a favourite teacher or tutor (rarely our parents) when we are young, and maybe a spouse or partner, a person in authority, an admired author or public figure. I distinctly remember, as a very young woman, using larger words (attempting instead of trying, for example), and more complex and pedantic grammatical constructions when I was ploughing admiringly through the (extensive) complete works of a favourite author, who happened to be (and to speak like) an Oxford don!

Moving from one part of the country to another, or to a different Anglophone country, can bring about changes in accent, vocabulary and grammar. Even those whose accent seems to remain faithful to their place of origin are likely to acquire the idiom of the new environment. There are likely to be at least some modifications to the accent; many people, returning to another Anglophone country after some time in the UK, are told that they sound very 'English', even if their English friends think they do not.

Some of us are very influenced by linguistic environment; we adapt our speech patterns to those with whom we are talking: accent, intonation patterns, even sentence constructions and use of idiom. It is unconscious, not deliberate, and difficult to control. 'Linguistic chameleons' are often those whose ears are well tuned to speech sounds, and such people often switch speech patterns between sentences, depending on who spoke to them last. In some people the changes are slight and subtle; in others they are more extreme, and they may happen almost immediately or only after prolonged exposure, such as a fortnight's holiday in Cornwall or Scotland.

Accent and dialect

Regional variations

This brings us neatly on to a discussion of accent and dialect. Accent is a phonological issue; the same words and grammar are used as in standard English, but their pronunciation will vary from region to region. Much of the variation in accent is carried on the vowels: /bă/ in the north, /bah/ in the south for example, in the word *bath*. The word *cup* has a different vowel sound in different parts of the country: compare the received pronunciation (RP) vowel /ʌ/ with that in the north, which sounds like the *u* in *put*, and that in the south-west, where it is more like the vowel sound in *bird*. There is even a distinction in vowel length between Devon and east Cornwall, on the one hand, and west Cornwall (where the vowels are shorter), on the other.

Another common feature of regional accents is the inclusion of the /r/ sound, in the south-west and in Scotland, for instance. In RP *car* and *bath* have the same vowel sound, but in Scotland /car/ has the /r/ pronounced. In the USA these vowels are very different from each other: /car/ with the /r/ pronounced in *car*, and for *bath*, the vowel sound resembles the RP sound /air/.

The letter l, /l/ is another variable regional pronunciation. In RP we use a slightly different /l/ at the beginning and at the end of a syllable. Try saying 'lip, pill'. Can you hear and feel a difference? The back of the tongue is higher in the final /l/, which is known as 'dark *l*'. However, in Liverpool dark *l* is used in both positions, and in Wales 'clear *l*' (the one we use at the beginning of a syllable) is used in both positions. You can hear this in the speech of Michael Howard, currently (2005) leader of the UK Conservative Party, who was brought up in Wales. Most of the consonants remain constant throughout the range of English accents.

We tend to think that the acceptance of a range of regional accents, on the BBC for example, is a new phenomenon. As I have already suggested, regional accents were quite usual in the nineteenth century; by the end of that century, judgements were starting to be made about people on the basis of accent, as communications got better and people began to travel more widely between regions. This seems to have gone full circle now, with regional accents back where they belong, respected as part of the rich variety of English. However, one effect of mass communication and movement of populations is to reduce the extremes of regional accents, so that for example, young Cornish people tend to sound less Cornish than their parents.

English in other Anglophone countries

When we talk about variations in English, we have to look further than Lands End to John O'Groats, for we have to include North America, Australia, New Zealand, West Indian English, and the Englishes of all the other former colonies, including those in Africa and on the Indian sub-continent. English is the language of government and even of education in many countries where it is not the first language spoken by any of its people. Many people use English, but as their second or third language.

In Tanzania, for instance, English is the language of government and of secondary education. Kiswahili is the main common language of the pop-ulation, and is used in primary education (where English is taught as a foreign language, but in classes of 80, with no books and poor facilities). Those lucky enough to go on to secondary education (which has to be paid for) have all their lessons, still in those huge classes, in English. Additionally, most people speak their local language, which would be used at home. We do have an easier time of it in the English-speaking world.

Dialect

It is almost always possible for English speakers with different accents to be able to understand each other. Some differences can arise when the intonation patterns change, for example in some north-east England accents such as Geordie, or in some West Indian and African accents.

However, communication can become difficult when the differences go beyond accent or pronunciation. When different vocabulary is used, or different grammatical structures, this ceases to be an accent and becomes a dialect. A *bairn* in Scotland, and a *tacker* in Cornwall mean the same as a *child* in standard English, for instance. In the West Country 'where's he to?' means 'where's he gone', and additional auxiliary verbs may be used, 'I do like' for 'I like', for example. In Yorkshire, and other parts of the north and east Midlands, *mardy* is the adjective used to describe some-one who is sulking or in a bad mood. On Tyneside, a *fret* is a sea fog. In Liverpool, to 'cut up a jigger' requires no scissors; it means to take a short cut through a back alley.

Dialect variations are not confined to regions, but also to activities, trades and professions: 'Aye, aye Captain' or 'ready about' would be unlikely to be heard on dry land, for instance. Again, modern communi-cations, especially television and film, mean we are familiar with many of the context-specific languages of groups other than those we belong to. Were it not for police and medical dramas, for instance, our familiarity with the terminology of crime and illness would not be so widespread.

Newly created languages

Pidgin

Moving on from dialect to a more distant relation of standard English, we come to consider pidgin. A pidgin is a restricted language that arises when people who have no language in common have to communicate with each other. There are a number of these, based on English, spoken in places such as Papua New Guinea. Many of the words are borrowed from English; others come from the local language. Let us look at an example. The pidgin for an eclipse of the sun is something like this: 'Hurricane-lamp bilong Jesus Christ gone baggerap.' A literal translation might be 'The sun is broken'. If you are wondering where they got *bag-gerap* from, convert the /ă/ sounds to /ŭ/; the original was two words, but not the sort of English used in polite society! The word, in pidgin, means broken, wrecked, collapsed, as in 'Ka bilong yu i baggerap' (your car's broken down).

Typically, in pidgin, one word is made to do several jobs, its meaning made specific by context as in the case of hurricane lamp (lamp, light, or in this case, the sun).

Creole

If two people, whose only common language is pidgin, marry and there-fore their children learn it as a first language, it is called Creole. In this case, something interesting happens; the very restricted pidgin (which is a language of limited structure and vocabulary for limited purposes, often originally trade) grows in complexity and vocabulary. If this happens in a community, it is not long before a new 'proper' language has developed. It seems that people need linguistic complexity, and if we don't have it, we very soon create it. Studies of pidgin and Creole systems and their changes give fascinating insights into how languages develop, often over a relatively short time span.

Language and society

Gender differences

Some linguists have looked at how language behaves in society, and the differences in use between different groups of people. A recent area of study is in language differences between men and women. One interesting thing to emerge from the research is that, contrary to popular belief, men seem to talk more than women. Women tend to speak more closely to the pattern that is considered 'standard' or 'best' than men. No one has explained why this should be so. In recent years the differences between the speech of men and women seem to be decreasing, with the gradual disappearance of the features in women's language that demonstrated uncertainty and powerlessness. These characteristics are now seen to come from people of either sex who are, or feel themselves to be, relatively powerless. They include a tendency to question rather than make statements, and to use more empty, non-specific adjectives. This is unsurprising in view of recent changes in society, particularly in relation to gender issues.

Language and 'social class'

There was some very controversial research in the 1960s by a linguist called Bernstein while studying for a PhD. Many of the papers appeared in journals but the thesis as a whole was never published. His comments on language and social class would now be considered not at all politically correct, but his findings are worthy of attention from education professionals. He proposes that there are two linguistic codes: a formal and an informal code. Some people have equal access to both (Bernstein would say those in the upper social classes), while others (the rest of the social classes) have access only to the informal code. The labels he uses are **an elaborated code** and **a restricted code**.

The less formal code, Bernstein claims, is used by all of us at home, with familiars, and in informal situations; I do not think we would find that controversial. But those who have access to the more formal code use it in the workplace, in formal exchanges (such as with doctors, the boss, in business dealings, at the bank and so on) and it is the language used by teachers in school. This means that those who do not have access to the formal code are disadvantaged.

The way researchers divided people up into class bands and put labels on them is now considered offensive, but from experience, those in education can recognize that there are important and significant differences in the environmental influences on children's language, which cannot be ignored. While we may not like Bernstein's terminology (but remember he was of a different time), his observations may have some application in language and literacy teaching.

The perception of syntactic structures

One thing we have not covered in previous chapters is the issue of how, and at what stage, we understand a syntactic structure. We might call it the 'I thought you were going to say ...'. phenomenon. People start to predict the pattern of a sentence as soon as they begin to hear it; we tend to impose a subject-verb-object structure on what we are hearing, and so can be misled until further information proves us wrong and we have to adjust. Consider this example:

Anyone who cooks ducks ...

This conjures up a mental picture of ducks roasting in the oven, but could be misleading. The whole sentence reads:

Anyone who cooks ducks out of the washing up.

Ducks is the main verb of the sentence, not the object. In practice, we often have to hold quite a lot of information in the 'pending tray' until we can make complete sense of a sentence. We make up our minds what a sentence is going to mean before it is finished. This phenomenon, of understanding the whole from the incomplete, is closure, which we have already looked at in Chapter 3 on language acquisition.

Sign languages

An important kind of language that we have no time to consider in detail is sign. Sign language is much more than just gesture. It has a wide vocabulary and syntactic structures, typified by associated hand movements and facial expressions, and the use of different spatial areas to make the signs, to give the necessary range of meanings, such as questions, negation, and so on.

While some signs are iconic (and therefore recognizable by the rest of us, which is analogous with onomatopoeic words in spoken language), most are not. Sign is subject to linguistic change in the same way as spoken language and, interestingly, therefore, different sign languages are used in different parts of the world, though these do not follow the same geographical spread as spoken languages. So, for example, British Sign Language and American Sign Language are different, and not understood by each other, though the speaking populations both use English. Other systems, based on the systems used in spoken and written language (finger spelling, for example) have been created, and many deaf people have access to more than one system.

The influence of Chomsky

Finally, we cannot end a piece of work on spoken language without a word about modern linguistic theory, and in particular the work of the celebrated linguist, Noam Chomsky, who published his first work, *Syntactic Structures*, in 1957.

We learned, when looking at theories of language acquisition, that Chomsky introduced the idea of a universal grammar. The implications of this for mature language are that we make sentences by making 'transformations' to the surface structure of our chosen language (usually the mother tongue). These transformations come from the 'deep structure' – the abstract, the meaning, the universal. To perform these transformations, we need three components: a phonological component (sounds), a semantic component (meaning) and a syntactic component (grammar). This is where Chomsky differs most radically from other linguists; the syntactic component consists of a base, a deep structure and a series of transformations, to bring it to an appropriate surface structure. Many linguists have spent many years trying to write down all the transformations or rules, to account for all the possible syntactic structures in (in this case) English.

There are various possibilities:

- The same deep structure with different surface structures:

  (active and passive: *The dog bit the snake. / The snake was bitten by the dog.*)
  (*Her husband was ill. / Her husband was not well. / It was her husband who was ill.*)

- Different deep structures with the same surface structure:

  (identical sentences such as *Rolling stones can be dangerous.*)
  (similar sentences such as *She is anxious to please. / She is hard to please.*)

Chomsky's model takes account of the difference between meaning and the realization of that meaning. We can see from the examples how the same structure can be used to produce sentences with different meanings, and how the same meaning can be conveyed in different ways.

Confusingly, Chomsky has adapted and developed his ideas since the 1960s, and of course many other linguists have joined in. The work continues. Jean Aitchison (1987a) quotes an anonymous (well-known) linguist thus: 'There are three things you must never run after: a bus, a woman and a theory of Transformational Grammar. There will be another one along in a minute.' If you are interested in pursuing any of these ideas, please consult the Bibliography.

Summary

In this chapter we have looked at:

- how language became gradually more like the form we use today
- the development of accents
- how language change happens: historical, geographical, individual changes
- English regional variations
- English in other Anglophone countries
- dialects
- pidgin and Creole languages
- language differences between genders and between social groups
- how syntax is perceived
- sign languages
- Chomsky and transformational grammar

PART 2
WRITTEN LANGUAGE

CHAPTER **11**

The history of spoken language

Overview

Part 2 will cover aspects of the structure of written language and the ways in which it can be described. Teachers of students with literacy difficulties should know about the history and structure of words, the regularities and patterns in words and sentences, in order to organize the learning for the students. All speakers and writers of English benefit from understanding more about the words they use every day. The study of it will hopefully inspire them with an interest and sense of wonder about our language.

The changing nature of spoken English has been discussed in previous chapters. Let us look at the historical events which have influenced these changes. The development of language is neither steady nor simple. The influences on language are complex, and the development of new vocabulary is patchy. Geography, travel, trade, war, power struggles and education all affect developing language. This chapter contains a brief and necessarily simplified background to changes in language, and the expansion of the lexicon. It will track the origins of the English language in its spoken form and Chapter 12 will consider the main points of change affecting written language.

The users of English

At present, English is used as a major means of communication around the world (see Figure 11.1). It is estimated that about one-third of the world's population in over 70 of the world's territories is exposed to and required to speak or understand English. Apart from those in Britain, millions of people in the USA have English as their mother tongue, as do the populations of Canada, Australia, New Zealand and South Africa. The estimate is of 300 million mother tongue speakers. But if we consider only these English speakers, they account for just the tip of the iceberg of English learners (Crystal, 1988b). There are millions of others in countries such as India, Kenya and Nigeria for whom English is the 'official' language, used to carry on the affairs of government, education, commerce, the media and

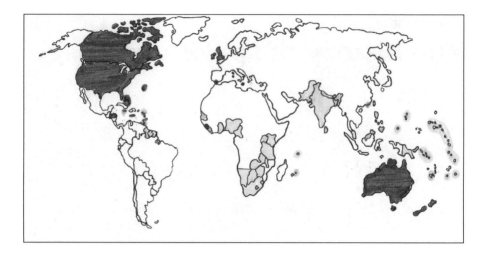

Key:  Territories where the main language is
     English: this includes dual-language
     areas, such as Quebec.

     Territories where English has a 'special
     place': these include those where
     English is an official language, and
     where Creole is used.

Figure 11.1 English speakers around the world.

the legal system. These speakers learn English as a second language. Their
countries had usually been embroiled in the rise and fall of British imperi-
alism: countries where, even after independence, English was maintained
as a common neutral language. Often this occurred in situations where the
existence of competing tribal factions would have made choosing a local
language impossible.

The rest of the numbers of English speakers in the lower part of the
language-learning iceberg (Crystal, 1988b) relate to people who learn
English as a 'foreign' language in schools and institutes of higher education, or absorb it socially through pop music and American films.

And English is in the ascendancy. With the globalization of communication and the invention of new technologies and because of Bill Gates
and his Microsoft computer empire, English is the main language for anyone wanting to use the Microsoft operating system, and English is the
most effective language for extracting information from the world wide
web. The shift here is that it is American, not British, English that is the
form of the language which is proliferating most extensively.

The English language has been forged by wars and attempts to avoid
them, by three invasions and a cultural revolution. As an oral language it
springs from our need to communicate events, feelings and abstract ideas.

The roots of English

The cradle of about a third of the world's languages is thought to originate from an Indo-European common source, probably originating from a people living near the Black Sea, who, at some time between 3500 and 2500 BC, began to travel east and west. From this common Indo-European language have come the Slavic language Russian, the Celtic and Gaelic languages, the European descendants of Latin, French and Spanish, as well as German and its offshoots, Danish, Dutch and English (see Figure 11.2).

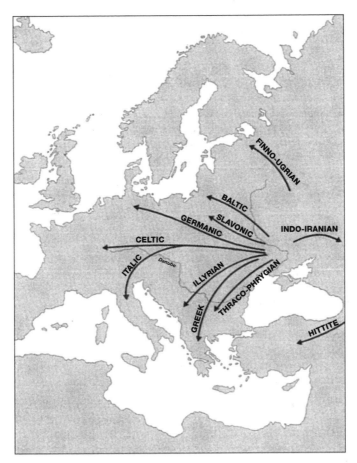

Figure 11.2 The home of the Indo-Europeans.   Source: McCrum et al., 1986.

At some time between 3500 and 2500 BC, the Indo-European community, which was probably based in Central Europe, began to travel east and west. Today the Indo-European family of languages stretches from the Hebrides in the west to the Indian sub-continent in the east, and includes descendants of Latin, like French and Spanish, the Slavic languages of European Russia, the Celtic languages of Ireland, Wales and Scotland, and the German tongues, like Danish, Dutch and English.

Philologists, in comparing words in Latin, Greek and ancient Sanskrit, discovered striking similarities in words. For instance, there are similarities between numbers, and the Sanskrit for father and mother 'pitar' and 'matar' corresponded very closely to the Latin 'pater' and 'mater'.

These relationships were pointed out in detail by the German philologist and renowned collector of fairy tales, Jakob Grimm and were embodied in 'Grimm's Law'. Grimm indicated the relationship between certain consonants in Germanic languages and their originals in Indo-European, which consistently linked to letters in Latin and Greek. Grimm demonstrated the link between the Latin letter *p*, and the letter *f* of German and English, which we see in words with the same meaning such as the word for fish: in Latin *piscis*, in German *Fisch*, and in English, *fish*. Similarly the *v* appears as *f* in connected words. Sanskrit *pitar*, Latin *pater*, German *vater*, and English *father*. This is used to show that these languages therefore all share a common ancestry in a language which has disappeared.

Table 11.1 Families of languages

Modern English	Old English	Gothic	Old High German	Old Norse
stone	stan	stains	stein	stein
bone	ban		bein	bein
oak	ac		eih	eik
home	ham	haims	heim	heimr
rope	rap	raip	reif	reip
goat	gat	gaits	geiz	geit
one	an	ains	ein	einn

Source: Barber, 1964.

Further links can be seen in families of languages (see Table 11.1). You may have noticed similarities between words in modern European languages, and these links are shown in Old English, Gothic (the language of the Goths who invaded the Roman Empire), Old High German (ancestor of modern German) and Old Norse (the early form of the Scandinavian languages).

Within the English language is preserved the history of mainland Britain which, sitting as an offshore island to Europe, was a constant irritant and curiosity to its neighbours, and was therefore subject to invasions. Each of the invaders brought with them their culture, customs and their language.

Events affecting the language

Figure 11.3 gives a brief chronology of some of the significant events which have shaped our language. You may find it useful to bookmark this

Language use	Period	Date	Event	
Latin for scholarship and instruction in schools	CELTIC	55 BC	Julius Caesar arrives in Britain	
		AD 43	Roman invasion of Britain under Emperor Claudius	
			Building of Hadrian's Wall	
	ANGLO-SAXON OLD ENGLISH	436	End of Roman withdrawal	
			Angles, Saxons and other Germanic tribes arrive	
		449	Invasion by Angles, Saxons and Jutes	
		450–480	OLD ENGLISH inscriptions in runic letters	
		597	Augustine brings Christianity to Kent	
		700	First manuscript records of OLD ENGLISH	
		787	Viking raids begin	
		871	Alfred becomes King of Wessex	
			Later translates Latin texts into ENGLISH	
		1000	Approximate date of epic OLD ENGLISH poem *Beowulf*	
French for gentry	MIDDLE ENGLISH	1066	Norman Conquest, William the Conqueror defeats Harold at Battle of Hastings	
		1150–1200	First surviving texts of MIDDLE ENGLISH	
English used in Church, Law Courts; **Latin** for scholarship and in universities		1362	English first used at the opening of Parliament	
		1375–1400	Geoffrey Chaucer writes *The Canterbury Tales*	
		1348	John Wycliffe's ENGLISH translation of the Latin Bible	
		1400–1450	The Great Vowel Shift, affecting pronunciation of English words	
		1476	William Caxton sets up printing press at Westminster and publishes *The Canterbury Tales* (1478)	The Renaissance
		1492	Christopher Columbus discovers the New World	
	EARLY MODERN ENGLISH	1549	Bishop Thomas Cranmer produces Book of Common Prayer of the Church of England	
		1558–1603	Reign of Elizabeth I	
		1582	Robert Mulcaster, *The First Part of the Elementarie*	
		1590–1616	William Shakespeare's main work written	
		1600	East India Company establishes trading outposts in India	
		1607	First permanent English settlement in America	
		1609	First permanent English settlement in the Caribbean	

continues over

EARLY MODERN ENGLISH	1611	Publication of authorized edition of King James version of the Bible for use in Protestant services
	1620	The *Mayflower* arrives in the New World. ENGLISH competes with Dutch, French, Spanish and Portuguese as a colonial language.
	1712	Jonathan Swift in Dublin proposes an English Academy to 'fix' the language.
	1755	Publication of Samuel Johnson's *Dictionary of the English Language*.
	1762	Publication of Robert Lowth's *Short Introduction to English Grammar*
	1776	Declaration of Independence and start of American War of Independence, which created the United States of America, having ENGLISH as its principal language
	1783	Webster's *The American Spelling Book*
LATE MODERN ENGLISH	1780–1900	British colonization of Canada, New Zealand, Australia, Ceylon, Trinidad, India and parts of Africa, Hong Kong and Singapore
	1828	Publication of Noah Webster's *American Dictionary of the English Language*.
	1901...	Most former British colonies gain independence
	1922	Establishment of the BBC.
	1926	Publication of Henry Fowler's *Dictionary of Modern English Usage*
	1928	Publication of Murray's dictionary *The Oxford English Dictionary*
	1930	First television programme with synchronized sight and sound broadcast by the BBC.
	1934	British Council created to teach English as a foreign language.
	1951	Launch of first two working business computers in the UK and the USA.
	1971	Invention of the microprocessor, a revolutionary development in computing.
	1975	Bill Gates designs Microsoft computing company
	1977	Spacecraft Voyager travels into deep space carrying a message in English
	1991	Timothy Berners-Lee created the World Wide Web enabling world-wide connectivity between all computers.

Figure 11.3 Some events affecting the English language.
Source: compiled from McArthur (1992) and Crystal (1988).

chart so you can refer back to this chronology as you go through this chapter and the next.

We will look first at how these historical events can offer us some insight into the development of English, particularly our vocabulary.

Latin

At one time the Celtic languages dominated what is now modern Britain. Julius Caesar's military expedition to Britain in 55 BC was the beginning of the influence of Latin on those Celtic languages. The Roman invasion under the Emperor Claudius began more than 400 years of control over much of the island, pushing the Celtic speakers beyond Hadrian's Wall in the north, and into Wales in the west.

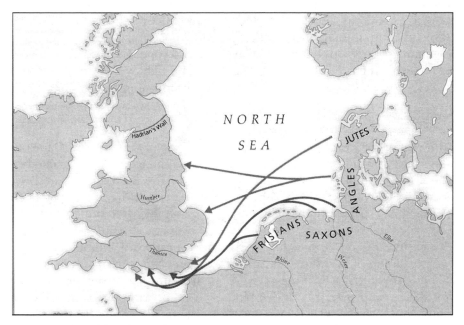

Figure 11.4 AD 449: The Anglo-Saxon invasion. Source: Crystal (1995).

Then in AD 449 the island was subjected to the terror and violence of the Angles, Saxons and Jutes, who inflicted their language on the native Britons at the point of a sword.

Anglo-Saxon/Old English

As the Anglo-Saxons began to settle and to farm the land, they used their own familiar vocabulary for everyday farming words such as *sheep*, *shepherd*, *ox*, *earth*, *plough*, *work*, *wood*, *field* and *work*. They lived in places ending in 'ham' meaning a settlement (as in Dagenham); 'ing' (Worthing);

'stowe' (Hawkstowe), 'sted' (Oxted), and 'ton' (Brighton). Besides farming words and place names they also bequeathed to us our 100 most common words. The words *you, here, there,* and *is* are all of Anglo-Saxon origin.

These early Germanic settlers were referred to in Latin as *gens anglorum* and this was the beginning of the word *English* for the both the people and the language. So in this broad view of history, Anglo-Saxon and Old English are synonymous.

The coming of Christianity to Britain brought a new wave of culture and language. When St Augustine arrived from Rome, in Kent, in 597 he was welcomed by a sceptical, but tolerant King Aethelbert, and was allowed to carry on his mission. The building of churches and monasteries soon followed with their monks as teachers, giving instruction in poetry, astronomy and arithmetic. They also recorded the words of the Bible in Latin, in magnificent illuminated manuscripts.

Church words thus entered our language and concepts, and allowed people to express more subtle ideas. The monks brought words from Latin and Greek – *disciple, angel, martyr, shrine, psalm* and from Hebrew, *Sabbath*.

Vikings

The year AD 865 brought the Vikings, Swedes, Norwegians and Danes to the north-east and with them the Old Norse language. In their raids, they sacked and plundered the gold and silver of the monasteries, and left instead a legacy of place names. The place names of the north-east often betray their Viking origins. The endings *-by, -wick, -thwaite* and *-thorpe* are characteristic of Scandinavian origins: Grimsby, Keswick, Micklethwaite and Grimesthorpe. The Yorkshire word 'riding', as in the 'North Riding of Yorkshire', is an Old Norse word meaning a third part.

Old Norse and Old English were at that time fairly similar, and the speakers could probably understand each other without too much difficulty, much as modern Danes and Norwegians can. Some of the Viking words that have survived are: *awe, egg, skirt, scrub, loose, take, anger, ill* and *bread*. Nine hundred of these Scandinavian words, used in the territory of the Danelaw are still in our lexicon; mainly plain and single syllabled: *get, hit, leg, low, root, skin, same, want* and *wrong*.

The Vikings, however, came up against the young King Alfred and his English-speaking Saxons. Alfred was trying to reunite the country, which was separated by region and by language into many factions.

He decided that unification could best be achieved by rebuilding the monasteries and schools, and by initiating a campaign to promote English as the national language. At the age of nearly 40, Alfred learnt Latin so that he could supervise the translation of some key texts, notably Bede's *History of the English Church and People*. He translated these texts into

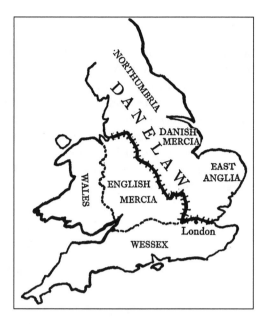

Figure 11.5 The division of England between King Alfred and the Danes in 886 AD. Alfred held England south and west of the hatched line. Source: Barber (1964)

English, and became the saviour of the English language and the founder of English prose, thus gaining his title 'Alfred the Great' for the profound effect he had on our language.

Alfred's Old English was a highly inflected language. Common words like *king* relied on word endings to convey the meaning. So 'the king' as subject of the sentence was 'se cyning' but 'to the king' was 'thaem cyninge'.

The Saxons and Vikings could understand each other's speech, as they bought, sold and gave instructions. However, as people from the Viking north and the Anglo-Saxon south strove to trade, do business and understand each other, the subtleties of the word endings began to be ignored. So it was that the need for co-operation and commerce provided a strong motivation for simplifying the language, and the inflexional word endings began to be dropped.

In about AD 1000 the Old English epic poem *Beowulf* was written down. Its 3000 lines formed the greatest single work of Old English literature and epitomized the fusion of the Saxon and Viking languages and cultures, with its rhythmical alliterative form, and its lauding of heroic retribution. These Viking values were combined also with a Christian perspective. The written version of this important poem has given us an insight into the oral tradition which underpins our cultural heritage.

Middle English

With 1066 and the Battle of Hastings came William the Conqueror complete with the French language from Normandy. William set out to win over and unify the whole country. Like Alfred the Great, William believed that the instrument for change was language. Norman French was to be spoken at court and in the main rooms of the castles, which were built by William's French-speaking noblemen. We can imagine, for instance, inside the castle the joints of meat prepared by English speakers in the kitchen were called *sheep*, *ox* and *pig*. But when they arrived upstairs on the plates of the French-speaking gentry they were named *mouton*, *boeuf* and

Titles of rank (in their modern spelling) include:	Words to do with administration	Words concerned with the law:
• sovereign • prince • peer • duke • marquess • count • baron However, we did retain the English words: • king • queen • lord • lady • knight	• government • crown • state • parliament • council • chancellor • nation • people • country	• justice • court • judge • prison • verdict • sentence • attorney • plea • accuse • crime • punish
Ecclesiastical words: • religion • service • saviour • virgin • saint • relic • abbey • friar • clergy • parish • prayer • sermon	Arts and fashion: • fashion • dress • costume • apparel • art • beauty • colour • column • paint • music • chant • poem • romance	Military terms: • armour • battle • castle • tower • war Abstract nouns: • cruelty • obedience • courtesy • mercy • charity

Figure 11.6 Medieval French loan words.

porc, words which were later anglicized to *mutton, beef* and *pork*. The forced adoption of such French loan words reflected the subjugation of the native Britons and the beginning of the loss of many English words. About 85 per cent of Old English words are no longer in use today. For 300 years, French was the language of the ruling class and filtered into Old English to create Middle English with a stronger French flavour. Nearly a half of modern English comes from Latin and French as a result of the huge influx of an estimated 10,000 French loan words in the twelfth and thirteenth centuries. Look at the examples in Figure 11.6. There are words dealing with rank, administration, the law and fashion.

However, William decreed that Latin would continue to be the language of the Church and school. It wasn't until 1348 that English replaced Latin as the medium of instruction in schools, though students at Oxford and Cambridge continued all their studying in Latin. Many Latin words entered the lexicon at this time, in their entirety, or with adaptation. By 1362 French was no longer used as the main language of the law, and English could be spoken in the law courts.

The year 1384 saw the publication of John Wycliffe's translation of the Latin Bible into English, making the language of the church more accessible to the common man.

Around 1400 The Great Vowel Shift had begun, leading to changes in pronunciation, particularly of the vowel sounds. For 400 years, vowels had been vulnerable to change. When an extra consonant or syllable was added to a word with a long vowel sound, the addition of the extra material shortened the vowel sound:

keep – kept; deep – depth; five – fifth; sheep – shepherd; child – children.

We know from the rhymes in poetry at the dawn of Early Modern English in the fifteenth century, that all the vowel sounds seemed to shift in a fairly symmetrical chain reaction. Before the shift, *keep* had been pronounced more like *cape, hide* like *heed*, and *boot* like *boat* (see Pinker, 1994).

In 1476 the first English book was printed by William Caxton, on his own printing press in Flanders, and so opened up literacy to a wider audience. But it also demonstrated just how many dialects there were in English at the time, when he recorded the story of the travelling merchant asking for eggs – *eggys* – from a woman who could not understand what he wanted, as she would have used the word *eyren*. In trying to solve this problem when he came to decide which dialect to print, Caxton, having set up his press in Westminster, chose the speech of the London area, which therefore became 'standard' speech. By the end of the fifteenth century, social distinctions between 'central' and 'provincial' life were firmly established. These were partly defined by differences in speech, between 'standard' and 'regional'. The former was thought of as correct, proper and educated; the latter as incorrect, careless and inferior: a view which has not completely disappeared today.

The Renaissance

So we arrive at the Renaissance. The Renaissance from the time of Caxton until about 1650 was a period of enormous expansion in science, medicine and the arts. New words had to be coined for the new concepts, techniques and inventions. This period of history had a huge effect on the vocabulary of English.

Look at the Latin words which were adopted wholesale at the time to express some of the new concepts (Figure 11.7). Many of them came or were created from Latin and Greek and from their European origins in

Some of the words were taken over bodily in their Latin form, with their Latin spelling, like:	Other words however, were adapted, and given an English form. For example, the Latin ending -atus is sometimes replaced by -ate as in:
• genius (1513) • species (1551) • cerebellum (1565) • militia (1590) • radius (1597) • torpor (1607) • specimen (1610) • squalor (1621) • apparatus (1628) • focus (1644) • tedium (1662) • lens (1693) • antenna (1698)	• associate • culminate • decimate • desperate • dominate • exterminate • originate • nominate • participate • procrastinate • rejuvenate
	Some are mathematical, like: • area • radius • series • calculus
Many of these Latin words are scientific terms like: • pollen • vacuum • equilibrium • momentum	There are everyday words too, like: • album • miser • circus
A number are legal terms, like: • alias • caveat • affidavit	But in general these Latin terms are the kind of words that are introduced into a language through the medium of writing rather than in speech.

Figure 11.7 Latin loan words.

French, Italian, Spanish and Portuguese. In Early Modern English, the trickle of Latin loans becomes a river, and by 1600 it is a deluge.

At the same time traders and explorers set off to other continents including the New World. From their travels they brought back jewels, fabrics, spices and words. Words came into English from over 50 other languages, and attracted bitter criticism from many quarters as do imported words even today. But the purists had little influence, and English was enriched by the influx of the new vocabularies.

The publication of religious texts had a great influence on the rhythms and vocabulary of the language. The first version of the Book of Common Prayer was published by Thomas Cranmer, Archbishop of Canterbury, in 1549. The constant repetition of this language in church services embedded itself in the memory of ordinary parishioners, so that many of the phrases gained broader currency and achieved the status of idioms: *holy wedlock; read, mark, learn and inwardly digest; wilt thou have this woman to thy wedded wife; earth to earth, ashes to ashes, dust to dust; renounce the devil and all his works; as it was in the beginning, is now, and ever shall be: world without end, Amen.*

Seventy years later came the enormously influential publication of the Authorised King James' Version of the Bible, for use in Protestant services in England, Scotland and Ireland (see Figure 11.8).

Again, it had a far-reaching influence on the general population and on the whole language. The translation was designed to be read aloud from the pulpits of the land, so careful attention was given to the rhythm and balance of the verses. These memorable rhythmic phrases have become the cornerstone of much English idiom, reused by writers, poets and singers in many ways over the years. Table 11.2 lists some of the phrases that entered the language currency as idioms from the King James' Bible, but their origins often are unnoticed in our present secular society.

Figure 11.8 King James' Bible.
Source: The British Library.

Table 11.2 Biblical idioms

Phrase	Book and chapter
my brother's keeper	Genesis 4
a good old age	Genesis 15
eye for eye	Exodus 21
to spy out the land	Numbers 13
the apple of his eye	Deuteronomy 32
a man after his own heart	1 Samuel 13
how are the mighty fallen	2 Samuel 1
a still small voice	1 Kings 19
the skin of my teeth	Job 19
out of the mouth of babes	Psalm 8
at their wit's end	Psalm 107
a lamb brought to the slaughter	Jeremiah 11
can the leopard change his spots?	Jeremiah 13
eat sour grapes	Ezekiel 18
the salt of the earth	Matthew 5
cast your pearls before swine	Matthew 7
the strait and narrow	Matthew 7
if the blind lead the blind	Matthew 15
in the twinkling of an eye	1 Corinthians 15
money is the root of all evil	1 Timothy 6
fight the good fight	1 Timothy 6
the patience of Job	James 5
rule with a rod of iron	Revelation 2

Of course one of the greatest single influences on the language was Shakespeare. With the publication of the first folio of his plays in 1623, a richness of concept, imagery and phraseology entered the language from a single author of prolific talent and imagination. The list of phrases we use from Shakespeare is endless; a few of them are listed in Table 11.3.

Table 11.3 Shakespearean idioms

Expression	Play, Act, Scene
salad days	Antony and Cleopatra I v
beggars all description	Antony and Cleopatra II ii
[play] fast and loose	Antony and Cleopatra IV xii
it's Greek to me	Julius Caesar I ii
what the dickens	The Merry Wives of Windsor III ii
as good luck would have it	The Merry Wives of Windsor III v
wear my heart upon my sleeve	Othello I i
a foregone conclusion	Othello III iii
in my mind's eye	Hamlet I ii

Table 11.3 Shakespearean idioms (contd.)

Expression	Play, Act, Scene
to the manner born	Hamlet I iv
brevity is the soul of wit	Hamlet II ii
to be or not to be – that is the question	Hamlet III i
a tower of strength	Richard III, V iii
cold comfort	King John V vii
at one fell swoop	Macbeth IV iii
double, double toil and trouble	Macbeth IV i
all our yesterdays	Macbeth V v
with bated breath	The Merchant of Venice II iii
love is blind	The Merchant of Venice II vi
all the world's a stage	As you Like it II vi
I have not slept one wink	Cymbeline III iv
we band of brothers	Henry V, IV iii

These publications – The Book of Common Prayer, The Authorised Bible and Shakespeare's canon – have given us a common reference point for many extant concepts and idioms.

As we teach students, their appreciation of the depth and richness of the language is increasingly enhanced by learning new words in context, and relating them to the context in which they were originally coined.

Modern English

The Renaissance had thus ushered in Early Modern English. We can read texts of the time, and the vocabulary, syntax and grammar are so similar to modern English that the text is usually comprehensible.

The English we can recognize today was being spoken and written. As England became a major power in the world, with its empire extending to all corners of the globe, it continued to absorb into itself new words, for example *tea, khaki, bungalow, turkey, tobacco, kookaburra, koala, hello* and many more. All these words continued to enrich our vocabulary. Because English has absorbed words from many other languages, its vocabulary is huge, its dictionaries are voluminous and we have a wide range of words for expressing a single idea.

English is rich in synonyms. Many synonyms carry their histories within them. As Old English gave way to Latin and French, new words came into the language allowing people to express ideas with slightly different shades of meaning.

The Old English *doom* can be expressed by the French word *judgement*. A person may receive a *hearty* slap on the back in Old English, but a more elegant *cordial* greeting in French. The synonyms *rise, mount* and *ascend* are used with slightly different shades of meaning or context. A walker may *ascend* a hill, but not *rise* up it.

You may be interested in considering some of these in the next task.

Task 11.1

Match the synonyms across the three columns. The first one has been done for you, but the rest need to be rearranged. Cover the answers until you are ready to check.

	Old English	Latin	French
1.	kingly	royal	regal
2.	house	inform	contribution
3.	ask	initiate	commence
4.	tell	conserve	sanctify
5.	stop	perambulate	save
6.	start	turbulence	create
7.	bless	consent	promenade
8.	keep	donation	mansion
9.	walk	domicile	question
10.	think	interrogate	luminous
11.	make	consecrate	contribution
12.	shining	cogitate	tantalize
13.	gift	terminate	dictate
14.	agree	manufacture	finish
15.	storm	radiant	imagine
16.	tempt	labour	perceive
17.	gift	agriculture	pasture
18.	see, watch	seduce	accept
19.	work	donation	tempest
20.	field	observe	occupation

A

1.	kingly	royal	regal
2.	house	domicile	mansion
3.	ask	interrogate	question
4.	tell	inform	dictate
5.	stop	terminate	finish
6.	start	initiate	commence
7.	bless	consecrate	sanctify
8.	keep	conserve	save
9.	walk	perambulate	promenade
10.	think	cogitate	imagine
11.	make	manufacture	create
12.	shining	radiant	luminous
13.	gift	donation	contribution
14.	agree	consent	accept
15.	storm	turbulence	tempest
16.	tempt	seduce	tantalise
17.	gift	donation	contribution
18.	see, watch	observe	perceive
19.	work	labour	occupation
20.	field	agriculture	pasture

Did you find that in general the Old English word is usually more common, the French word is more literary and the Latin word more learned? When Winston Churchill wished to appeal to the hearts and minds of English men and women during the second world war, he did it with the short, plain words for which Old English is noted: 'We shall fight on the beaches, we shall fight on the landing grounds, we shall fight in the fields and in the streets, we shall fight in the hills, we shall never surrender.' Only the last word *surrender* is of foreign Norman-French origin. If he had used French or Latin based words, *combat, pastures, mountains*, the speech would have lost the strong impelling rhythm of its essential English vocabulary, and its appeal to patriotism.

Neologisms

The etymology of the language is fascinating and it also gives us an insight into the history of our language and the concerns of our society. The language continues to grow, change and expand. Indeed it may be argued that, with global mass media and communication, the language is undergoing change at an unprecedented rate right now. In the Renaissance, a time of huge increase in vocabulary, it may have taken years for a new word to travel from London and be understood by people in the north. Now, with communication through the internet and the mass media of radio, television and daily newspapers a word can be adopted by millions of people in several countries in the space of weeks.

A neologism is a newly invented word or a new sense of a word; the origins of new word-coinings are usually worth discovering. Neologisms may be formed in various ways, and for people with an interest in words, it is useful to classify the ways in which this happens. Here are some of the ways in which new words may be formed:

- borrowings
- abbreviations: acronyms and clippings
- compound words
- portmanteau words
- eponyms

Borrowings

These are complete words which are adopted into English from another language. They usually refer to exotic items or native equivalents. Borrowing occurs when there is close contact in multilingual situations, or when there is a need to draw from one language to another for such purposes as education or technology. The Cannon Corpus of new English words shows transfers from other languages into English. Most words were from

European languages (French, Spanish, Italian, Greek, German and Latin) but there were also some Japanese words.

Look at the following list for examples of some of these borrowings, which are usually the result of trade, travel and the importing of new products and ideas. You can quickly see that these words refer to articles and concepts which were not native to Britain, and for which new words were needed. English people of course borrowed the label from the country where the item originated as they first encountered, for instance, *chipmunks, apricots, tea* and *leprechauns.*

The Corpus of new English words 1987–1989, lists 1029 transfers from 84 other languages, including:

The Americas from Native America: *chipmunk, hickory, pow-wow, wigwam;* through Spanish: *avocado, cocoa, chocolate, tomato, pampas.*

African: *outspan, chimpanzee, zombie, mumbo-jumbo, voodoo, yam, jazz.*

Arabic in Asia: *apricot, alcohol, algebra, mohair, monsoon, syrup.*

Hebrew: *camel, cherub, messiah, Sabbath.*

Persian: *arsenic, azure, magic, paradise, talc.*

Southern and SE Asia: *bungalow, dinghy, dungaree, gymkhana, shampoo, chutney, crimson, sugar, yoga, mantra.*

Chinese: *china, chopsticks, ketchup, tea, bonsai, futon, tofu.*

Celtic languages: *druid, hooligan, leprechaun, smithereens, glen, loch, corgi.*

Dutch: *brandy, coleslaw, drill, easel, skipper, yacht.*

German: *dachshund, frankfurter, hamburger, kindergarten.*

Norse: *anger, bloom, dirt, egg, leg, muck, root, skill.*

Greek: *analysis, charisma, cinema, criterion, diagnosis.*

Latin: *area, complex, formula, inertia, peninsula, referendum.*

Abbreviations

Shortened versions are a popular way of forming new words. Perhaps because they are short and zippy, this makes them memorable and attractive to say. Abbreviations can be made by creating acronyms or by producing clippings.

Acronyms

An acronym is an abbreviation formed from the initial letters of a series of words, and pronounced as one word. Here are some with which you may be familiar. See if you can remember the words from which the initial letters are derived.

Acronyms provide a verbal shorthand, simplifying a string of terms into an easily pronounceable single word. An acronym may also make a challenging concept more easily accessible.

Task 11.2

Look at the acronyms in the left-hand column, and write the full titles. Cover the answers in the right-hand column until you are ready to check.

NATO	North Atlantic Treaty Organization
Unicef	United Nations International Children's Emergency Foundation
radar	radio detection and ranging
ASH	Action for Smoking and Health
GIGO	Garbage In, Garbage Out (computer term)
Nimby	Not In My Back Yard
BUPA	British United Provident Association
scuba	Self-Contained Underwater Breathing Apparatus
twoc	Taking Without Owner's Consent (vehicles)

Clipping

A clipping, or clipped word, is an abbreviation formed by the loss of some of the word, usually dropping some of the syllables. We may clip the end of the word, just leaving the beginning. Examples are *pro* from professional, *gent* from gentleman, *ad* from advertisement and *chimp* from chimpanzee. Different parts of the word may be dropped, leaving behind the most significant part. So, the beginning of the word may be clipped, leaving *burger* instead of hamburger; *bus* in place of omnibus; and *phone* instead of telephone. Words may even be clipped before and after, with only the middle syllable remaining. So *'tec* is the abbreviation of detective, and *'flu* for influenza. Names are often clipped, as a sign of familiarity or friendliness: Cath(erine), Dom(inic), Ben(jamin), (Eliza)Beth, (Al) Bert, Tone (Anthony).

Compound words

These are words which originated as two words, but are now written as one, such as *football, teapot, blackbird, handbag, shortcut* and *database*. Some compound words have not yet achieved single-word status, and are still written with a hyphen; *dry-clean, sun-dry, back-up, catch-all*. It will probably just be a matter of time and use before these are treated as whole words.

Portmanteau words

These are also called blend words. They were named by Lewis Carroll, to describe a word formed by fusing elements of two other words. A portmanteau is a bag with two compartments. Carroll created the word *slithy* from *slimy* and *lithe* in his poem *Jabberwocky*.

Here are other examples of portmanteau words for you to unpack.

Task 11.3

Look at the portmanteau words in the left-hand column (below) and decide what the original words were. Cover the answers in the right-hand column until you are ready to check.

A

Portmanteau word	Original words
Oxbridge	Oxford/Cambridge
hi-tech	high/technology
brunch	breakfast/lunch
smog	smoke/fog
heliport	helicopter/airport
Eurovision	European/television
motel	motor/hotel
geep	goat/sheep
motorcade	motorcar/cavalcade
toytoons	toys/cartoons
Chunnel	Channel/tunnel

To our students, these may be very familiar words, having landed fully formed into their spoken vocabulary. Students usually enjoy and are helped by finding out about the origin of words. It gives them insight into the growth of the lexicon, helps them to refine the meaning of the word, and probably explains the reason for the spelling too.

Eponyms

An eponym is formed when we name an object after a person such as:

Wellington (after the Duke of Wellington who wore long boots)

Stetson (after the nineteenth-century US hatter)

Parkinson's law (after the twentieth-century British economist)

the eponymous Mr Hoover, which is a back reference to the inventor from the object.

All of the above are ways of creating new words when we need them, and neologisms are constantly being invented.

Recent neologisms

The following are examples of neologisms which were absorbed into English in the fairly recent past. These are from the 1970s and 1980s.

There are examples of borrowings, eponyms, but also the use of phrases with familiar words, used to convey a new meaning.

Depending on your age, you may remember the story behind their adoption. Family members, friends or colleagues may be able to help. Answers are not provided for this task.

Task 11.4

Can you remember the news story, political or social events which relate to the adoption of these terms?

1970s	1980s
boat people	cash point
bottom line	couch potato
downsize	Filofax
ecocatastrophe	glasnost
empty-nester	golden handshake
flexitime	gridlock
gas-guzzler	home shopping
junk food	kiss-and-tell publication
Legionnaire's disease	necklacing
nouvelle cuisine	telemarketing
shuttle diplomacy	whole foodie
Watergate	yuppie

In our present world with its rapidly expanding areas of new technology and mass media, neologisms are constantly being coined. It is an interesting exercise to jot down any novel words and consider how they have been formed. There is a proliferation of reference books about phrases and idioms currently available which often give intriguing insights into the social and political origins of new phrases.

Many children are fascinated to discover the stories behind words. They may readily start to invent their own words, in poetry and descriptions. If they do so, it is a sign that they are becoming more aware of words and the language.

Measuring vocabulary

The English language has a very rich history: it has absorbed words from many varied sources; it has a huge lexicon, the fattest dictionaries and a great number of synonyms. Writers and communicators who use English have the ability to convey subtleties and shades of meaning in a way that few other languages can. It is therefore impossible to know the meaning of all the words in the dictionary, but it is interesting to find out the possible range of one's own vocabulary.

It would be difficult and time-consuming to try to detect the number of words in a person's lexicon. There are obvious problems about how the words should be counted. Should we count different forms of the same word as one word or more: *think, thinks, thinker, thought*? Should we measure the words of a person's receptive vocabulary, the words that are understood; or should we measure only the words in a person's expressive vocabulary, the words a person uses?

Despite these difficulties, some academics have devised tests to measure the size of a person's vocabulary.

Although such a test may not be completely reliable, it can be fun to do if the results are not taken too seriously. The task below is a test you can try for yourself to find out roughly the extent of your own vocabulary. It was devised some time ago by Hunter Diack (1975).

Task 11.5

Test your vocabulary. You need a sheet of paper or a pencil. Beginning at word number 1, read through the words of the first test below in the order numbered. As you come to a word you do not know, write the number of the word on your sheet of paper. Carry on in this way until you have ten numbers on your sheet. At that point stop, whether or not you know the next word. That is to say, you read through the test until you have met ten words that you do not know the meaning of. Now you must show that you really do know the words you claimed to know. It is enough if you show that you can give a correct meaning to the last five words you claimed to know – that is, the last five words whose numbers you did not write down. You can do this in each case by making a small sketch to illustrate the meaning, by writing about the meaning, or by showing in a sentence how the word is used.
Repeat this process for Tests 2 and 3.

Test 1

Level 1	Level 2	Level 3	Level 4	Level 5
1. abroad	11. abandon	21. abridge	31. abhorrent	41. abscissa
2. boulder	12. ballot	22. aggregate	32. amorphous	42. badinage
3. dawdle	13. chaos	23. bivouac	33. crustacean	43. cartel
4. expedition	14. contraband	24. chronology	34. declivity	44. daemon
5. horizon	15. excavate	25. credulous	35. emaciated	45. dendrite
6. jangle	16. fatigue	26. hireling	36. fabrication	46. exordium
7. limit	17. laboratory	27. indolent	37. galaxy	47. inchoate
8. pattern	18. manual	28. nomadic	38. heretical	48. moraine
9. rate	19. purchase	29. accidental	39. igneous	49. rubric
10. stroke	20. shuttle	30. somnambulism	40. nomenclature	50. soutane

Task 11.5 *continued*

Test 2

Level 1	Level 2	Level 3	Level 4	Level 5
1. abbey	11. accelerate	21. acrid	31. baroque	41. abreast
2. abundance	12. aquatic	22. aftermath	32. cabal	42. atavistic
3. boast	13. celebrity	23. centrifugal	33. Charybdis	43. claque
4. convenient	14. identical	24. circuitous	34. dorsal	44. dharma
5. decimal	15. latitude	25. faction	35. ephemeral	45. flagellum
6. happiness	16. martial	26. interim	36. fiscal	46. gerrymander
7. invisible	17. rotary	27. nautical	37. invective	47. haptic
8. somersault	18. teem	28. retrograde	38. lymphatic	48. imbroglio
9. torpedo	19. terminate	29. splice	39. mandible	49. janissary
10. undergrowth	20. veteran	30. vehement	40. palliative	50. phrenetic

Test 3

Level 1	Level 2	Level 3	Level 4	Level 5
1. absence	11. abode	21. admit	31. acquiesce	41. accidie
2. agriculture	12. barricade	22. alabaster	32. agrarian	42. burette
3. blizzard	13. bulletin	23. bigotry	33. bullion	43. coruscate
4. crescent	14. climax	24. circumvent	34. clandestine	44. contumely
5. downpour	15. crouch	25. culminate	35. desultory	45. desuetude
6. fragment	16. export	26. fallacious	36. eradicate	46. frustum
7. hemisphere	17. flimsy	27. mediocre	37. fluted	47. haulm
8. reach	18. hospitality	28. nutritious	38. homogeneous	48. imago
9. sheaf	19. longitude	29. parry	39. larynx	49. mandragora
10. triangle	20. rustic	30. rancour	40. overt	50. normative

The mark in each test is the number of words known in that test up to the tenth unknown word. The total vocabulary is the average score in three tests multiplied by 600, e.g. average score 25 = total vocabulary 25 x 600 = 15,000 words. You may find this hard to believe but extensive tests have shown this to be a very accurate estimate of how many words a person knows. So, multiply your average score (i.e. total over 3 tests (3) by 600, to find out how many words you know.

So, how many words do you know?

Conclusion

In this chapter, we have considered the growth of vocabulary in spoken English. A person's spoken language, his lexicon and dialect, is influenced by his local concerns, his trade, his geographical location, as well as by political, and social and cultural changes. In the next chapter we will consider the development of written English.

Summary

- History of spoken language
- English: now a world-wide language
- Origin: one-third of all languages, from near the Black Sea?
- Similarities between Old English, Gothic, High German and Norse
- Events affecting language
- The growth of English

55 BC	Latin
AD 450	Anglo-Saxon/Old English
	King Alfred translated texts into English
1000	*Beowulf*
1066	Middle English
	French influence on vocabulary
	Canterbury Tales, Caxton printing press
1550s	Early Modern English
	Elizabeth I, King James' Bible, Shakespeare
	The Renaissance
	Modern English
	Webster's *Dictionary*

- Neologisms
- Measure your vocabulary

CHAPTER 12

The history of written language

Introduction

Having looked at the influences on English spoken vocabulary, let us look now at English and its written form. To go back to basics, we need to ask why and how writing was invented. It seems probable that speech arose at the same time as tool-making, and was an aid to human co-operation and communication. There are still many theories and controversies surrounding the origins of the development of speech and oral language. But when we turn to written language we are on firmer ground, as fragments of evidence survive. Writing is a further development of speech. It is a visual representation of speech, devised for communicating at a distance of time or place. For instance, a nomadic group who had moved away from an area may wish to leave a message for another group who would pass by later. Records needed to be kept too, in permanent visual form. Primitive people often used systems of knots tied in rope, or notches in sticks, as a record and an aid to remembering crop yields, days journeyed, etc. Before writing was invented, all cultural traditions had to be memorized and handed down orally, but there is a limit to the amount that can be memorized. No very serious expansion of knowledge can take place until some of it can be committed to a permanent written record. So, people began to communicate in written form, first by means of pictures. These can tell a story independently of language.

Picture writing

Picture writing was used, for example, by early Native Americans, with images scratched or painted on birch bark or animal skins. The picture writing in Figure 12.1 was left on a tree by scouts of the Micmac tribe to warn those following that ten men of another warring tribe had been seen in canoes on the lake, going towards the outlet. The fish is the tribal emblem of the enemy tribe, and the lake with the arrow is a map of the tribe's movements. The message depicts a whole situation and is

185

unrelated to a specific language. It could be understood by another tribe speaking another language.

Figure 12.1 Micmac picture writing. Source: Barber (1964).

Similarly, in modern times we use conventional signs or logograms as a means of universal communication. The sign for men's and women's toilets, road signs that indicate a bend or a bridge ahead, can all be understood by speakers of other languages and by non-readers.

Writing developed out of these pictograms in two ways. First, the pictures were simplified and conventionalized, so they were no longer recognizable pictures. Second, the symbols were made to stand directly for linguistic items, first words, then syllables, and finally sounds or phonemes. So emerged the beginning of an alphabet.

The conventionalization of the symbols depended on the materials for writing. If the symbols were pressed into clay the writing may be wedge-shaped and angular, as in the cuneiform writing of the Sumerian scribes between 4000 and 3000 BC.

When scribes wrote with pen or brush on leather or papyrus, curves were easy to make. The script of the Egyptians from 3000 BC was pictorial, and is referred to as hieroglyphic writing. It was usually carved and used for religious purposes. For everyday use a quicker form known as 'hieratic', or priestly, writing, was devised, and this in turn developed in about 700 BC into a script called 'demotic' or popular writing. Chinese has a similar history of pictograms.

The alphabet

Our alphabet, like all those of Western Europe, is derived from the Latin alphabet, which in turn came from Greek, and this can be traced back to Egyptian hieroglyphics.

Originally, a picture of the sun was drawn to represent the concrete object *sun* or associated words such as *bright, day* or *time.* Finally, other symbols came to stand for the sound of the word.

Figure 12.2 shows the origin of some of our alphabet as it is thought to derive from the hieroglyphic ideogram into the West Semitic syllabic system, and finally by the Greek into a symbol representing a single phoneme.

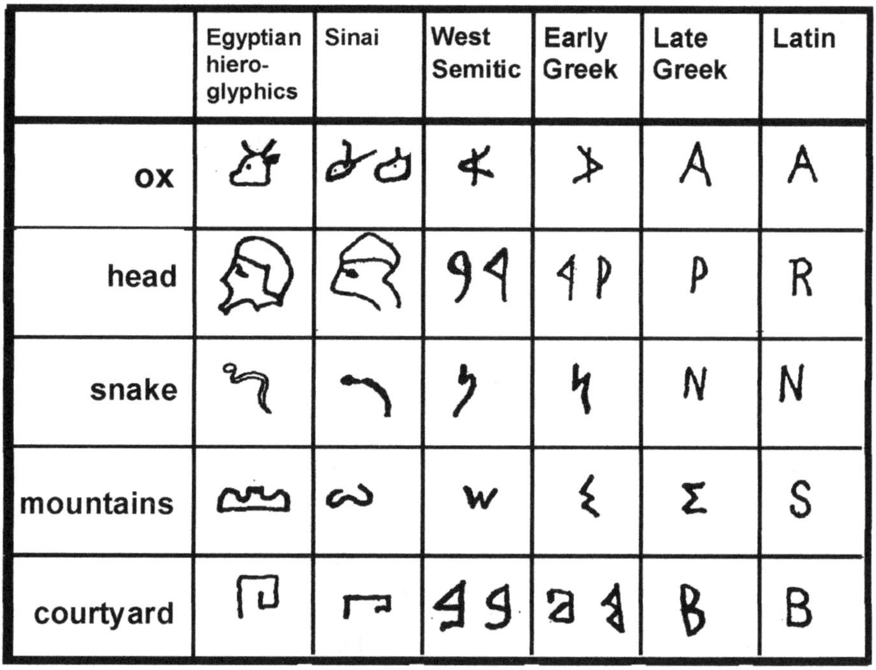

	Egyptian hiero-glyphics	Sinai	West Semitic	Early Greek	Late Greek	Latin
ox					A	A
head					P	R
snake					N	N
mountains					Σ	S
courtyard					B	B

Figure 12.2 English alphabet origins. Source: Barber (1964).

Previously, writing had been the secret religious code, to which only priests, after years of memorizing, were privy. Old English was first written using the runic alphabet which was used in Northern Europe and Scandinavia from about the third century AD. The name *runes* means *secret* and the runes-master imbued the symbols with magical or mystical significance to convey secret information. In the twentieth century J.R.R. Tolkien uses runes in his *Lord of the Rings* trilogy, to convey an impression of mystery and secrecy.

Figure 12.3 shows some of the Old English runes, with the alphabetic equivalent for each in Anglo-Saxon and the probable meaning of each rune before it came to symbolize only the first sound of the word. The original runic alphabet consisted of just 24 symbols, each of which had a name, and the whole alphabet was called the futhorc, an acronym of the names of the first six letters. The Old English alphabet had the 31 runes seen here, as extra ones had to be added to cope with the sounds of Old English. Runes were formed from straight lines, as they were designed to be engraved on stone, wood, metal and bone. Runes have been identified mainly on monuments, weapons and jewellery from the fifth and sixth centuries, where they were used to state the name of the craftsman or owner.

Rune	Anglo-Saxon	Name	Meaning (where known)
ᚠ	f	feoh	cattle, wealth
ᚢ	u	ûr	bison (aurochs)
ᚦ	þ	þorn	thorn
ᚩ	o	ōs	god/mouth
ᚱ	r	rād	journey/riding
ᚳ	c	cen	torch
ᚷ	g [j]	giefu	gift
ᚹ	w	wyn	joy
ᚻ	h	hægl	hail
ᚾ	n	nied	necessity/trouble
ᛁ	i	is	ice
ᛄ	j	gear	year
ᛇ	3	ēoh	yew
ᛈ	p	peor	?
ᛉ	x	eolh	?sedge
ᛋ	s	sigel	sun
ᛏ	t	tiw/tir	Tiw (a god)
ᛒ	b	beorc	birch
ᛖ	e	eoh	horse
ᛗ	m	man	man
ᛚ	l	lagu	water/sea
ᛝ	ng	ing	Ing (a hero)
ᛟ	oe	eþel	land/estate
ᛞ	d	dæg	day
ᚪ	a	ac	oak
ᚫ	æ	æsc	ash
ᚣ	y	yr	bow
ᛠ	ea	ear	?earth
ᚸ	g [ɣ]	gar	spear
ᛣ	k	calc	?sandal/chalice/chalk
ᛤ	k̄	(name unknown)	

Figure 12.3 Development of letters from runes. Source: Crystal (1995).

Phoneticization

The change from pictures to symbols which represented phonemes was a really crucial development, when the symbol came to represent a sound. The great advantage of this system was that it needed a relatively small number of symbols to represent the sounds of a language and therefore anything that could be said, could be written. Furthermore, when a simple phonetic system of transcription is devised, people are able to write words which they may not have learned in written form before. It is no longer necessary for the priestly elite to spend many years learning the hieroglyphics, runes or other pictograms. Phoneticization makes written language accessible to a greater number of people. It creates the possibility of universal literacy. With greater literacy comes the availability of more knowledge, and so we find the beginnings of democracy.

The runic alphabet was probably available to a very small elite in Anglo-Saxon England, but the arrival of Christian missionaries brought the rapid introduction of the Roman alphabet. The ecclesiastical writing of the time was in Latin, painstakingly transcribed. Monastic scribes used trimmed quill feathers from the wings of large birds to write with ink on parchment skins, as the only way of reproducing a manuscript.

The Lindisfarne Gospels, written at the monastery on Holy Island between 724 and 740, had richly illuminated lettering using bright colours and gold leaf. They were enclosed in a jewel-encrusted case: a precious and revered manuscript using the Latin alphabet. The Latin alphabet was established and supreme.

Unfortunately these Roman letters could not represent all the sounds of English, so when the native tongue was being written down, some runes were included in the Old English alphabet. There are some, but not a great many texts left from the Anglo-Saxon period. The writings of King Alfred (849–899) and the epic poem *Beowulf* (around 1000 AD) (Figure 12.4) are amongst the extant writings of the period, using the Old English alphabet. The Anglo-Saxon Chronicle was a compilation of various texts written in Old English from AD 1 to the twelfth century. All these texts are unusual, as very little was written in the vernacular, and they give scholars an important insight into the writing of those times.

Capital letters were not used. The alphabet was a mixture of Latin letters and runic symbols. It had an elongated *s* (ſ), the letter *j* had a different form *eoh* (ȝ) (see Figure 12.3) and the letter *v* was spelled *f*. The letters *q*, *x* and *z* were rarely used. The letter *w* was printed using the runic symbol *wyn* Ƿ and the voiced and unvoiced sounds for *th* were written with two different symbols, *thorn* (þ) and *edh* (ð), as can be seen in Figure 12.4 and in the transcription of The Lord's Prayer in Figure 12.5.

'HWÆT WE GARDE
na in geardagum þeodcyninga'

Lo! praise of the prowess of people-kings

Figure 12.4 *Beowulf.*
Source: Resources for Studying, www.georgetown.edu/irvinemj/english016/beowulf/
beowulf.html

Fæder ūre,
þū þe eart on heofonum,
sī þīn nama gehālgod.
Tō becume þīn rīce.
Gewurþe ðīn willa on eorðan swā swā on heofonum.
Ūrne gedæghwāmlīcan hlāf syle ūs tō dæg.
And forgyf ūs ūre gyltas, swā swā wē forgyfað ūrum gyltendum.
And ne gelæd þū ūs on costnunge,
ac ālȳs ūs of yfele. Amen

Figure 12.5 The Lord's Prayer.

The word *the* was represented by (þᵉ) *thorn* and the letter *e*. Later the
thorn was written slightly differently and became confused with *y*, which
is the basis of mock-archaic writing such as Ye Olde Coffee Shoppe, below.

Ꝥe Olde Coffee Shoppe

Spelling varied greatly reflecting the preferences of individual scribes.

Spelling

Up until the 1500s, spelling was a lottery, for both the writer and the reader. The spoken language consisted of many dialects, and these were

reflected in the written language. Writers spelled words as they spoke them. After 1066 and the Norman Conquest, spelling gradually began to change. Norman scribes heard English words and began to spell them using French conventions. So *qu* was used instead of *cw* (*queen* for *cwen*); *ou* instead of just *u* in *house*. They used *c* before *e* instead of *s* in *cercle*. Because of the script used, words with *u*, *v*, *n*, and *m* were difficult to read, as they looked very similar, so the Norman scribes changed the *u* to *o*, giving us the present spelling of *come*, *love*, *one* and *son*, with the vowel *o*. So by the beginning of the fifteenth century, English spelling was a mixture of two systems, Old English and French. The consequences plague English learners still.

Middle English writing is dominated by the breadth and variety of the poetry and narrative of Chaucer, who lived from around 1345 to 1400. Chaucer used a whole range of writing styles, from simple domestic chat to high-flown rhetoric, and is best known for writing the 24 stories of *The Canterbury Tales*.

Whan that Aprille with hise shoures soote,	When April with its sweet showers
The droghte of March hath perced to the roote	Has pierced the drought of March to the root
And bathed every veyne in swich licour,	And bathed every vein in such liquid
Of which vertue engendred is the flour;	From which strength the flower is engendered
Whan Zephirus eek with his sweete breeth	When Zephirus with his sweet breath
Inspired hath in euery holt and heeth	Has breathed upon in every woodland and heath
The tender croppes and the yonge sonne	The tender shoots and the young sun
Hath in the Ram his half cours yronne,	Has run his half-course in the Ram
And smale fowules maken melodye,	And small birds make melody
That slepen al the nyght with open eye	That sleep all night with open eye
So pricketh hem nature in hir corages	(So nature pricks them in their hearts)
Thanne longen folk to goon on pilgrimages...	Then people long to go on pilgrimages...

Figure 12.6 The Prologue to *The Canterbury Tales*. Source: The Huntingdon Library, California.

In Figure 12.6, The Prologue to *The Canterbury Tales*, the original text shows the care and skill that went into the illumination of the first letter. Capital letters and spaces between words were being used by this time. The writing, partly because of its poetic form, contains many variations in word order with the noun appearing before the adjective, for example, 'shoures soote', and the verb being placed before the subject in 'engendered is the flour'.

Scholars suggest that the *ight* in *night* is pronounced as in the German word *nicht* and that the final e on words at this time is also pronounced: *soote, sonne*. English writing as we know it is starting to emerge, with familiar syntax, fewer inflexional endings and some recognizable vocabulary. It is the vowels in the words that cause the difficulty. Chaucer was writing before the Great Vowel Shift had taken effect, and this is what makes his writing harder to read than that of Caxton or Shakespeare who wrote when the pronunciation of the vowels was more consistent. Even so, with all three authors, the same word was often spelled in different ways.

The beginning of standardized spelling

Some standardization of spelling came, however, with the royal Chancery records. The scribes who kept records for the King were much more consistent in their spelling, and gave us the modern form of *such, can, could, shall, should*. They produced vast numbers of documents in the 1430s, and modern standard English has been shaped by the dialects of the Central and East Midlands and London, which were used by the Chancery scribes and Caxton.

William Caxton established his printing press near Westminster Abbey in 1478. His spelling, too, was inconsistent, as he tried hard to make his English understandable to a broad range of people speaking different dialects. His punctuation was also very idiosyncratic and did little to aid conformity in written English. Printing itself brought its own difficulties. Sometimes letters were left off to make the print fit into the line. Some of the printers were foreigners, and proofreaders were not always educated. However, Caxton did have an effect on subsequent spelling. He fixed the spelling of *might* and he was instrumental in the dropping of the letter thorn in favour of *th*. Nevertheless, there was a great deal of criticism of the chaotic nature of the writing system at the time.

It was another 100 years before any consensus about spelling emerged. The great age of Elizabethan literature brought unprecedented growth in English vocabulary. Between 1530 and 1660 many new words entered the language from other cultures, old words took on new meanings, and there were many complaints that the language was changing too rapidly, and that in particular spelling and punctuation should be regularized.

At the end of the sixteenth century Richard Mulcaster, a scholar, school-master and liberal educational theorist, published *The First Part of the Elementarie* (1582), a teaching manual which was the period's most significant pronouncement on spelling. It contained a table of recommended spellings for 9000 words. Vowels became more predictable: long vowels were spelled with a double vowel (*oo*, *ee*) or with the addition of a final *e*, (*name*). Consonants were doubled to indicate a preceding short vowel as in *sitting*, the letters *v* and *u* stopped being interchangeable and similarly *j* and *i*. Mulcaster took a firm but liberal stand in the controversy about *inkhorn* terms: ostentatious words from Latin or Greek which were beginning to appear in some writing. He loved the English of his mother tongue but defended the right to borrow terms from other languages. Thus he led the movement for spelling reform, and he also issued the first call for a comprehensive dictionary of English. During the seventeenth century many spelling guides were produced, but not the gathering of all the words into a dictionary which Mulcaster had called for. It was 170 years later when Samuel Johnson came into the picture, a teacher and writer, the son of a provincial bookseller. In 1755 Johnson published his *Dictionary of the English Language*, an authoritative treatment of 40,000 words which he had gathered over a period of seven years.

Johnson paid attention to the different senses of a word, used copious quotations as illustration and identified the parts of speech. The subjectivity of some of his definitions has become famous:

excise: a hateful tax levied upon commodities

oats: a grain, which in England is generally given to horses, but in Scotland supports the people

His was the first attempt at a truly principled lexicography and his approach has influenced English dictionaries ever since.

With the publication of the dictionary, spelling and meanings of words had become fixed and, as eighteenth-century notions of correctness emerged, poor spelling became increasingly stigmatized.

Consequently, with concerns over spelling largely answered, scholars then turned their attention to grammar. Bishop Lowth's *Short Introduction to English Grammar* (1762) became a standard textbook of prescriptive grammar. He illustrated his grammar rules with errors to be found in the Bible, and he advised against ending sentences with a preposition. Although he based his grammar on the Latin model, he modified it so that it described English well.

The novelist Jane Austen (1775–1817) is famed for her careful, skilled use of language. She would have arrived for her two years of tuition at

Abbey School in Reading, when Bishop Lowth's approach was well established, and correct grammar would have been a concern of her tutors. Jane Austen frequently made alterations to the grammar in subsequent editions of some of her novels, demonstrating her concern for grammatical accuracy.

In America in 1783, Noah Webster published *The American Spelling Book*, a book with a distinctive blue cover which sold a million copies a year – the most popular school book ever written. In it, Webster incorporated some elements of spelling reform such as dropping the *u* out of *favour* and the *k* off the end of *musick*. He substituted *-er* for *-re* (theater), *se* for *ce* (defense), *k* for *que* (check), and a single *l* before a suffix (traveling).

When he was 70 years old in 1828 Webster finished and published his *American Dictionary*, which decided and fixed American English spelling.

English: an alphabetic-phonetic system

The spelling of English is based on an alphabetic-phonetic system, in which sounds are represented by letters, but it is not a transparent system. A transparent system of orthography has a 1:1 grapheme–phoneme (letter–sound) correspondence, in which each letter, or group of letters, consistently represents a sound.

Languages such as Italian or Swahili are transparent. Once a child has learned the system of letter–sound links, she can read, that is, pronounce, any word in that language, but may not know the meaning of the word or understand the sentence. It is easy for an English reader to pronounce the Kiswahili words *jambo* or *hakuna matata*, but she would need to have had experience of the language to know that the words meant 'hello' and 'that's no problem'.

Because of its history, English, though phonetic, is not a transparent language. Written English has a more complex set of patterns and spelling rules. But it is not a totally erratic and irregular language. Crystal (1995) reports that only 3 per cent of everyday English words are so irregular that they have to be completely learned by heart and that there seem to be fewer than 500 words in English whose spelling is wholly irregular. These are words such as:

> although, answer, autumn, climb, cough, could, debt, dough, eye, once, people, said, shoe, sugar, talk, who.

Unfortunately several on this list are amongst the most frequently used words in the language. However, he also states that 80 per cent of English words are spelled according to regular patterns, leaving us only about

15 per cent of words to argue about. As teachers, we must be aware of the spelling patterns in those 80 per cent of regular words and teach those letter groups. Such consistency will give our students confidence.

When students are faced in school or college with new technical terms and specialist vocabulary, these words, though often long, do usually conform to general spelling rules. The vocabulary, which our secondary school students have to learn may be in science subjects, with words such as *respiration, photosynthesis, carbon dioxide* and *gravitational pull*. It may be in history that they must learn to spell *reformation* and *historical*. These words comply with well-established spelling patterns. As teachers, we must know the patterns and know how to teach them.

Despite the efforts of spelling reformers, and the creativity of text messaging on mobile phones, English spelling for formal writing seems at present to be fixed. The 15 per cent of awkward words probably includes the spellings of words such as *debt* and *plumber,* which contain reminders of their former origins and pronunciations. The *y* in *martyr* and the silent *p* in *psalm* are reminders of the long, and for some people, precious, history of our words. For some scholars, the argument for preservation of traditional spelling has hinged on this notion that words should retain their history in their spelling. English vocabulary and spelling will continue to be an area of concern, interest and argument.

From the point of view of teaching the English language, we have a less than perfect spelling system. There are some irregularities because the language is organic, has altered with time and will continue to change. But because of this, the English language provides us with a rich and effective means of expressing ourselves. We must ensure that we as teachers know enough about our own language to pass on to our students both our knowledge and our enthusiasm.

Summary

- History of written language
- Picture writing: conveys ideas
- Alphabet: conveys words
      began with runes
      phoneticization
- Writing used Latin letter forms + O.E. symbols (e.g. thorn þ)
- 1066>   Norman scribes used French symbols cw > qu, u > o (love), u > ou (house)
- 1300s   Chaucer's writing: vowels and syntax different from Modern English Great Vowel Shift
- 1430>   Royal Chancery Records used dialect near London as standard
- 1478   Caxton printing press: letter thorn became *th*

- 1582   Richard Mulcaster's spelling manual
- 1755   Johnson's *Dictionary*, fixed spelling
- 1762   Louth's *Short Introduction to English Grammar*
- 1783   Webster's *Dictionary*, fixed American spelling
- English spelling: not transparent, but phonetic. 80 per cent regular.

CHAPTER 13

Grammar 1: syntax

What is grammar?

Chapter 11 dealt with meaning of words and the size of a person's vocabulary, as these are necessary precursors to comprehending written text. But another aspect of language is equally important: our sense of grammar.

The word 'grammar' has struck terror into many a schoolboy's heart in the past. It was a subject that he often didn't understand and couldn't get right; a source of enormous frustration to some:

> [of his primary school teacher] On one occasion, when she had been irritating me over some little question of English grammar, I bit her arm right through to the bone, an action which I have never for an instant regretted.
>
> Noel Coward (1937) *Present Indicative* (in Crystal and Crystal, 2000)

A traditional British education was renowned for teaching pupils to speak and write grammatically. Indeed there were 'grammar schools'. Good grammar was the mark of a gentleman:

> In those days the English language was supposed to come to an English gentleman naturally, without effort, like clean-living or an aptitude for ball games.
>
> A.P. Herbert (1935) *What a Word!* (in Crystal and Crystal, 2000)

Good grammar was a painful prerequisite for anyone wanting advancement in society:

> Grammar, n. A system of pitfalls thoughtfully prepared for the feet of the self-made man, along the path by which he advances to distinction.
>
> Ambrose Bierce (1911) *The Devil's Dictionary* (in Crystal and Crystal, 2000)

The radio station BBC Radio 4 regularly receives letters complaining about any grammatical gaffes made by its presenters and interviewers: someone using a split infinitive or saying 'different than' or 'between you and I' is certain to attract adverse comment. As a nation we are aware of and interested in grammar, and the subject still rouses strong emotions. The respected Ernest Gowers (1962) stated:

> The old-fashioned grammarian certainly has much to answer for. He created a false sense of values that still lingers...Too much importance is still attached to grammarians' fetishes and too little to choosing the right words. But we cannot have grammar jettisoned altogether: that would mean chaos.

The word grammar derives from Greek, through Latin, from the word *gramma* meaning a letter and *ars grammatica* meaning 'the craft of letters'. In Anglo-Saxon and Old French a related word meant occult learning, and a book of magic. Grammar is related to the word *glamour* used by Sir Walter Scott to mean a magic spell, that is 'to cast a glamour over someone'. So through the ages when we have used the word grammar, it has had connotations of mysterious learning, something hallowed and scholarly. Grammarians have taken years of study to master the techniques and terminology. A great mythology has grown up around the notion of 'knowing about grammar'. But in a simple and fundamental way grammar is easy. It is simply the rules which govern the way we communicate. It is all to do with making sense. We all grow up with an awareness of grammar. We learn to put words together in the right order to make sense, and we add the correct endings onto words. If we heard the utterance 'Drove he car up motorway the', we would recognize immediately that it sounded wrong and did not make sense. To that extent, we know English grammar, because we would never form an utterance in that way. By the age of five most children would be able to express that thought as 'He drove the car up the motorway'. Acquiring grammar is an unconscious process which a normal human being learns. Noam Chomsky, the American linguist, stated that we have a genetic predisposition for language, and we can generate and transform sentences to produce an infinite number of utterances. The modern linguist Steven Pinker develops Chomsky's idea in his book *The Language Instinct* (1994). Pinker believes that humans have a biological adaptation to communicate information in the same way a spider has an urge to spin webs and a competence to succeed.

However knowing *about* English grammar is a metacognitive process, which helps us reflect on how we communicate and how we understand the rules for constructing sentences. To do this we need to master the terminology such as **clause**, **phrase**, **noun** and **adjective** in order to talk about the grammar of a sentence.

It is not enough to have a comprehensive lexicon and know the meaning of many words. Unless we can put the words we need into the right order and with the right endings on them, we will not be able to communicate effectively with anyone. For example, the words *John*, *went*, *house*, *me*, conjure up some images, but they are not meaningful until they are put into a sentence such as 'John went into the house before me'. This now gives us information about the time the event occurred and the relationship between the other elements in time and space. We are talking about John (he's the subject of the sentence); it happened in the past (*went* is the past tense of the verb), and we know the order in which the two people went into the house (the preposition *before*).

Grammar is the systematic study and description of a language. It can also be defined as the set of rules and examples dealing with the syntax (word order) and morphology (word parts) of a standard language. Linguists may distinguish between a descriptive grammar, which carefully describes the grammatical elements of the language as it is used by a range of people, and a prescriptive grammar, which pronounces what is good and bad grammar. It is the latter, the prescriptive grammar, which teachers are expected to know and dispense. Grammar books in schools tell children how sentences should be formed, the way words should be used, and the terminology to describe the process.

The history of grammar

Classical grammar, in the Greek tradition, has influenced the study of English grammar. The Greek philosophers Plato (422–347 BC) and Aristotle (384–322 BC) took a close interest in language, because it was the vehicle for their main interest, logic and rhetoric. In 100 BC Dionysius Thrax wrote *The Art of Letters*, describing the nature of letters, syllables, words and sentences.

In the texts of the time, there were no spaces between words, and hardly any punctuation, so reading depended on seeing patterns in the unbroken lines of print. Writing was a mystery to the general population so grammarians who could copy, edit and understand works such as the epics of Homer were sometimes considered to be sorcerers.

In more modern times, grammar has sometimes been regarded as an esoteric area of knowledge. But some grammarians have been very influential and respected. Henry Fowler brought humour and common sense to English grammar with his *Modern English Usage* (1926). This useful guide has long acted as a bible for those concerned with disputed points of grammar. More recently, in 1990, Sidney Greenbaum and Randolph Quirk published *A Student's Grammar of the English Language*, which has clear parallels with traditional grammar, with the difference that half the book is devoted to syntax, demonstrating that English is now being described in its own terms, where word order is very important to the communication of meaning.

Modern grammar

Modern English grammar is usually regarded as having two major constituents: morphology and syntax. We deal with syntax here and morphology in the next chapter.

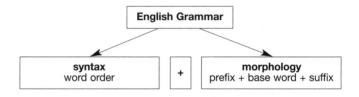

Syntax

Syntax deals with the order of words: the way in which words combine into such units as a phrase, a clause and a sentence:

A **sentence** consists of one or more clauses.

A **clause** consists of one or more phrases.

A **phrase** consists of a group of words.

A **word** consists of one or more **morphemes**.

Morphemes will be discussed in Chapter 14 on morphology. This chapter will deal with the syntactic aspect of grammar, and the attributes of sentences, clauses and phrases.

Word order

Word order is at the heart of syntax, and most modern English grammar is taken up with the rules governing the order in which words and clusters of words can appear. Mother tongue speakers never think twice about them, because, as children, we absorb these rules in our speech. Consider the following alternatives. The first one sounds fine but the second one is unacceptable:

I walked to town.   I to town walked.

She switched it off.   She switched off it.

In some languages, Latin for instance, word order is not crucial, as the endings of the words indicate the relationships between the elements of the sentence. But in English, word sequence is very important. If we change the order of the words, the meaning may be altered fundamentally:

The dog bites the cat.	The cat bites the dog.
She can come in.	Can she come in?
Naturally, I stood up.	I stood up naturally.

In the last pair, the first one means 'Of course I stood up, it was the expected thing to do'. Whereas the second one means 'I stood up naturally, not awkwardly'.

Here is a short exercise on syntax, which you may find interesting.

Task 13.1

Look at the sentences. Alter the order of the words to change the meaning. Cover the answers below until you are ready to look at possible solutions.

The man swallowed the fish.
Her husband saw her with her lover.
Sideboard for sale by local lady with Queen Anne legs.
Show me the last three pages.
Happily, the final competitor finished at 5.00 pm.

A

Here are some examples of changes in word order, which result in a different meaning:

The fish swallowed the man.

Her lover saw her with her husband.

Sideboard with Queen Anne legs for sale by local lady. (This time, the sideboard, not the lady, has bowed legs.)

Show me the three last pages. (i.e. the last page of each of three documents. The original sentence referred only to one document.)

The final competitor finished happily at 5.00 pm. (The competitor is happy. The original sentence expresses general relief that the competition was over before 5 pm.)

In the first sentence, the fish may have been sardine-sized, but when changed became whale-sized and you were probably reminded of the biblical story of Jonah. In the second sentence you were forced to switch attention to the new subject. In the third sentence, you may have been embarrassed that a lady was writing an advertisement, mentioning her bowed legs. The changed fourth sentence results in a different number of books, and in the last sentence, the changed syntax shifts the perspective from the organizers to the competitor.

Changes in word order can result in either vast or subtle changes in meaning. Faulty arrangement of words can lead to unintentional absurdities:

There was a discussion yesterday on the worrying of sheep by dogs in the House of Commons.

After your instructions about claiming my benefit, I have given birth to twins in the enclosed envelope.

Spoken and written syntax may differ. Spoken language is 'on the hoof', with no time to plan and polish before uttering the words. Oral sentences are characterized by false starts, hesitations, interruptions, forgotten words and lost conclusions and this has been discussed in earlier chapters. Conversations are sometimes delivered in sentences, but also in phrases and fragments of a sentence. When writing, we have time to think, plan, change our minds, redraft and proofread; so written sentences are more carefully crafted.

The sentence

The sentence is the chief syntactic structure. The word *sentence* is still difficult and controversial to define. The traditional definition of a sentence is 'a complete expression of a single thought', but this can be problematic. The following expressions may express a single thought but are not, in the traditional sense, sentences: 'Taxi!', 'Lovely day!', 'Cup of tea?'

The following sentence expresses more than one thought: 'For Christmas, Ian would like a computer game, a skateboard and a visit to a theme park.' So it, too, does not conform to the definition.

Numerous definitions of a sentence have been tried and found wanting. The sentence is the largest structural unit treated in grammar. In written language the sentence is signalled by punctuation, primarily by a full stop, and contains one or more clauses.

```
sentence = clause(s) + .
```

Sentence types

Sentences may be simple, compound or complex. A **simple sentence** consists of only one main clause:

The baby cried.

The drain has been repaired.

The policeman negotiated with the kidnapper.

A **compound sentence** has two or more main clauses linked by the co-ordinators *and, or, but*.

> The baby had cried *or* his sister had demanded attention all afternoon.
>
> The drain has been repaired, *but* the contractors will still be returning tomorrow.
>
> The policeman negotiated with the kidnapper all day, *and* other experts continued through the night.

A **complex sentence** consists of one main clause within which there are subordinate clauses. Let's continue with the crying baby and others. The main clause is typed in bold:

> **The baby**, who had cried all afternoon, **was happy and playful at bedtime**.
>
> **The drain**, which has been broken for years, **has now been repaired**.
>
> **The policeman negotiated with the kidnapper** after the building had been surrounded.

Complex sentences are sometimes difficult to understand because of their length. If the main clause can be identified, the meaning is easier to ascertain. Despite the best efforts of the campaigners for plain English, long sentences like this can be found. It is necessary to acquire the skill of unpacking the sentence to discover the main clause. Can sentence analysis help the recipient to make sense of part of this letter from a telephone company?

> I regret that the survey officer who is responsible for the preliminary investigation as to the technical possibility of installing a telephone at the address quoted by the applicant has reported that owing to a shortage a spare pair of wires to the underground cable (a pair of wires leading from the point near your house directly back to the local exchange) is lacking and that therefore it is a technical impossibility to install a telephone for you.

The main clause is:

> the survey officer ... has reported that ... it is a technical impossibility to install a telephone for you.

The disappointed recipient can then investigate the other clauses, in order to make sense of all the asides and explanations that the writer feels obliged to convey. A subordinate clause is indicated by the word *who*. The writer elaborates on the survey officer's job, the address and the wires. If we try to represent this visually, it may unpack as in Figure 13.1.

The structure of the sentence opens up, revealing its meaning, or in this case, most of its meaning. It is still unclear whether *shortage* refers to

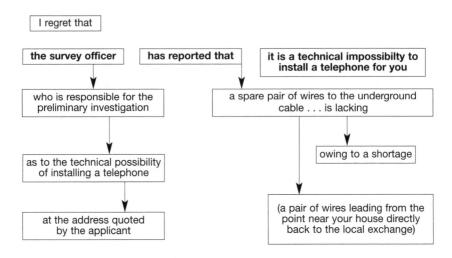

Figure 13.1 The main clause revealed.

the lack of sufficient wires within the cable, or the shortage of further wires which could be dug into the ground. The unfortunate applicant, lacking a telephone, obviously could not ring up to find out what the letter meant. The meaning would have more clearly expressed if it had been divided into several sentences.

However there are times like this, or when reading academic or legal papers, when we need to understand long sentences. This skill is dependent not only on the reader's knowledge of the subject, but on his knowledge of sentence structure too.

Try the next task on sentences.

Task 13.2

See if you can identify whether each sentence is simple, compound or complex.

Cover the answers overleaf and then check.

1. Mrs Harris, that good soul, always visited the sick on Sunday afternoon.
2. She went to the butcher's and then caught the bus into town.
3. During the night, the dog, which had been very restless, began to howl.
4. Matthew liked a big bowl of cornflakes and cream for his supper.
5. The florist screamed but nobody heard her.

Task 13.2
continued

6. Yariv was always riding his bike or playing on his video game.
7. As she had seen the film previously, she didn't want to see it again.
8. The idiosyncratic speech of Mrs Gamp was evidently one of Dickens' own favourite creations.
9. The author lived in the country, where most of his novels were set.
10. Justin was in a splendidly good humour and set them all laughing.

A

1.	Mrs Harris, that good soul, always visited the sick on Sunday afternoon.	Simple
2.	She went to the butcher's and then caught the bus into town.	Compound
3.	During the night, the dog, which had been very restless, began to howl.	Complex
4.	Matthew liked a big bowl of cornflakes and cream for his supper.	Simple
5.	The florist screamed but nobody heard her.	Compound
6.	Yariv was always riding his bike or playing on his video game.	Compound
7.	As she had seen the film previously, she didn't want to see it again.	Complex
8.	The idiosyncratic speech of Mrs Gamp was evidently one of Dickens' own favourite creations.	Simple
9.	The author lived in the country, where most of his novels were set.	Complex
10.	Justin was in a splendidly good humour and set them all laughing.	Compound

Functional categories of sentence

Sentences can also be classified according to their dominant function in discourse, according to the kind of communication they are. That is, whether they state something, ask a question, give a command or exclaim. These are referred to as:

- declarative
- interrogative
- imperative
- exclamatory

Each type of sentence can be either affirmative or negative.

The **declarative sentence** is a straightforward statement:

(Affirmative)   The cat ran up the curtains.
                                Most teenagers like pop music.
                                Sharon went to the nightclub with her friends.
(Negative)   He did not come in the door.

The **interrogative sentence** asks a question:

(Affirmative)   Has the dog caught the rabbit?
                                Is Mark in?
                                Where did Hitler die?
(Negative)   Didn't he arrive at the chateau?

Note the syntactic structure of an interrogative sentence. When forming a
question in English, the verb usually comes before the subject.

The **imperative sentence** commands the hearer to do something:

(Affirmative)   Fetch that bone.
                                Consider the problem carefully.
                                Look both ways before you cross the road.
(Negative)   Don't touch that switch.

The **exclamatory sentence** is usually punctuated by an exclamation mark:

(Affirmative)   Ouch, that hurts!
                                The heavens opened!
(Negative)   Wasn't it marvellous!

The clause

The clause is a component of a sentence. A sentence can be made up of
one or more clauses. A **clause** contains a verb, and usually a subject, and
a predicate:

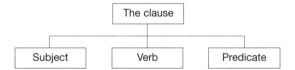

In the clause 'Nobody moved', *nobody* is the subject, and *moved* is the
verb. In 'Shaun took my typewriter', *Shaun* is the subject, *took* is the verb,
and *my typewriter* is the predicate. In 'I like my coffee strong', *I* is the subject, *like* is the verb, *my coffee strong* is the predicate. In the clause 'Has
Derek arrived yet?', *Derek* is the subject, *has arrived* is the verb, and *yet*
is the predicate.

Modern clause analysis recognizes that the predicate needs to be analysed further, and so a clause may have five elements: subject, verb, object, complement and adverbial.

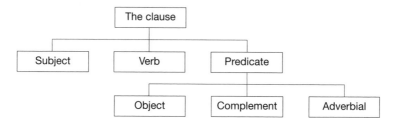

All of these elements appear in the sentence 'Sharon paid Fred the milk-man on Monday, as usual'.

- The **subject** usually identifies the theme or topic of the clause: *Sharon*.
- The second element is the **verb** which expresses a wide range of meanings, such as actions, sensations or states of being: *paid*.
- The third element is the **object** which identifies who or what has been directly affected by the verb: *Fred*.
- The fourth element is the **complement**. This complements and adds further information about another clause element usually following the verb for example *the milkman*.
- The fifth element is **adverbial** *on Monday, as usual*. There may be an indefinite number of these in a single clause. They express a wide range of meaning such as manner, place and time. For example:

She stayed	at home,	quietly,	all day
	(place)	(manner)	(time)

The main elements to identify in a clause are the subject, verb and object. If your students can do this they will get a better feel for sentence construction, and more control over sentences. So try this exercise yourself.

Task 13.3

Identify the three main elements (if present) in each of the clauses below: subject, verb and object. Cover answers overleaf and then check.

The apprentice engineer moved the lever.

On-going criticism would have undermined his effectiveness even more.

Task 13.3
continued

My cousin's wife used to make delicious marmalade.

During the siege many of the people in the castle starved to death.

The shopping list had clearly become too long.

In the middle of the night the old oak tree was split in two by lightning.

Have they gathered in the harvest yet?

A

subject	verb	object
The apprentice engineer	moved	the lever
On-going criticism	would have undermined	his effectiveness
My cousin's wife	used to make	delicious marmalade
many of the people in the castle	starved	
The shopping list	had become	
the old oak tree	was split	
they	have … gathered in	the harvest

You will have noticed that in several cases the subject may be expressed in several words: the apprentice engineer; on-going criticism; my cousin's wife. The verb is the most obligatory part of a clause and may consist of one word (moved) or several words (would have undermined; used to make).

In the examples above, each clause was a main clause and so formed a sentence. We have seen above that clauses often contain groups of words which form phrases. Let us now consider the phrase.

The phrase

A phrase consists of a group of words within a sentence or clause. It is a small group of words which function as a grammatical unit. In traditional grammar a phrase did not have a finite verb, but in the list of phrases, here, note there is a **verb phrase**, which neatly describes the several words which together form the verb in a sentence: *has been running*; *would have brought*.

The National Literacy Strategy defines phrases as 'two or more words, which act as one unit' and gives five types of phrase, named after their main word. They are listed here, with examples:

noun phrase The black dog; hot buttered toast; a very bright light.
verb phrase has run; won't have been listening; has been talking.

adverbial phrase expands the verb; answers the questions how? when? where?: quite casually; terribly slowly; very happily indeed, and also time phrases such as: as quickly as possible; quite often; very soon.

adjectival phrase a phrase with adjective and an intensifier: extraordinarily happy; not too awkward; cold enough; easy to please.

prepositional phrase starts with a preposition and explains the relationship between two nouns in a sentence: in the garden; by her chair; with the red beard; in our city.

You can 'grow your own' noun phrases. Look at the example in Figure 13.2.

							Buns						are	for	sale.
						The	buns						are	for	sale.
					All	the	buns						are	for	sale.
				All	the	currant	buns						are	for	sale.
Not	quite	all	the			currant	buns						are	for	sale.
Not	quite	all	the	hot	buttered	currant	buns						are	for	sale.
Not	quite	all	the	hot	buttered	currant	buns			on	the	table	are	for	sale.
Not	quite	all	the	hot	buttered	currant	buns	on	show	on	the	table	are	for	sale.
Not	quite	all	the	many	fine,										
					interesting-looking, hot-buttered home-made	currant	buns, which Gran cooked	on	show	on	the	table	are	for	sale.

Figure 13.2 Growing a noun phrase. Source: Crystal (1995).

The noun *Buns* in the first sentence 'Buns are for sale', gradually expands to 'Not quite all the many fine interesting-looking hot-buttered, home-made currant buns, which Grandma cooked on show on the table are for sale'. This is just an expansion of that first noun, and the whole noun phrase still forms the subject of the sentence, even when it includes a subordinate clause, 'which Grandma cooked'.

This is also a good exercise to give to children to encourage them to use more expressive language in their writing. Try the three tasks below yourself.

Task 13.4

Growing noun phrases

Extend the first noun into a long and interesting noun phrase that will fit the rest of the sentence. There are no answers of course, as the length of the phrases is governed only by your vocabulary and imagination.

Books .... will be put back into the bookcase.

Farmer .... went to round up the sheep.

Kitchen .... filled with people.

Task 13.5

Adverbial phrases

Use these verbs (choose your own subject and the form of the verb) and add on an adverbial phrase. e.g. The rabbit ran *very erratically.* Cover the answers below, which provide suggestions.

move
emerge
prove
settle
whisper

If you got stuck, here are some adverbs and intensifiers from which you could have permed some suitable phrases. Choose one from each column until you have a satisfactory adverbial phrase.

Intensifier	Adverb
very	elegantly
quite	breathlessly
most	comfortably
endearingly	confidentially
extraordinarily	clumsily
almost	emphatically
as ...	as possible

Task 13.6

Adjectival phrases

Cover the answers overleaf, which provide suggestions.

Make up to five different sentences by adding an adjectival phrase:

He/she was ....
....
....
....
....

Task 13.6
continued

Put an adjectival phrase before these nouns:

A/an ....baby

....teenager

....politician

....actor

....castle

....cloak

A

If you got stuck, here are some adjectives and intensifiers from which you could have permed some suitable phrases. Choose one from each column to get you a satisfactory adjectival phrase.

Intensifier	Adjective	
very	small	
quite	argumentative	
most	lazy	
not too	bucolic	
extraordinarily	tyrannical	
almost	voluminous	
fairly	opinionated	
amazingly	pink	
impossibly	friendly	
extremely	talented	
	large	
	imposing	
	impregnable	
as ...	voluble	as possible

Conclusion

So within English grammar, knowledge of syntax is important. Meaning is transmitted through the order of words in phrases, clauses and sentences. In some other languages, the parts of speech are recognizable by the endings of the words. English has fewer inflexional endings, so we need to arrange words according to received usage in order to make sense. The terminology in this chapter has necessarily referred to some word classes, or parts of speech, such as noun, adverb and preposition. Parts of speech will be dealt with more fully in Chapter 15.

In the present chapter we have been describing and dealing with groups of words, and the order in which they appear. Next we will shift our examination to word level, and consider the meaningful segments of words. Morphology is the other aspect of grammar, to which we will turn in the next chapter.

Summary

- Grammar: the study and description of language.
- Modern grammar: Syntax (word order) + Morphology (prefix/base/suffix)
- Syntax: order of words in a:
  sentence
  clause
  phrase

- Word order is important as English does not have word endings to indicate a word's function in a sentence.

- Sentence: Types: simple, compound, complex.
  Function: declarative, interrogative, imperative, exclamatory.
- Clause: consists of subject, verb, predicate
  Predicate has object, complement, adverbial.
- Phrase: a unit of two or more words
  Types: noun, verb, adverbial, adjectival, prepositional.

CHAPTER 14

Grammar 2: morphology

What is morphology?

Morphology and **syntax** are the two aspects of grammar. Syntax has been dealt with in the previous chapter, so now we turn to morphology.

The term morphology is used in linguistics. The Greek word *morphe* means form, and *logos* means word. You may remember the television artist Tony Hart's Morph, which was a little clay man that could easily change shape. We are looking here at word structure, the shape of the word. So morphology is the study of the form of words.

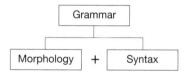

For example, look at the word *please* (Figure 14.1) and the number of words which can be made from it by the addition of one or more morphemes.

What is a morpheme?

A morpheme is the smallest unit of grammar. The word *unkind* has two morphemes: *un* and *kind*; *unhappiness* has three: *un*, *happy*, and *ness*, and even the one-syllable word *dogs* has two morphemes *dog* and the final *s*. So when we divide a word into morphemes we are splitting it into units of meaning, and into grammatical units. This normally means splitting it into parts which include the base word, with additional affixes, that is, prefixes and suffixes.

The division of the word into morphemes may coincide with syllable boundaries, as *un-help-ful* or *dis-place-ment*. But this is not always the case: in *renationalize* there are five syllables but only four morphemes:

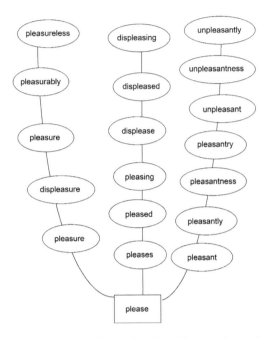

Figure 14.1 Words formed from 'please' by the addition of morphemes.

*re-nation-al-ize.*The next task will provide you with some practice with the morphological elements of words.

Task 14.1

Divide the following words into morphemes. Cover the answers (overleaf) until you are ready to check.

Separate the prefixes, base words and suffixes into columns. There may be more than one entry in each column, for example:

	Prefix	Base word	Suffix
unreclaimed	un re	claim	ed

Here are the words:

1. listless
2. impossibility
3. subconscious
4. extraordinary
5. antiseptic
6. punishment
7. hopefulness
8. nationalization
9. arrival
10. submariners
11. unrealistic
12. antidisestablishmentarianism

Check your answers overleaf.

Task 14.1

continued

			Prefix	Base word	Suffix
A	1.	listless		list	less
	2.	impossibility	im	possible	ity
	3.	subconscious	sub	conscious	
	4.	extraordinary	extra	ordinary	
	5.	antiseptic	anti	septic	
	6.	punishment		punish	ment
	7.	hopefulness		hope	ful ness
	8.	nationalization		nation	al ize ation
	9.	arrival		arrive	al
	10.	submariners	sub	marine	er s
	11.	unrealistic	un	real	ist ic
	12.	antidisestablishmentarianism	anti dis	establish	ment arian ism

Within morphology, linguists actually make a further distinction, which will be mentioned here. It is not necessary as far as ordinary teaching is concerned, but may be of personal academic interest to you. Morphology can be divided into inflexional morphology and derivational (sometimes called lexical) morphology.

Inflexional morphology

This studies the way words vary in their form to make grammatical contrasts. This usually involves the use of suffixes; *dogs* has the plural -*s*, and the suffixes in *hops*, *hopped*, *hopping* are only there to make the grammatical distinctions of number or tense: 'three hops', or 'John hops'; 'we hopped' (past tense), or 'they are hopping' (present continuous tense). These inflexional suffixes are formed with grammatical endings, which are well known and familiar. In fact these grammatical endings do not come and go, and have hardly changed for centuries. Inflexional suffixes are not usually listed in most dictionaries, as they do not make a difference to the meaning of the word, just to its grammatical use.

As an aside, it is often just these words, base words with added suffixes, that students have difficulty in spelling, and if a student wants to look up *hopped*, *hopping*, or *ridiculed*, *ridiculing*, then he needs to consult a spelling dictionary, which lists not only the headwords but those words with the suffixes too.

Derivational morphology

Derivational morphology, on the other hand (sometimes called lexical morphology), studies the ways new items of vocabulary can be made up out of a combination of elements, as in *in-describ-able*, or *mis-place* or *descend-ant*. The meaning of these words is different from the meaning of the base word on its own. The dictionary deals with these suffixed words in quite a different way. Words with derivational suffixes are usually found as separate entries in the dictionary as they require a separate definition from that of the base word. So if you wanted to look up the word *formed* in a dictionary, you would look up the word form as a verb, and not expect to see all versions of the verb listed, as this is merely an inflexional suffix. However, if you wanted the word *deform* that would be listed as a separate entry.

We often make up new words by adding new suffixes.

Example

When the powerful word *Watergate* entered the language in 1973, with its strong overtones of political and moral scandal, it was not long before newspapers were coining new words using *-gate* as a suffix to convey the uncovering of information which would besmirch reputations: *Irangate*, *Thatchergate* and *Camillagate*.

So suffixes can be purely grammatical in function, or they can change the meaning of a base word.

The distinction between derivational and inflexional morphology will not be dwelt on here. It is enough for teaching purposes to know that morphology is concerned with morphemes, which consist of prefixes, base words and suffixes.

For good readers and spellers, words seem to fall quite naturally into separate units of meaning and grammar, *un-know-ing*, *un-friendl(y)-ness*, *pre-determin(e)-ism*. The fact that most of us can easily segment words into morphemes demonstrates that we have a good understanding of both the meaningful elements and the grammatical units that go to make up words.

So adept are we at this that some humour relies on the moving of morphological boundaries: splitting and joining the morphemes in different ways. The Knock-Knock jokes make extensive use of this.

Knock, knock.
Who's there?
Soup.
Soup who?
Souperman.

Mrs Malaprop was mistress of the misplaced morpheme. Malapropisms often involve attaching the wrong prefix to the root word: 'Illiterate him, I say, quite from your mind,' ordered Mrs Malaprop; 'Make no delusions to the past'; 'Sure if I reprehend anything in this world, it is the use of my oracular tongue'. These linguistic games all tap our awareness of the morphemes in words.

Affixes: prefixes and suffixes

Let us consider the effects of suffixes and prefixes in a text.

Task 14.2

This passage is written without suffixes. How many times must you read it to put the suffixes in correctly? How many suffixes were missing? Cover the answer section until you are ready to check.

Profess Binns was look at her in such amaze, Harry was sure no student had ever interrupt him before. The profess peer at Hermione as though he had never seen a student proper before. But the whole class was now hang on his ever word. He look dim at them all, ever face turn to his. Harry could tell he was complete throw by such an unexpected show of interest.

A

Profess**or** Binns was look**ing** at her in such amaze**ment**, Harry was sure no student had ever interrupt**ed** him before. The professor peer**ed** at Hermione as though he had never seen a student proper**ly** before. But the whole class was now hang**ing** on his ever**y** word. He look**ed** dim**ly** at them all, ever**y** face turn**ed** to his. Harry could tell he was complete**ly** throw**n** by such an unexpect**ed** show of interest.

Did you get all 16 suffixes? There were nine different ones: *-or, -ing, -ment, -ed, -ly, -ing, -y, -n* and *-ed*.

Task 14.3

This passage is written without prefixes. How many times must you read it to put them in correctly?

Cover the answer overleaf and list the missing prefixes.

The men on the marine could not have had time to pare for the plosion that wrecked their vessel. The national cry that followed focused on the sident's judgement in not rupting his holiday in order to vise the rescue.

Task 14.3
continued

A

Check your answer:

The men on the **sub**marine could not have had time to **pre**pare for the **ex**plosion that wrecked their vessel. The national **out**cry that followed focused on the **Pre**sident's judgement in not **inter**rupting his holiday in order to **super**vise the rescue.

There were six different prefixes: *sub-*, *pre-*, *ex-*, *out-*, *inter-* and *super-*.

In these tasks, you probably found it harder to work out which prefixes were missing than which suffixes. When the suffixes were missing you would find that you understood the general gist of the passage, but it sounded a bit odd, that is, ungrammatical. But when the prefixes were missing, you had to work quite hard before the meaning became clear.

Morphological units

Now we will look separately at each of these morphological items: prefixes, base words and suffixes.

Base words

Base words are called root words in some literature. Words which have the same base, or root, are often linked, but are difficult to look up in a dictionary if the common element is not in the initial position. So while it is easy to look up words starting with *omni-* or *aqua-* it is more difficult to find words which all contain the base word *fix*.

Some specialist dictionaries list groups of words alphabetically on the basis of the functional elements they contain. So words ending in *-archy*, are listed together, and when searching for words which contain the morpheme fix we would unearth *affix*, *crucifix*, *infix*, *prefix*, *suffix* and *transfix*.

However, with the introduction of computerized forms of dictionaries on CD or online, such as the *New Shorter Oxford English Dictionary*, such search facilities are making thousands of words and morphemes much more accessible to the interested amateur as well as scholars of philology and linguistics.

Suffixes

A suffix is a letter or letters added to the end of a base word to change its function or meaning. Suffixes can sometimes be divided by the function they perform. Some suffixes specifically form nouns, such as the *-age* in *mileage*; *-hood*, as in *childhood*; and the *-ism*, as in *nationalism*. Other examples are listed in Table 14.1.

Table 14.1 Suffixes which form nouns

Suffix	Example	Suffix	Example
-age	package, wastage	-hood	childhood
-al	perusal	-ing	building
-ant	dependant	-ism	optimism
-(a)tion	administration	-ist	optimist
-(c)ian	magician Parisian	-ite	socialite
-dom	freedom	-ity	acidity
-ee	employee	-let	leaflet
-eer	engineer	-ling	duckling
-er	teacher	-ment	enjoyment
-(e)ry	chivalry	-ness	happiness

There are other suffixes which signify an adjective, such as *-able*, in *washable*. See Table 14.2 for others with examples.

Table 14.2 Suffixes which form adjectives

Suffix	Example	Suffix	Example
-able	comfortable	-ive	restive
-al	comical	-less	hopeless
-ed	striped	-like	childlike
-esque	statuesque	-ous	famous
-ful	wonderful	-some	troublesome
-ic	romantic	-worthy	trustworthy
-ish	childish	-y	sticky

Foreign suffixes can cause problems for English speakers, and these are carefully listed in most dictionaries. So, the English endings of *-s* and *-es* may be used on some foreign words, to make a plural, but on other words (particularly if the vocabulary is more technical or formal) the suffix of the original language is usually used. Examples of those which have the anglicized *s* or *-es* are the plurals: *circuses, viruses, areas, sopranos*. But the following words retain the plurals of their original language: *stimuli, larvae, bacteria, crises, graffiti*. Table 14.3 gives examples taken from David Crystal's *The Cambridge Encyclopaedia of the English Language* (1985b), showing words whose plurals are anglicized or foreign.

However, there seems to be no consensus about the plural form of many such foreign words, and the following may be found taking a plural

Table 14.3 Endings of foreign words

		Anglicized plural		Foreign plural	
		Singular	Plural -s / -es	Singular	Plural (original language)
Latin-based endings	-us	plus	pluses	locus	loci
		campus	campuses	stimulus	stimuli
	-a	drama	dramas	larva	larvae
		panorama	panoramas		
	-um	album	albums	datum	data
				curriculum	curricula
Greek-based endings	-es	suffix	suffixes	index	indices
		complex	complexes	matrix	matrices
	-is			analysis	analyses
				thesis	theses
				neurosis	neuroses
	-on	proton	protons	criterion	criteria
		horizon	horizons		
Italian-based words	-o	soprano	sopranos	mafioso	mafiosi
		piano	pianos		

ending of either formation, the anglicized one or the foreign one: *formulas* and *formulae*; *curriculums* and *curricula*. In some such cases the meanings of the different forms have diverged: (spirit) *mediums*; (mass) *media*: *appendixes* (in bodies or in books); *appendices* (in books only).

Suffixing rules

The rules for adding suffixes are the most reliable of English spelling rules, so they are worth learning and teaching. There are basically four. Before considering the rules, we should first look at the suffixes themselves.

Task 14.4

Look at these two columns of suffixes and decide the criterion by which they have been sorted into two types:

-able	-ful
-al	-less
-ed	-ness
-er	-ly
-ic	-ment
-ing	-some
-ous	-hood
-al	-let

You probably knew or spotted that there are two types of suffixes, those that start with a vowel (in the left-hand column) and those that start with a consonant (in the right). So we can refer to a suffix as a vowel suffix or a consonant suffix, classifying it by the first letter of the suffix.

In many cases, when adding a suffix to a word, the two morphemes are just joined together, for example, *childhood, strained, counting*. This gives us the simplest rule, the 'add rule'. But this is not always the case. Apart from just adding the base word and suffix together, there are three other rules which are used.

Task 14.5

Add the following words and suffixes and try to identify any modifications which you have to make in the spelling of the completed word.

Cover the answers below until you are ready to check.

Can you identify the four rules?

Base word	Suffix	Base word	Suffix
child	hood	balance	ing
stop	er	slop	y
shake	ing	subdue	ed
steady	er	happy	er
strain	ed	train	s
hug	ed	ease	y
rob	ed	merry	ment
trade	er	grip	ing
crazy	ly	hid	en
count	ing	sand	er
absolute	ly	copy	ed
baby	es	rehearse	al

(+ between the two Base word/Suffix pairs)

A

The words can be classified like this:

Add	Double	Drop	Change
childhood	stopper	shaking	steadier
strained	hugged	trader	crazily
counting	robbed	balancing	babies
absolutely	sloppy	subdued	happier
trains	gripping	easy	copied
sander	hidden	rehearsal	merriment

You probably identified some words with no modification; some words which drop the *e*; those which double the middle consonant; and those in which the *y* at the end of the base word was changed to *i*.

From that exercise you would discover the four rules:

- add
- double the middle consonant
- drop the e
- change the ending of the base word

Let us consider each rule in turn.

The add rule

Many suffixes can just be added to the base word without any trouble, as in, for example, *trains*, *sander* and *absolutely*. In fact most consonant suffixes can be slotted on to a base word without any more ado.

So the rule for using 'add' is the default position: use it for joining most base words and suffixes, except if any other rule is needed.

Therefore if many suffixes just add on, we'll have to look at the exceptions.

The doubling rule

For the present, let us consider only base words of one syllable. It gets more complicated with longer words. In the instances where you had to double the final consonant of the base word in the task above, as in *stopper*, *hugged*, *robbed* and *sloppy*, the base word had one syllable, ending in a short vowel, followed by one consonant (stŏp, hŭg) and the suffix you were adding was always a vowel suffix (*-er*, *-ed*).

In some American spelling books, this is called the 1-1-1 rule; that is, a word of ONE syllable, with ONE short vowel, followed by ONE consonant. Such words will double that final consonant if a vowel suffix is being added. All these attributes need to be in place before the rule applies.

1 syllable	1 short vowel	1 consonant	+	vowel suffix
hid	ĭ	d		ĕn

For example:

vc		**v**		
stop	+	ing	=	stopping
vc		**v**		
pat	+	ed	=	patted
vc		**v**		
rob	+	ed	=	robbed
vc		**v**		
slop	+	y	=	sloppy

The advanced doubling rule

The doubling rule above only applies to words of one syllable. Now we come to the more complicated rule: the doubling rule in longer words. If the base word has two syllables or more, take care, as you will need to consider another attribute: you need to identify the stressed syllable in the word.

If you wish to spell words such as *referring* or *targeted*, speak the word aloud and listen for the stressed syllable, which is the one with most volume and emphasis. In the case of these two words, the stressed syllable in each is in bold: re-**fer**-ing and **tar**-get-ed.

Some people find this difficult, and if so, it is best to try stressing (shouting) the different syllables in a word, until you hear the one that sounds right.

Which sounds most like *terminal*, as in 'terminal exam'?

ter - min - al ✓

ter - **min** - al

ter - min - **al**

The stress is on the first syllable of terminal. Once you can identify the stressed syllable in the word you want to write, the rest is easy. If the stress is on the last syllable of the base word, then treat that syllable as if it were a one-syllable word, and double the middle consonant if the 1:1:1 rule applies:

vc   **v**

re-**fer** +   ing   =   referring

vc   **v**

ad-**mit** +   ance   =   admittance

If the stress is on the first syllable, do not double the final consonant:

vc   **v**

tar-get +   ed   =   targeted

vc   **v**

con-fer +   ence   =   conference

Task 14.6

Add these base words and suffixes and decide whether you need to double or not, according to the stress in the completed word. Cover the answers until you are ready to check.

Task 14.6
continued

Base	+	Suffix		Base	+	Suffix
admit	+	ing		commit	+	ed
permit	+	ed		confer	+	ing
visit	+	ed		confer	+	ence
upset	+	ing		forget	+	ing
prefer	+	ed		rivet	+	ing
occur	+	ed		develop	+	ed
benefit	+	ed				

A

Base	+	Suffix	=	Rule	Result
ad**mit**	+	ing	=	double	admi**tt**ing
per**mit**	+	ed	=	double	permi**tt**ed
visit	+	ed	=		visited
up**set**	+	ing	=	double	upse**tt**ing
pre**fer**	+	ed	=	double	prefe**rr**ed
oc**cur**	+	ed	=	double	occu**rr**ed
benefit	+	ed	=		benefited
com**mit**	+	ed	=	double	commi**tt**ed
con**fer**	+	ing	=	double	confe**rr**ing
confer	+	ence	=		conference
for**get**	+	ing	=	double	forge**tt**ing
rivet	+	ing	=		riveting
de**vel**op	+	ed	=		developed

The stressed syllables have been typed in bold, and it can be seen that in five of the examples, the stress is not on the final syllable of the base word, so the suffix is just added to the base word.

The -ll rule

There is an extra, and happily easy, suffixing rule which applies to British English, but not to American English. If the base word ends in the letter *l*, it is doubled before a vowel suffix:

Base	+	Suffix	=	British English	American English
travel	+	ing	=	travelling	traveling
cancel	+	ed	=	cancelled	canceled
rival	+	ed	=	rivalled	rivaled
libel	+	ing	=	libelled	libeled

The drop the e rule

This is a very familiar rule which you may have taught or remember being taught. Again you need to be sure you have all the elements together before you apply the rule. The rule of course is that you drop the final *e* of a word (of whatever length) if you are adding a vowel suffix. This rule will stand you in very good stead for most occasions.

		v		
dance	+	ing	=	dancing
		v		
time	+	er	=	timer
		v		
enhance	+	ed	=	enhanced
		v		
slime	+	y	=	slimy

There are a few exceptional words in which the *e* is not dropped. Where they do occur, the *e* needs to be kept for some other reason. For example, the *e* may be needed to soften a *c* or a *g* as in *traceable* and *spongeable*, or to make a distinction with another word which would otherwise be identical, as in *singing/singeing*, and *dying/dyeing*.

In summary, the main exception to the 'drop *e*' rule is, retain the *e* to keep *c* or *g* soft:

trace	+	able	=	traceable
change	+	able	=	changeable

The change rule

This is the most complex rule, and admits of several exceptions, but it is nevertheless worth knowing and applying in a large number of cases.

For this rule, we need to look first at the ending of the base word. If the base word ends in the letter *y*, beware when adding suffixes. If there is a consonant before the *y*, for the most part you change the *y* to *i* and add the suffix. And this time it doesn't matter what kind of suffix it is: it can be a vowel suffix or a consonant suffix.

c		**v**		
try	+	ed	=	tried
c		**v**		
deny	+	al	=	denial
c		**c**		
merry	+	ment	=	merriment
c		**v**		
marry	+	age	=	marriage

If you want to add the suffix *-s* in this case, you add *-es* instead. One of few parroted spelling rules that used to be taught in school was the 'change the *y* to *i* and add *es*', and you may have learned that one.

cry	+	s	=	cri + es	cries
deny	+	s	=	deni + es	denies
supply	+	s	=	suppli+ es	supplies

These two guidelines work nicely with the words above and with *babies*, *happier*, *copied*, *happiness* and *merriment*. They don't work with *trying*, *defying* or *Toryism* because in these words, if the *y* of the base word were changed to an *i*, there would be two *i*'s together in the word, which is not permissible in English. (The word *skiing* is the lone exception with double *i*, but that's a Norwegian word and we can't legislate for foreign words.) Therefore when adding a suffixing beginning with *i*, to a base word ending in *y*, just add it on without any change.

study	+	ing	=	studying
reply	+	ing	=	replying
copy	+	ist	=	copyist

If the *y* at the end of the base word is part of a vowel digraph, such as *ay*, *oy* or *uy* then leave it alone. This results in words such as *stayed* in which the suffix is merely added to the base word. Vowel digraphs ay, ey, oy, uy:

spray	+	er	=	sprayer
journey	+	ed	=	journeyed
toy	+	ed	=	toyed
buy	+	er	=	buyer

There are one or two more exceptions or alternatives for words ending in *y*, so that for instance both forms of some words are used, for example *drier/dryer* and *crier/cryer*.

The change rule works well if you can remember it, but it is a bit complex, and these are exactly the sorts of words for which a spelling dictionary is designed.

The other kind of affix is the one that comes at the beginning, not at the end of words, and this of course is the prefix.

Prefixes

Although the function of the suffix is both grammatical and semantic, the function of a prefix is semantic: a prefix, attached to the beginning of a word, changes the meaning of the word: *popular* becomes *unpopular*; *complete* becomes *incomplete*; a *husband* may become an *ex-husband*; and a *circle* halved becomes a *semicircle*. Each has a different meaning from the original base word.

New words may be coined using prefixes, and new prefixes are sometimes created. In the 1980s the prefixes *mega-* and *loadsa-* were used as in *megatrendy*, *megaworry*, *megacity*, and *loadsamoney*, *loadsaspace*, *loadsapeople*.

David Crystal (1995) identified 57 varieties of prefix and grouped them according to meaning (see Table 14.4). Some prefixes appear more than once in the list because they have more than one meaning.

Table 14.4 57 varieties of prefix

Negation		Location and distance	
a-	-theist, -moral	extra-	-terrestrial, -mural
dis-	-obey, -believe	fore-	-shore, -leg
in-	-complete, -decisive	inter-	-marry, -national
non-	-smoker, -medical	intra-	-venous, -national
un-	-wise, -helpful	pan-	-African, -American
		super-	-script, -structure
Reversal		tele-	-scope, -phone
de-	-frost,-fraud	trans-	-plant, -atlantic
dis-	-connect, -infect		
un-	-do, -mask	**Time and order**	
		ex-	-husband, -president
Disparaging		fore-	-warn, -shadow
mal-	-treat, -function	neo-	-Gothic, -classical
mis-	-hear, -lead	paleo-	-lithic, -botany
pseudo-	-intellectual	post-	-war, -modern
		pre-	-school, -marital
Size or degree		proto-	-type, -European
arch-	-duke, -enemy	re-	-cycle, -new
co-	-habit, -pilot		
hyper-	-market, -card	**Number**	
mega-	-loan, -merger	bi-	-cycle, -lingual
mini-	-skirt, -bus	demi-	-god, -tasse
out-	-class, -run	di-	-oxide, -graph
over-	-worked, -flow	mono-	-rail, -plane
sub-	-normal, -conscious	multi-	-racial, -purpose
super-	-market, -man	poly-	-technic, -gamy
sur-	-tax, -charge	semi-	-circle, -detached
ultra-	-modern, -sound	tri-	-maran,-pod
under-	-charge, -play	uni-	-sex, -cycle
vice-	-chair, -president		

Table 14.4 contd.

Orientation		Grammatical conversion:	
anti-	-clockwise, -social	*Verb to adjective*	
auto-	-suggestion, -biography	a-	-stride, -board
contra-	-indicate, -flow		
counter-	-clockwise, -act	*Noun to verb*	
pro-	-socialist, -consul	be-	-friend, -witch
		en-	-flame, -danger

All of these prefixes can be divided into two kinds, consonant prefixes and vowel prefixes. Examples of the former would be: *in-*, *un-*, *con-*, *inter-*, which end in a consonant, and examples of the latter would be *re-*, *pre-*, *pro-*, *intro-*, which end in a vowel.

You may be relieved to find that there are only two prefixing rules: add and change. This time it is the prefixes ending in a vowel which are easy to combine with a base word, as they can just be added onto the beginning of the base word. This results in words like *resit*, and *react*; *presume* and *pre-empt*, *produce* and *proactive*.

Many of the consonant prefixes can just be added to the base word too. We can cite words such as *unwise*, *disobey* and *superstructure*.

Change rule

However, some of the consonant prefixes, particularly those of Latin origin, change their last letter to match the first letter of the base word. This makes ungainly constructions such as *in+legal* and *ob+fer* and *con+rupt*, much easier to pronounce as *illegal*, *offer* and *corrupt*. The prefixes *ad-*, *con-*, *in-*, *ob-*, *sub-*, *dis-* and *ex-* may all change their final letter. When the prefix *in-* is followed by *l*, *r* or *m*, it is likely to change and produce double letters (illogical, immortal, irregular). However, when *in-* or *con-* precedes a *p* as in *in+prove* or *con+pel* euphony demands that the *n* is pronounced like an *m*, and so it has become assimilated, so we say and write *impossible*, *important* and *compel*. Interestingly though, this change has not yet occurred with the computer jargon word *input*, but in time it will probably be spelt with an *m* too. The prefix *ex-* may change (ex+fort=effort) or just drop the *x* (ex+ migrate= emigrate).

If we know that consonant prefixes have a tendency to change, it makes us much more aware of the possibility of and reason for double letters in these words. Of course the vocabulary here tends to be more advanced, and often depends on the ability to spot a Latin base word. Look at the examples in the task below.

Task 14.7

Split the words into the original prefix and base word
e.g. *immobile = in / mobile*. You may also find a suffix or two.
Use a piece of paper to mask the answers in the last three
columns, and expose each answer after you have decided
on the word.

A

	Prefix	Base word	Suffix
innumerable	in	numer	able
immortal	in	mortal	
illuminate	in	lumin	ate
impartial	in	part	ial
irreplaceable	in, re	place	able
account	ad	count	
announcement	ad	nounce	ment
collecting	con	lect	ing
corrected	con	rect	ed
occurred	ob	cur	ed
oppose	ob	pose	
suffix	sub	fix	
supported	sub	port	ed
effective	ex	fect	ive
ejected	ex	ject	ed

Because of the length and difficulty of the words, this prefixing rule is one which you would teach to students who already had fairly secure and sophisticated spelling skills.

Conclusion

In this chapter, we have covered the segmentation of words into morphemes, the smallest units of meaning and grammar. Students with literacy difficulties may have great problems in seeing, hearing and being aware of these units. We need to help them to identify these morphemes as an aid to understanding the meaning of new words, and to spelling the words they need to write. The spelling rules for adding suffixes are clear and reliable, and need to be understood and used well.

Summary

```
              ┌──────────────┐
              │   Grammar    │
              └──────────────┘
        ┌──────────┴──────────┐
  ┌──────────────┐   +   ┌──────────────┐
  │  Morphology  │       │    Syntax    │
  └──────────────┘       └──────────────┘
```

■ Morpheme: the smallest unit of grammatical analysis
　unhappiness {un} {happ(y)} {ness}
　dogs　　　　{dog} {s}

■ Morphemes consist of:
　base words (lexical words) + affixes (= prefixes + suffixes)

■ Morphology: the study of the form of words
　Inflexional:　　　　　　　　dogs　　　　　hops　　　hopped hopping
　Derivational (lexical):　　{descend} {ant}

■ Suffix types: vowel suffixes and consonant suffixes

■ Suffixing rules
　Add:　　　　default position
　Double:　　1:1:1 rule in words of one syllable + vowel suffix
　　　　　　　i. 1:1:1 rule in longer words if stress is on last syllable of base word
　　　　　　　ii. Letter l always doubles before a vowel suffix (British English only)
　Drop e　　before a vowel suffix: any length of word
　Change　　if a word ends in consonant + y, change y to i and add suffix

■ Prefixes
　Prefixes change word meaning
　Prefixing rules:
　Add:　　　　default position
　Change:　　if prefix ends in a consonant, it may change to first letter of base
　　　　　　　word, esp. if m, l, r

■ Conclusion
　Knowledge of morphemes is important for understanding the meaning of
　words, for grammar and for spelling.

CHAPTER 15

Parts of speech/word classes

Where do parts of speech fit into grammar?

The grammar of a language is made up of syntax and morphology. In English syntax, word order is important in the phrase, clause and sentence so that meaning is communicated clearly. The words within sentences have meaning but they also have a grammatical function, and in order to describe these we need to refer to their parts of speech.

In the previous chapter on morphology, parts of speech were referred to in considering how suffixes affect a word.

What are parts of speech?

The traditional grammarians of English list eight parts of speech based on Latin and Greek grammatical analysis. Modern grammarians, since the development of structural linguistics, prefer to use the term 'word class' rather than 'parts of speech' but by and large the terms are interchangeable. The main parts of speech are:

1. noun
2. verb
3. adjective
4. pronoun
5. preposition
6. adverb
7. conjunction
8. interjection

Also jockeying for a place in the list are the terms **participle** and **article**. Participle is now usually a sub-category of the verb. The term article is utilized in English for two words: *the* (the definite article) and *a* or *an* (the indefinite article), which occur before a noun in a sentence. You will often also find that, in some grammar books, these are called determiners.

A part of speech is determined by the use of a word in a particular sentence. Most dictionaries identify the part of speech of words along with their use and meaning.

One word may have different meanings according to its part of speech, e.g. 'These shoes *match* your dress' (verb); 'The best team won the *match*' (noun). These would be listed as different parts of speech, and with different meanings in the dictionary. However, contemporary usage in speech or writing may alter a class of word. For example, the word *party* is usually used as a noun (a birthday party, the political party) but may sometimes be used as a verb (she will party all night). So the part of speech is determined by its use and position in a sentence.

Students are used to understanding the meanings of words but they may have difficulty in classifying words according to their function in a sentence, and therefore, they may find grammatical terms meaningless and hard to memorize. All of these eight terms for parts of speech should be known by 11-year-old children at the end of Key Stage 2, according to the National Literacy Strategy. Children may have heard them during literacy lessons, but be unable to understand or remember the terms or the concepts.

If you are an educator, as you go through each term and the examples for it, think how you could make the term meaningful and memorable for your students. The following task is a short pre-test to determine your own level of confidence with the terms.

Task 15.1

Test your own present knowledge of parts of speech. On paper, write the definition you would use, give two or three words as an example, and put them into a phrase or clause to demonstrate their use. The table, with answers, is provided as a summary at the end of the chapter.

Part of speech	Definition	Example	Use
noun			
verb			
adjective			
pronoun			

Task 15.1
continued

Part of speech	Definition	Example	Use
preposition			
adverb			
conjunction			
interjection			

The noun

A **n**oun is a **n**aming word (the alliterative definition can help some students). The word noun originally derived from the Latin word *nomen* meaning a name. Nouns are used mainly as the subject or the object in a sentence, and often in combination with the definite article (*the* girl, *the* house, *the* invention) or with the indefinite article (*a* car, *a* mountain or *a* decision).

There are several subclasses of nouns and the National Literacy Strategy uses these four terms:

* proper nouns
* common nouns
* collective nouns
* abstract nouns

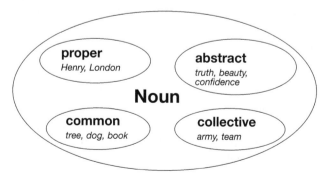

Figure 15.1 Noun subclasses.

Other terms for nouns are **concrete**, **countable** or **uncountable**. Concrete nouns refer to objects which can be seen and touched, as in *paper, glass, door*. Countable nouns are words such as *book, student, pebble*, whereas uncountable nouns are words such as *information, earth, jewellery*.

The four main categories in Figure 15.1 are worth closer consideration.

Proper nouns

Children can most easily understand proper nouns using their own names as an example. Proper nouns start with a capital letter (Emma, Matthew, Shahid, Smith and Manchester). They are the names of specified people, places, times, occupations, events, publications and so on. They are not usually preceded by an article. (We don't say *a* London, *the* America, *the* July.)

Common nouns

Common nouns are most other nouns. They are usually used with an article, so we say *a* book, *a* hat, *the* church, *the* game, *the* waiter. Most common nouns can be used in the singular or plural: *cat/cats, farmer/farmers*.

Collective nouns

Collective nouns name a group of people or things such as *army, flock, crowd, committee, team* and *government*. These words refer to one thing, even though it may contain several members or items.

In a prescriptive grammar these words should be treated as a singular noun, so we should say (and in particular, write) 'the government *is*', 'the committee *was*', 'the team *has* arrived'. Complainants often criticize broadcasters for misusing collective nouns, when they say 'the committee *were* deciding', 'the team *have* come'. The speaker in such cases may have been thinking of the individual members of these collective nouns, and therefore used the plural form of the verb. As teachers we should guide students towards using the singular verb with a collective noun.

Abstract nouns

An abstract noun refers to a concept, an event, a quality or a state, an action, such as *beauty, inspiration, happiness, health, acting*. Abstract nouns are difficult for children to identify, but important for older students to recognize and refer to, when analysing literature or poetry.

Gender

Traditional grammarians would describe other attributes of nouns such as gender and case. In French and Italian, for instance, all nouns are masculine or feminine, but this is not so in English. In addition, the influence of recent political correctness has meant that the few nouns in English which assign a particular gender are used less frequently (authoress, poetess; chairman, chairwoman). However, some words still exist which are masculine or feminine such as *host/hostess*, *prince/princess*, *waiter/waitress*.

Case

The case of a noun refers to the set of forms it may take, dependent on its use in the sentence. Latin was an inflectional language, in which the case of a noun was denoted by differences in ending of the word:

homo fecit mensam

fecit homo mensam

mensam homo fecit

All of the Latin sentences above mean 'the man (*homo*) made (*fecit*) the table (*mensam*)'. It is the ending of the word which denotes whether it is the subject or the object of the sentence. Word order is irrelevant.

In Table 15.1 the Latin word *homo*, meaning *man*, is declined to show how the change of word ending denotes its case. There were six cases in Latin.

Table 15.1 Latin declension of *homo* ('man')

Case	Word	Use
Nominative	homo	subject of the sentence: **The man** made ...
Vocative	homo	the form of address: **O man!**
Accusative	hominem	object of the verb: He hit **the man.**
Genitive	hominis	possession: **the man's** table
Dative	homini	indirect object: He gave it **to the man**; **for the man**
Ablative	homine	**by, with** or **from, the man**

Modern English depends on the syntax of the sentence, that is, the place of the noun in the sentence, to indicate its function. Changes in word order can radically affect the meaning. If the position of the noun is changed, its function as subject or object of the sentence is changed, as shown in 'The man ate the fish', or 'The fish ate the man'. As you can see in Table 15.1, the case of a noun in modern English is dependent also on the use of prepositions.

However, one case is still indicated on nouns in modern English and that is the genitive or possessive case which is signalled by use of the apostrophe *s*, as in 'Tom's', in a phrase such as 'Tom's coat'. Similarly, 'the men's books', 'the cat's paw' and 'the traveller's story'.

Singular and plural

Most nouns occur either in the singular (one coat, a baby, a garden, a dog) or in the plural (several coats, babies, gardens and dogs). Plurals are regularly formed by the addition of an *s* to the singular form. But some nouns have an irregular plural. Young or immature children often overgeneralize this rule and apply the suffix *s* rule to irregular plurals such as *mouse, foot, man* rendering them as *mouses, foots* and *mans*, instead of *mice, feet* and *men*. The same may occur with nouns whose plural is the same as the singular such as *sheep, deer* and *salmon*.

Some nouns may look like plurals because they end in the letter *s*, but they behave as singular nouns. Examples of these are *physics, mumps, billiards* (we say physics *is* a difficult subject, or his mumps *has* disappeared).

Conversely there are nouns which appear only as plurals. You would never say 'her jeans *is* too tight' even though you are talking about one garment, or 'the scissors *is* lost'. Both of these take a plural verb 'jeans *are* tight' and 'scissors *are* lost'. The words *outskirts, dregs, remains* and *tropics* are dealth with similarly.

The verb

A verb is a word or group of words, which names an action or state of being. It is commonly described as a 'doing' word. The verb is the most important, compulsory part of the sentence. Verbs can be divided into full verbs such as *hears, held, listened*, and auxiliary verbs. The auxiliary verbs are the ones such as *to be, to have, to do*, which help out with some tenses. They appear in constructions such as 'he *is* mending', 'they *have* replied', 'I *do* like her'. The other auxiliary verbs are the modal verbs such as *may, can, will*, which change the mood of the statement. They make the verb less definite, or qualify the action in some way: 'I may come later'; 'he could drive'; 'she will think about it'.

Full verbs can be divided into regular verbs, which have a predictable form in the past tense, and irregular verbs, which have to be learned.

Tense

The shortest sentence in the Bible is 'Jesus wept', using the past tense of the verb to weep. The tense of the verb shows the time at which the action of the verb takes place, in the past, the present or the future.

The past tense may be expressed as 'I walked', 'she jumped', 'they thought', or the verb *to have* may be used with the verb to form the perfect tense as in 'I have walked', 'she has jumped', 'they have thought'.

The present tense may be expressed as 'I walk', 'he thinks', 'they laugh' or using the verb *to be* to form the continuous present: 'I am walking', 'he is thinking', 'they are laughing', to indicate that the action is still continuing.

The future tense is formed with *will* or *shall*: 'I shall meet', 'she will cook', 'they will invade'.

Most reports or narratives are written in the past tense and so this is a form which children must quickly master in order to write their news or a story.

The present tense is used for timeless statements or eternal truths as in 'oil floats on water' and 'beauty is in the eye of the beholder'. The present is used more in speech than writing, although it may be used for dramatic effect in a narrative as the action reaches a climax:

> The door yields and bursts open: suddenly a stench fills the air, rats scurry across the floor, flies buzz round her head, she sees the body and screams.

Person

The action of the verb has to be performed by someone, so a person usually precedes the verb. In standard English the first person is the speaker or writer denoted by *I* or *we*, the second person is the person or persons being addressed *you*, and the third person are others being referred to *he*, *she*, *it* or *they*. The grids in the next task tabulate this clearly, showing singular forms and plural forms.

Regular verbs

Regular verbs are predictable in the forms they adopt during changes in tense.

Task 15.2

Choose a regular verb from the following list and go through each table according to the tense given, using the correct pronoun and form of the verb. Make a note each time the verb form changes with the addition of a suffix.

Cover the answers (overleaf) until you are ready to check

to walk, to turn, to hop, to pack, to rush, to buzz

Task 15.2
continued

Present tense

Singular		Plural	
Person		**Person**	
1			
2			
3			

Present continuous

Singular		Plural	
Person		**Person**	
1			
2			
3			

Past tense

Singular		Plural	
Person		**Person**	
1			
2			
3			

A

How many alterations to the base word have you made?

Present tense

Singular		Plural	
Person		**Person**	
1: I	turn	we	turn
2: you	turn	you	turn
3: he/she/it	turns	they	turn

Task 15.2

continued

Present continuous

Singular		Plural	
Person		**Person**	
1: I	am turning	we	are turning
2: you	are turning	you	are turning
3: he/she/it	is turning	they	are turning

Past tense

Singular		Plural	
Person		**Person**	
1: I	turned	we	turned
2: you	turned	you	turned
3: he/she/it	turned	they	turned

In many languages the base form of the verb changes using different endings according to the person and the tense. However, these endings have been largely, but not entirely, dropped in English.

As you probably quickly discovered from that exercise the regular English verb has four forms.

- First, the base form (or infinitive) with no endings (*to walk, turn, lift, buzz*, etc.).
- Second, the base form with the addition of the suffix *s* (or sometimes *-es*) used for the third person singular in the present tense (*he walks, she turns, it buzzes*).
- Third, the *-ing* form, or participle, made by adding *-ing* to the base word. This is used in the present continuous (*she is walking, he is hopping*) and also in the past continuous (*she was walking, he was hopping*).
- Fourth, and finally, the *-ed* form which is the most common way of forming a past tense (*I lifted, it happened*).

Note that in the addition of *-ing* and *-ed* there is sometimes a spelling change. We will deal with these spelling rules in Chapter 17.

Irregular verbs

The exercise you just completed used regular verbs of which there are thousands in modern English. There are also some irregular verbs, but according to David Crystal (1995) fewer than 300 of these. These irregular verbs are the surviving members of the strong verbs of Old English. They use the -s and -ing endings in the same ways as regular verbs but they often have an unpredictable past tense, or an unpredictable past participle form.

The example below contains a few irregular verbs whose change is not predictable.

Base	Past	Past participle
send	sent	sent
take	took	taken
swim	swam	swum
keep	kept	kept

Many of these verbs change the vowel in the past tense. The past tense of a few verbs have the alternative endings, -t or -ed (*burned/burnt*, *learned/learnt*, *spelled/spelt*, *spoiled/spoilt*). In these words the *t* is rare in American English but is often used in British English.

Task 15.3

Try to sort out these verbs for yourself from the following alphabetical list (reading across). The base form is given to you. Think about the past and the past participle of each, as in the table above. First extract and jot down the regular verbs, and then write down each irregular verb with its past tense and past participle.

Cover the answers (overleaf) until you are ready to check.

be	beat	blink	blow
break	bring	burn	cut
drop	flick	greet	help
jump	knot	lie	lay
miss	sell	see	sew
spin	spring	sit	slay
tread	wink	yell	zip

Task 15.3
continued

A

Regular verbs

Base	Past tense	Past participle (has...)
blink	blinked	blinked
drop	dropped	dropped
flick	flicked	flicked
greet	greeted	greeted
help	helped	helped
jump	jumped	jumped
knot	knotted	knotted
miss	missed	missed
wink	winked	winked
yell	yelled	yelled
zip	zipped	zipped

Irregular verbs

Base	Past tense	Past participle (has...)
be	was	been
beat	beat	beaten
blow	blew	blown
break	broke	broken
bring	brought	brought
burn	burned (or burnt)	burned (or burnt)
cut	cut	cut
lie[1]	lay	lain
lay[2]	laid	laid
sell	sold	sold
see	saw	seen
sew	sewed	sewn
spin	spun	spun
spring	sprang	sprung
sit	sat	sat
slay	slew	slain
tread	trod	trodden

[1] intransitive – to lie on the bed   [2] transitive – to lay an egg

Some of those irregular verbs are tricky for adult speakers, and can certainly trip up teenage students. Some patterns were obviously emerging, but never very consistently, so it is difficult to extrapolate from one verb to another. We just get used to one pattern (*spring, sprang, sprung;* / *drink, drank, drunk*) only to find that the change of vowel doesn't work for *blink*, and that it's not *blink, blank, blunk* at all. You will need to be aware of these verbs to help out students who find them difficult in both speech and written work.

Fortunately, there is a limited number of these difficult verbs, and there have been no new additions recently. It seems to be strongly ingrained in us to regularize any new verbs that enter the language. So when the word *fax* was created from the *facsimile*, and then used as a verb, it became 'to fax', 'he faxed' (with the *-ed* suffix in the past tense) and 'he has faxed', treating it as a completely regular verb.

Voice

A final category relating to verbs is voice. English may be written in active voice or passive voice, and these affect both the verb and the sentence structure. Voice involves the relationship of the subject and the object in a sentence.

Active and passive

In an active sentence, the subject of the sentence performs the action: '*Susan* chose the furniture'; '*The cat* caught the mouse'. In a passive sentence the subject has the action performed upon it: '*The furniture was chosen* by Susan', and '*The mouse was caught by* the cat'.

The same meaning can be conveyed whether the sentence is written in the active or passive voice, but there are differences in style and emphasis. Passive sentences are usually more formal, and the passive is the preferred style for reports and academic work, using clauses such as: 'The phosphorus *was placed* in the test tube'; 'The client *was interviewed*'; 'This profile of skills *is considered to be* ...' and so on.

Children need to be able to use verbs correctly, and spell them correctly too. Verbs are very vulnerable to changes in spelling because they may have a change of vowel in different forms, or require the addition of suffixes. We can help our students by teaching the spelling rules which govern suffixes. We'll deal with this in Chapter 17. The choice of a suitable verb in a sentence can often greatly improve our students' writing, and this also needs opportunities for practice. It is therefore important that students learn to recognize and control the verbs in sentences.

Adjectives

Adjectives are much more simple than verbs, and form a sparkly addition to speech or written language. An adjective is commonly defined as a 'describing word'. It is a word or phrase which is added or linked to a noun to describe and qualify it. The adjective is said to qualify a noun or pronoun since it limits the word it describes in some way, by making it more specific. Thus, adding an adjective *red* to the noun *book* limits book since it means we can forget about books of any other colour. Similarly adding *little*, to make it 'little red book' means we can forget about books of any other size and colour.

Adjectives can come before the noun: a *red* house, a *gracious* lady, a *kind* gesture; or often after the verb as a predicate: the house was *white*, the sky turned *blue*, she is *angry*.

In the National Literacy Strategy, adjectives are divided into six types:

1 Number
  These occur, for example, in: *four* books, *three* wishes, she is *thirty*.

2 Quantity
  For example, she wants *more* soup, *all* members of staff, *many* students, *half* a loaf, *few* criminals.

3 Quality
  These are the most common and easily recognized adjectives. Qualities such as *beautiful, fragrant, sparkling, mean* and *miserable* are in this category, as well as words of colour and size such as *purple, yellow, large, tall*.

4 Possessive
  These are found in phrases such as *my* shoes, *your* dinner, *his* anorak, *their* plates.

5 Interrogative
  These often occur, as the name implies, in questions: *which* boy? *whose* house? *what* substance?

6 Demonstrative
  These seem to accompany a demonstrative gesture of the hand, pointing out *that* floorboard, *this* ceiling, *these* walls, *those* screws.

Adjectives can come in strings as in '*an enormous red-brick, Victorian* house' or '*a big, beautiful bouncing* baby'.

Task 15.4

Consider the clusters of adjectives with each noun, below. Write them as a string before the noun, in the order in which they sound best. See if any common sequence emerges. Cover the answers until you are ready to check.

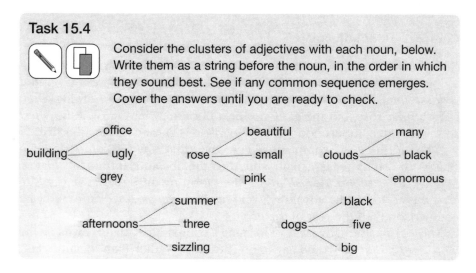

Task 15.4   You almost certainly found that in English we prefer to know
continued   the number or quantity first followed by size, quality, colour
                and classification.

A

Adjectives in strings are usually ordered:

Number	Quantity	Quality	Colour	Classification	
		ugly	grey	office	building
		beautiful, small	pink		rose
	many	enormous	black		clouds
three		sizzling		summer	afternoons
five		big	black		dogs

As native speakers we get a feel for the euphony of strings of adjectives, and would be surprised by phrases such as 'old three silly men'. We would want to rearrange it into 'three silly old men'. Younger children, or those with language problems, may still not be able to tell which sounds right.

Simple and derived adjectives

Adjectives can come in two forms: simple and derived. Simple adjectives would be those such as *red, tall, ugly, beautiful*. Derived adjectives are adjectives made from another class of word, usually with the addition of a suffix so the nouns *health, summer* and *pain* become the adjectives *healthy, summery* and *painful*. The verbs *to help, to jump, to hope* can become the adjectives *helpful, jumpy* and *hopeful*.

Comparison of adjectives

Comparison is a usual attribute of adjectives. If a quality can be ascribed to a noun, we can have more of it, or even the most of it as in *red, redder, reddest; long, longer, longest*. So I may grow a *fine* rose, you may insist you grow a *finer* rose, but the gardener next door, may have grown the *finest* rose in the neighbourhood. The comparison is carried in the adjective.

When forming the comparative adjective (that is when comparing two things) the suffix *-er* is usually added to the absolute form as in *bigger, happier, louder, madder, shorter*. When forming the superlative, the suffix *-est* is added to the absolute form *biggest, happiest, bravest* to indicate comparison with the rest of the group.

There is an alternative way of forming a comparative, that is by using the word *more* and we would say 'more beautiful' rather than 'beautifuller'.

Similarly, the superlative can be formed by using *most* as in 'most difficult' or 'most enormous'.

Task 15.5

Write the comparative and superlative forms of the adjectives given, and try to identify how you decide whether to use a suffix *-er or* -est, or to use *more* and *most*. Cover the answers until you are ready to check.

Absolute	Comparative	Superlative
nice		
tall		
regular		
deadly		
loud		
comfortable		
beautiful		
short		
mysterious		
realistic		
effective		
handsome		
clever		
magical		
good		
bad		
many		

A

	Absolute	Comparative	Superlative
1 syllable	nice	nicer	nicest
	tall	taller	tallest
	loud	louder	loudest
	short	shorter	shortest
2 syllables	deadly	deadlier	deadliest
		more deadly	the most deadly
	clever	cleverer	cleverest
		more clever	the most clever
3 syllables	regular	more regular	the most regular
	comfortable	more comfortable	the most comfortable
	beautiful	more beautiful	the most beautiful
	mysterious	more mysterious	the most mysterious
	realistic	more realistic	the most realistic
	effective	more effective	the most effective
	magical	more magical	the most magical
Irregular words	good	better	best
	bad	worse	worst
	many	more	most

That exercise on comparison of adjectives was for your own interest, but great consensus amongst natural English speakers is usually found. It seems that we are happy to use the suffixes -er and -est on words of one syllable, sometimes on words of two syllables, but when a word reaches three syllables or longer, we almost always use the words *more* and *most* to form the comparative and superlative. We have fine rules of language such as this, which are absorbed by native speakers.

The children and even adults whom we teach may have difficulty with these more subtle aspects of language. Some people confuse the two forms, and produce overkill in phrases such as 'more longer', 'the most beautifullest', which are clearly wrong. Children will need to be warned to avoid such constructions.

We are all bombarded at every turn with comparative and superlative adjectives, as advertisers jostle to grab our attention and persuade us that their product is better than the opposition's: *cleaner, fresher, softer, healthier, smoother, firmer, tastier, purer.* They may even claim that it is the best product on the market, with superlative adjectives such as *best, biggest, finest, brightest and tastiest.*

As teachers we encourage our students to write more vividly by using adjectives in their work. The students also need to recognize a writer's use of adjectives to persuade and influence the reader. When evaluating poetry, the student is often called upon to comment on the use of adjectives. As teachers we must do our best to help them spot these special sparkling, seductive parts of speech.

Pronouns

Our fifth part of speech is the pronoun. A pronoun is a word which stands in for a noun and so avoids repetition in a sentence: 'Peter has just come home. Peter is hungry.' With the use of the pronoun *he* this can be expressed as 'Peter has just come home. He is hungry.'

There are eight different types of pronoun listed here with examples.

Types of pronoun

Personal	*I, you, he, we, they*
Possessive	*his, hers, mine*
Reflexive	*myself, himself, themselves*
Reciprocal	*each other, one another*
Interrogative	*who? what? which?*
Relative	*who, whose, which, what, that*
Demonstrative	*that, these, this, those*
Indefinite	*any, some, many, anyone, somebody*

Personal pronouns

Personal pronouns are the main means of identifying the speaker, the person being addressed, and others. The first person refers to the person who is talking (*I* or *we*). The second person refers to the person to whom one is talking, *you*. The third person refers to a third party, not the one speaking or being spoken to: *he, she, it, they*. These personal pronouns can be in the singular referring to just one person: *I, you, he, she, it*, or in the plural, referring to more than one: *we, you, they*. *We* can refer to one person in the royal *we* as Queen Victoria's famous 'We are not amused'. The verb ending may change to agree with the person of the verb.

Pronouns do change according to *case*, that is whether they are the subject of the sentence, as in, *I* jumped, *you* jumped, *they* jumped, or if they are the object of the sentence. In the following sentences the pronoun is the object of the sentence: 'Ben saw *me*', 'Ben saw *you*', 'Ben saw *him*, or *her*, or *it*'. In the plural, the pronouns are *us, you, them*: 'Ben saw *us*', 'Ben saw *you*', 'Ben saw *them*' (see Table 15.2).

Table 15.2 Personal pronouns

Person	Singular Subject	Object	Plural Subject	Object
first	I	me	we	us
second	you	you	you	you
third	he/she/it	him/her/it	they	them

Students are urged to proofread their work for correct use of pronouns. Sometimes care needs to be taken, as colloquial usage is different from that expected in written English. Even though the sentences 'Me and my friend went to town' and 'Me and him were here first', are sometimes heard in everyday speech, in written speech the words *I* and *he* would be needed as the subject of the sentence: 'I went', and 'I am going on holiday', 'He is going on holiday'. So the sentences should be expressed as 'My friend and I went to town' and 'He and I were here first'. The order of the pronouns uses the polite convention of putting the other person first. The Queen, of course, always refers to 'my husband and I', unless of course she used the sentence 'It was given to my husband and me', when the pronoun follows a preposition. The other incorrect use of pronouns in a prescriptive grammar is the phrase 'between you and I'. The *between* is always followed by the object, and so the correct expression of the phrase should always be 'between you and me'.

Possessive pronouns

The possessive pronouns make similar distinctions. When speaking to Mary, instead of saying 'This coat is Mary's', I could use a pronoun and say 'This coat is yours'. Or if the speaker were referring to Mary across the room he could say, 'This coat is hers' (see Table 15.3).

Table 15.3 Possessive pronouns

Person	Singular	Plural
first	mine	ours
second	your	yours
third	his/hers/its	theirs

Note that none of these possessive pronouns has an apostrophe – yours, his and hers, all end in *s* but each is a word in its own right. There should be no apostrophe. Tables 15.2 and 15.3 refer to Standard English usage. Some dialects use pronouns differently. In Standard English the singular *you* is identical with the plural. There is no distinction in the word to identify whether the speaker is talking to one other person or several. But in Ireland, Liverpool or Glasgow you may hear the form *youse* as a non-standard plural form of *you*. However, the National Curriculum states that such non-standard forms are not acceptable in written English in school.

Reflexive pronouns

These always end in *self* or *selves* and they reflect the meaning of a noun or pronoun elsewhere in the clause: '*She* washed *herself*', '*He* built the house *himself*', '*They* fed *themselves*'.

Reciprocal pronouns

These are used to express a two-way relationship: They looked after *each other*. The boys help *one another*.

Interrogative pronouns

These are of course used in questions about nouns. If you were asking a question about a person you would use *who*: 'Who goes there?' 'Who did the washing up?' If the pronoun is the object of the sentence *who* changes to *whom*: 'Whom did you see?' (However, this form is frequently dropped in both spoken and written English. But the possessive form is still used: 'Whose is it?').

When referring to a non-personal noun, the interrogative pronouns *which* or *what* are used: 'Which has broken?' 'What has Tom done?'

Relative pronouns

These are used to link a subordinate clause to a noun in the main clause: 'He lived in the house, *which* he built himself'; 'There is the man *who* stole the money'; 'She is the person to *whom* I gave the book'; 'This is the infant *whose* mother ran a half-marathon'. A relative pronoun refers back to the word immediately preceding it. Did the woman in the following sentence buy the newspaper or the car? 'The newspaper carried an advert for the car, which she had bought.' If she only purchased the paper, the sentence should be rendered: 'The newspaper, which she bought, carried an advert for the car'.

Demonstrative pronouns

These are the words, *this*, *these* and *that*, *those*. They are used to express a contrast between near and distant as in: 'Take *this* here, not *that* over there'.

Indefinite pronouns

These express a notion of quantity, and many of these are compound words: *everyone, somebody, anybody, something*. Other items in this class are *much, many, more, most, less, some, neither*, as in: 'Much has changed'; 'Many will be going on holiday to Spain'; 'Neither could be trusted'.

The unknown author of 'That's not my job' cleverly uses four indefinite pronouns, everybody, somebody, anybody and nobody, as though they were indeed proper nouns.

'That's not my job'
This is the story of four people:
Everybody, Somebody, Anybody and Nobody.
There was an important job to be done and
Everybody was sure that Somebody would do it.
Somebody got angry about that, because it
Was Everybody's job. Everybody thought that
Anybody could do it, but Nobody realized that
Everybody wouldn't do it. It ended up that
Everybody blamed Somebody when Nobody did
What Anybody could have done.

Prepositions

A preposition is a word describing the relationship between two elements of a sentence, usually two nouns or a noun and a pronoun. They are often little words showing how the elements relate in time and space: *on, in, by, at, to, before, after, down, over, round, since, through, up, under*.
Prepositions can be classified thus:

Space	on, up, over, beside, under
Time	before, after, at, since
Complex prepositions	ahead of, in accordance with
Verb + preposition	to resort to
	to bring about
	to deal with

Figure 15.2 provides a visual representation of the many prepositions that relate, as the term suggests, to position in space.

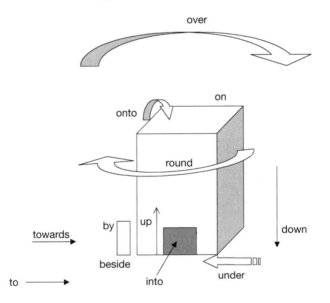

Figure 15.2 Prepositions.

Some words commonly used as prepositions can be also used as adverbs. In the sentence 'The student went down the road', the word *down* is clearly a preposition, as it is followed by a noun, showing the relationship between the student and the road. But in the sentence 'The student went down', the word *down* is an adverb.

There are obvious pitfalls in selecting the right terminology, so it is as well to be aware of them. Some complex prepositions consist of two words such as *ahead of* in 'Get ahead of the game'; 'They went ahead of us', and *in accordance with* in 'He acted in accordance with your instructions'.

Prepositions are often part of the verb as in 'to resort *to*'; 'to bring *about*' and 'to deal *with*' and these can cause some difficulties. Prescriptive grammar states that a sentence should not end with a preposition. So the sentence 'That was the man I gave the money to' should properly be rendered 'That was the man to whom I gave the money'. But by avoiding the preposition at the end, we can create some very unwieldy and inelegant sentences. When Winston Churchill's speech was changed by a civil servant to remove a preposition at the end of a sentence, Churchill famously penned the retort: 'This is the sort of English up with which I will not put'.

Children with language difficulties may not notice the little words like prepositions and may misuse them; may even omit them in speech and written language, or misunderstand them, confusing *before* and *after*, *over* and *under*. Some words take particular prepositions in English, which can cause difficulties for non-native speakers or those with language difficulty.

Task 15.6

Write the preposition which usually follows each of these words in a sentence.

Cover the answers until you are ready to check.

Word	Preposition	Word	Preposition
similar		to divide	(two)
bored		to divide	(many)
dependent		filled	
different		indignant	(something)
according		indignant	(somebody)
the invasion		suffer	
to agree	(somebody)	wait	(somebody)
to agree	(something)	write	(something)
to comment	(something)	disgusted	(something)

Task 15.6 Here are the prepositions which are usually paired with the above words:

continued

A

Word	Preposition	Word	Preposition	
similar	to	to divide	between	(two)
bored	with	to divide	amongst	(many)
dependent	upon	filled	with	
different	from	indignant	about	(something)
according	to	indignant	with	(somebody)
the invasion	of	suffer	from	
to agree	with (somebody)	wait	for	(somebody)
to agree	about (something)	write	about	(something)
to comment	on (something)	disgusted	about	(something)

Adverbs

An adverb is a word which modifies or adds to the meaning of a verb. It tells us how, when and where the action takes place: 'She cycled *slowly*'; 'He painted *beautifully*'. As you can see in those examples, many adverbs come after the verb and end in the suffix *-ly*: slow*ly*, quiet*ly*, sad*ly*, sympathetical*ly*'. But there are other words which perform as adverbs. In fact, the term began to be used as a dustbin for words which could not be classified in any other way. In an attempt to redress this, adverbs were categorized into groups and six types of adverbs have been identified.

Categories of adverbs

1. Manner: *quickly, slowly, happily, helplessly*
2. Time: *later, soon, daily, hourly, now*
3. Place: *far, near, here, there*
4. Degree: *rather, very*
5. Wh- adverbs: *when, where, why, how, whenever, wherever*
6. Sentence adverbs: *unfortunately*

The first four are the most common categories and these are listed in the National Literacy Strategy.

Manner

These tell us how the action was performed: 'She smiled *happily*', 'He moved *lazily*', 'She spoke *sadly*', 'He walked *slowly*', 'She collapsed *helplessly*'.

Time

For example, 'I'll come *later*', 'It will arrive *soon*', 'They spoke *daily*'.

Place

The third category is for adverbs of place telling us where the action was performed: 'She will go *far*', 'He drove *there*', 'He arrived *here*'.

Degree

This category modifies another adverb: 'He spoke *rather* slowly', 'He scrambled *very* quickly'. Sometimes an adverb of degree can also qualify as an adjective: 'He is a *very* old man', 'It is a *rather* handsome horse'.

Besides the four categories listed in the National Literacy Strategy, there are two others worth noting.

Wh- adverbs

This group covers the words *when, where, why, how*, and combinations *whenever* and *wherever*. They are used to introduce questions: '*Where* are they working?', '*When* did he come?'

Sentence adverbs

Finally, adverbs can be used to modify the sentence as a whole: '*Fortunately*, the cup did not break'.

Comparison of adverbs

Some adverbs, like adjectives, can be compared: 'The woman spoke *quickly*, her son spoke *more quickly*, the guide spoke *most quickly*'. In these examples the comparative and superlative are produced by adding *more* or *most* before the adverb, respectively. But some adverbs, as with adjectives, are formed by adding the suffixes *-er*, or *-est*, to the positive form: 'They came *early*; he came *earlier*; she came *earliest* of all'. Some adverbs have completely irregular forms as in: 'They sing *badly*, he sings *worse*, she sings *worst* of all'.

The common error many children make is trying to use both forms together: 'I worked more harder', 'I ran more faster'.

Task 15.7

If you feel you need practice or consolidation in categorizing adverbs, try this next exercise. Pick out the adverbs in these sentences and state how you would categorize them. Cover the answers until you are ready to check.

They lived happily in the cottage.
The choir sang most sweetly.

Task 15.7

continued

The gang ran far from the scene.
The cyclist fell awkwardly.
He arrived there, shaking badly.
He drove fastest on the motorway.
Ben swims the breaststroke very easily.
The stream bubbled rather gently over the pebbles.
The boss arrived earlier when the foreman was shouting loudly.
Where did you see the prisoner?
When did you hear the door bang loudly?

A		
They lived *happily* in the cottage.	manner	
The choir sang *most sweetly*.	manner, superlative	
The gang ran *far* from the scene.	place	
The cyclist fell *awkwardly*.	manner	
He arrived *there*, shaking *badly*.	*there*, place	
	badly, manner	
He drove *fastest* on the motorway.	manner, superlative	
Ben swims the breaststroke *very easily*.	degree, manner	
The stream bubbled *rather gently* over the pebbles.	degree, manner	
The boss arrived *earlier* when the	manner, comparative	
foreman was shouting *loudly*.	manner	
Where did you see the prisoner?	wh- adverb, place	
When did you hear the door bang	wh- adverb, time	
loudly?	manner	

Conjunctions

Conjunctions, as their name suggests are words which form a join between sentences or clauses, or they may be used to connect words within the same phrase, *and*, *but*, *whereas*. So they occur in phrases such as: 'The man *and* his dog'; 'Both the chairman *and* his wife'; 'Either British *or* American troops'; 'Neither my partner *nor* I'. Conjunctions can join two clauses of equal weight to form a compound sentence:

She went into the house *and* walked upstairs.

He was poor *but* he was honest.

The dog was pleased with the bone *and* wagged his tail.

The red team worked hard, *whereas* the blue team achieved very little.

Neither did he thank me, *nor* did he write a note.

Most conjunctions however connect a simple sentence with a clause with further information. In this case they are known as **subordinating conjunctions**:

He ran out of the house, *although* it was raining.

He came to the concert *because* his son was taking part.

The National Literacy Strategy lists four types of conjunction:

- cause
- opposition
- addition
- time

Cause: The first type of conjunction expresses cause or reason: 'He did it *because* he was angry', 'She was happy, *therefore* she was smiling broadly'.

Opposition: Examples of this type are: 'He spoke loudly, *but* his grandfather couldn't hear'; 'They travelled quickly, *but* did not arrive on time'.

Addition: The third group are conjunctions of addition: 'The students finished their work *and* left the room'.

Time: The fourth group are those of time: 'Wait here *until* I am ready'; 'He would play football *as long as* it was light'.

Concession: Another group of conjunctions that can be identified is that of concession: *although* or *even though* as in the sentence: 'He stood up to speak, *although* he was not prepared'.

Conjunctions can alter the relationship and therefore the meaning of a main sentence and its subordinate clause. Children can be encouraged to vary their writing and lengthen their sentences by use of conjunctions. The sentences: 'He studied hard', 'He went for a bike ride', could be rendered:

He studied hard *and* he went for a bike ride.

Because he had studied hard, he went for a bike ride.

When he had studied hard, he went for a bike ride.

After he had studied hard, he went for a bike ride.

As he had studied hard, he went for a bike ride.

Although he often went for bike rides, he studied hard.

Task 15.8

Here you can attempt, yourself, to use subordinating conjunctions of the type named. Think of, or write down, a suitable conjunction of the type named in each of the following sentences. Cover the suggested answers overleaf until you are ready to check.

Task 15.8

continued

Cause or reason

My uncle was angry (   ) his partner had deceived him.

You ask the question (   ) you know him.

Time

Wait there (   ) I have finished.

We have been here (   ) you left.

She read a book (   ) I wrote a letter.

Place

The faithful dog followed his master (   ) he went.

There was soft grass and flowers (   ) I sat down.

Concession

The lad is strong and healthy (   ) he is not tall.

We will go (   ) it rains.

Cause or reason

My uncle was angry *because* his partner had deceived him.

You ask the question *because* you know him.

Time

Wait there *until* I have finished.

We have been here *since* you left.

She read a book *whilst* I wrote a letter.

Place

The faithful dog followed his master *wherever* he went.

There was soft grass and flowers *where* I sat down.

Concession

The lad is strong and healthy *although* he is not tall.

We will go *even if* it rains.

Interjections

An interjection (from the Latin literally meaning 'thrown between') is an exclamation uttered by a listener which interrupts the speaker. It is punctuated by an exclamation mark, so it is very easy to spot on the page. Interjections express surprise *Oh!*, or pain *Ow!* or *Ouch!*, slight embarrassment *Oops!*, or it could be disgust as in *Yuck!* Greetings such as *Hello! Hi! Goodbye!* are interjections, as well as such exclamations as *Cheers! Hurray!*

Interjections are marginal items, not conventional elements of a sentence. They often take the form of a complete sentence in their own right. They rarely find a place in formal English writing but are liberally scattered in comic books with such onomatopoeic words such as *Crash! Wham! Whoosh! Whizz! Slurp! Sploosh!* The comic character Desperate Dan was apparently responsible for creating or preserving many interjections such as *Boing! Bop! Chomp! Wump! Blargh! Eek! Giggle! Gulp! Schucks! Yahoo!* and *Yeha!*

Identifying the part of speech

So there we have the main eight parts of speech: the noun, the verb, adjective, pronoun, preposition, adverb, conjunction and interjection. Unfortunately, a single word cannot always be classified as a particular part of speech because one word may be used with a different function. Some short words such as the word *go* may be used in different ways. In the sentence 'I go home', the word *go* is a verb. In the sentence 'Let me have a go', it is used as a noun, with the determiner *a* before it which would indicate a noun. As a single word sentence 'Go!' spoken in anger, the word becomes an interjection. Classifying words into parts of speech can be a tricky and bewildering for may children with language problems.

Conclusion

This chapter has been concerned with describing the words in sentences in terms of their use and function. Being able to use the terminology allows us to generalize ways of handling written language. So educators say: 'There must be a verb in every sentence'; 'Make sure that nouns and verbs agree'. These are the sorts of rules that appear in the prescriptive grammar which teachers are required to teach. The better the teacher understands the conventions, the more perceptive he/she can be in adapting them.

Similarly, when everyone concerned understands the terminology, it is easier to help students to improve their work: 'Can you think of some better adjectives to describe the dragon?'; 'Where is the main clause in this sentence?'; 'You should make sure that all your verbs are in the same tense'.

Knowing about parts of speech should not be regarded as a mere exercise. The knowledge is useful only if it helps writers to communicate meaning clearly and more precisely.

Answers to the pre-test (pp. 231–2) and summary

■ To summarize, here are some basic, simple definitions for the parts of speech
that were listed in the pre-test at the beginning of this chapter:

Part of speech	Definition	Example	Use
noun	a naming word	*book, John*	*London* is a big *city*.
verb	a doing or being word	*jumps, is*	The dog was *jump-ing* over the cat.
adjective	describing word	*red, big, delicious*	The *red* blouse was *beautiful*.
pronoun	stands in for a noun	*he, she, mine*	*Those* are *mine*, not *his*.
preposition	shows position in time and space	*on, over, before, after*	Put it *on* the table *before* dinner.
adverb	modifies a verb	*slowly, sadly, rather*	He drove there *slowly*.
conjunction	joining word	*and, but, because, although*	*Because* he was ill, he stayed off work *and* went to bed.
interjection	exclamation, interruption	*Hello! Bother!*	*Ouch! Help!*

CHAPTER 16

Orthography: reading

What is orthography?

Orthography is the study of correct spelling; of the way letters are arranged in words. There was a time when English spelling was very haphazard, but now English dictionaries provide us with a consensus on the conventional spelling of words.

The English system of orthography is a complex one because the history of the language has led to great variations in the pronunciation of words, and following that, great variability of spelling.

In this chapter we will consider conventional arrangement of letters in words in relation to reading: the patterns, sequences of letters and letter groupings that we need to observe when we are decoding, that is, reading words. In Chapter 17, we will turn to spelling to consider how we decide on the letter sequences we must write in order to spell correctly.

English orthography: a reader's nightmare?

The spelling patterns of English are ancient and intricate, and the source of much anxiety and confusion for those learning to read and write the language for the first time. Our orthography stimulates debate and is periodically the target of spelling reformers, who want to simplify it and make it more transparent. It has been argued that the complexity of English spelling leads to difficulties with the acquisition of literacy for our children in school, and for those learning English as an additional language. It has also led to great debates about the methods of teaching reading and spelling.

English is often ridiculed for the variety, erratic nature and contradictions of its spelling system. A Dutch observer of English, Dr Gerard Nolst Trenite, wrote a clever poem on English spelling called 'The Chaos', part of which is reproduced here. Try reading it aloud, listening for words with similar sounds that have different spellings or vice versa. By pointing out these apparent absurdities, the doctor is trying to construct an amusing indictment of English spelling.

The Chaos

Dearest creature in creation,
Studying English pronunciation,
I will teach you in my verse,
Sounds like corpse, corps, horse and worse,
It will keep you, Susy, busy
Make your head with heat grow dizzy,
Tear in eye, your dress you'll tear.
Queer, fair seer, hear my prayer,
Pray, console your loving poet,
Make my coat look new, dear, sew it!
Just compare heart, hear and heard,
Dies and diet, lord and word,
Sword and sward, retain and Britain,
(Mind the latter, how it's written).
Made has not the sound of bade;
Say, said, pay, paid, laid but plaid.
Now I surely will not plague you
With such words as vague and ague.

Dr Gerard Nolst Trenité (1870–1946) in McArthur (1992: 969)

There are several other such skits on English spelling, often in verse form, and you may well have your own favourite. It may be interesting to investigate others to see if they are making the same points.

The problems with English orthography

You probably noticed that most of the differences in the poem seemed to occur around the vowel sounds. Identically spelled words, homographs, were pronounced in different ways: *tear* and *tear*. Similarly, the same letter groups had different sounds in different words: the *-ord* of *lord* and *word*. We expect words with the same orthographic patterns at the end to rhyme, like *-amp* in *damp* and *stamp*, and the *-ean* of *bean* and *lean*. This poet deliberately chose homographs, words which look the same but which do not sound the same, to make his point (*tear/tear*) and words with the same ending which look as though they should rhyme but do not (*horse/worse*; *Susy/busy*; *paid/plaid*). Seeing the pairs of words together in the poem like this forces us to abandon one of the basic principles of reading, that of analogy. We cannot match the letter patterns with particular sounds, and that makes it harder to read.

Other words in the poem shared the same sound but not the same pattern; for example *verse/worse*; *busy/dizzy*; *heard/word*; *Britain/written*; *bade/plaid*. These sorts of words cause problems when spelling, rather than reading. The child who spells *verse* correctly, could perhaps be forgiven for spelling *worse* in the same way: 'werse'. She is, after all, using a fairly reliable spelling strategy, that of analogy.

The author is trying to convince us that there are no reliable patterns in English orthography, and that the system is chaotic. Few of the forced confusions here concern the consonants with the exception of the *sw* in *sword* with a silent *w* and *sward* where both letters are sounded. But on the whole, it is the vowels that cause most of the trouble.

The fixing of orthography

In Chapter 12 'The history of written English', we discussed some of the influences that account for the variability in our spelling system, and noticed that spelling was not fixed until 1755 with the publication of Samuel Johnson's *Dictionary of the English Language*. Before that, the letters in a word varied because of pronunciation and the availability of some letters which are now defunct.

In 1586 Elizabeth I wrote a letter to King James VI of Scotland spelling *desire* and *would* as *desair* and *wold*. When James replied he wrote the same words quite differently, and was not even consistent when writing them twice in the same document. Shakespeare is known for signing his name using several different spellings. Dr Johnson's dictionary may have fixed much of English spelling, but there was no consensus to form an Academy to watch over the language and establish a standard of spelling as happened in France. In English, words were absorbed into the language at different times and became fossilized, complete with their spelling. There was no formal guardianship to refuse entry to a word, or to anglicize the spelling. But by the eighteenth century, spelling became fixed by social consensus, born out of concern for the wild discrepancies that there were in English. The result was a lessening of variability, and a fossilization of forms that had come into existence at different periods of time. We can compare these to the formation of rock strata in geology, trapping fossils within the layers. In these orthographic strata, the lower layer is a vernacular substratum based on Anglo-Saxon, Danish and other Germanic material. Next comes a mid-stratum of Romance material,

(Norman-French often with a Latin base) and a super-stratum of newer Latin words and Latinized Greek.

Words written in these periods often became entrenched, with spelling which was not subsequently altered. Within each of these strata, room must be made for a smattering of 'exotic' items; that is, words that have been adopted completely from another language, such as *bazaar* (from the Persian) and *cello* (from Italian).

As you can see from Figure 16.1, the groups are characterized by the distinctive patterns of their spelling.

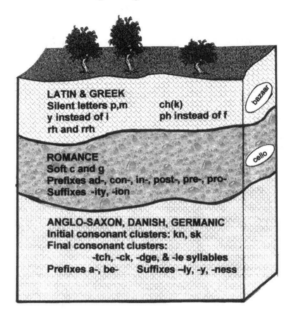

Figure 16.1 Orthographic strata.

Anglo-Saxon, Danish and Germanic

From the Anglo-Saxon, Danish and Germanic vocabulary we have acquired spellings with initial consonant clusters such as the *kn-* in *knee*, *knife*, *know*, *knuckle*, and the *sk-* in *skill*, *skate*, *sky*. Final consonant clusters which are of this time are the *-tch* in *batch*, *ditch*, *hutch*; the *-ck* in *back*, *deck*, *tick*, *lock*, *suck*; the *-dge* in *badge*, *hedge*, *midge*, *dodge*; and also the final *-le* syllable of words like *cattle*, *kettle*, *fizzle*, *bottle*. The prefix *a-*, was fossilized on words from this substratum such as *ablaze*, *alive*, *aglow*, *asleep*; similarly the prefix *be-* on *become*, *believe*, *belong*. Suffixes of this stratum are the *-ly* on *kindly*, *lordly*, *northerly*; the '*-y* of *sandy*, *slimy*, *wishy-washy*, and the *-ness* on words such as *darkness*, *slimness*, *wetness*.

Romance words

In the middle stratum of Romance words, words occur that originated from Norman French, but whose roots can often also be traced back to Latin. The spelling of these words is characterized by the soft *c* as in *cell* (as in prison cell, or blood cell), and the soft *g* as in *ginger* and *gelatine*.

There are also characteristic prefixes such as *ad-* as in *admit, adopt, advise*; the *con-* as in *conclude* and also in words such as *collide* and *commensurate* where the *n* of *con-* has been assimilated. The prefix *in-* occurs in *instinct, innate, investigate*; but the same prefix *in-* has a negative meaning in *indecisive, impossible* and *illiterate*. Again, in the last of these the *in-* has be assimilated into the root word.

Post- is another prefix from this period, and occurs in *postpone, post-date, pre-* in *prescribe* and *prevent*, and *pro-* in the words *progress* and *provide*. The suffix *-ity* is also characteristic of the Romance-style spelling in words such as *adversity, centrality*; and finally the *-ion* comes up in *condition, eruption, admission* and *propulsion*.

Greek-style spelling

The super-stratum of spelling contains Greek-style spelling, which has been transliterated from Greek letters into the Roman alphabet. It is characterized by the *ch-* with the sound (k) which occurs in *chaos, archetype, character* and *monarch*. There are consonants which appear at the beginning of words but are not pronounced such as the *p-* in *psychology* or *pterodactyl*, and the *m-* in *mnemonic*. The letter *y* is used instead of *i* in words like *analysis, psychology, synthetic*. For the sound (f), these words of Greek origin use *ph-* as in *pharmacy, amphibian, philosophical*.

And the rather strange-looking *r-* followed by *h* or even double *rrh* happens in this group. So we have *rhetoric* and *rhythm*, and *haemorrhage* and *catarrh*.

Awareness of the patterns

Each orthographic stratum has it own patterns of letters and consistencies, and literate users of English seem to be aware of the characteristics of the source language and pronounce words accordingly. How would you pronounce the word *chorology*? You may not be familiar with the word (it means the study of the geographical distribution of plants and animals) but you probably pronounced it correctly (kŏrŏˈləjĭ), because you recognize it as being in the same group of words as *chord* and *chronology*. So the *ch* was pronounced (k) not the (ch) sound as you would find in *child* or *chore*, from a different stratum of words.

Similar words

Because of the historical roots of our language, we have inherited some words which are very similar, but unrelated. It is these words which cause confusion and lead to our language being ridiculed. The words which make even good readers stop and think are homographs.

Homographs look the same but have a different pronunciation and meaning, like *bow* (ow) and *bow* (ō). These tend to be potentially difficult to read, relying as they do on context to provide their meaning, and therefore their pronunciation.

Task 16.1

Each of these homographs can have at least two different pronunciations and meanings. Jot down what they are. Cover the answers until you are ready to check.

row   lead   entrance   read   house   tear

A

Homograph	Pronunciation	Meanings
row	(rō)	propel a boat
	(row)	an argument
lead	(lēd)	to go in front
	(lĕd)	a heavy soft metal
entrance	entrance	the place to go in
	entrance	to bewitch
read	(rēd)	... a book, etc.
	(rĕd)	... past tense of above.
house	(hows)	a place to live (noun)
	(howz)	to give shelter
tear	(tēr)	... from crying
	(tair)	to rip apart

If you could do the task, it shows that you are well aware that groups of letters in English can represent different sounds. So awareness of orthography tends to be a virtuous spiral. The more you read, spell and notice words, the better you become at spotting these subtle patterns and differences.

It is estimated that there are patterns in English orthography, and that over 80 per cent of words are spelled according to a regular model. If this is the case, it means that it is a worthwhile task to group, categorize and learn the regularities of English orthography.

How does the reader decode English orthography?

Can we identify the regularities of English orthography when we read it? How predictable are the letters on the page? Can we rely on their sounds with any certainty? Do we have a basically alphabetic-phonetic language or is it totally haphazard and chaotic? Can we identify the elements which make up the 80 per cent or more of regular words?

Reading involves the recognition of patterns of letters on the page. English is not a logographic language like Chinese. It has basically an alphabetic-phonetic script and is based on the transcription of sounds into letters so new words can be decoded. But the 26 letters of the alphabet cannot directly represent, in a 1:1 correspondence, the 44 sounds which we have in English. The relationship is more indirect, and therefore more complex.

What must a reader do in order to read in a basically phonic script?

Reading is the process of extracting meaning from text. The first step of this process is to decode, to translate the letters into sounds, or the graphemes into phonemes. A learner must therefore first master the sounds of all the letters of the alphabet. Our word alphabet comes from the Greek alpha and beta, the first two letters of the Greek alphabet. These two letters have come to mean the whole series of letters, just as when we say, 'She can say her ABC', we mean that she can recite the whole alphabet.

Let us dispense with the basic information about the alphabet first. Of the 26 **letters**, five are true **vowels** (*a*, *e*, *i*, *o* and *u*) and the rest are **consonants**. Two letters can fall into both camps, the letter *y* is sometimes used as a vowel, and the letter *w* can be used after another vowel to create a vowel digraph. The word digraph is used for two letters which make one sound, and these may be a configuration of two consonants to create a **consonant digraph** such as *sh*. Alternatively there may be two vowels together such as *ai* representing a single sound (ā), and this is termed a **vowel digraph**.

Another piece of useful information concerns the letter *r* which can have a strong effect on any vowel which precedes it. We hear this when we read *ar* in *mark* as (ar̂), and not as (ă) (r). The **modifying r** can affect any of the vowels which it follows.

Reading choices

When a beginner-reader looks at a group of letters on a page, he has to decide what sounds to say. Sometimes there may be more than one sound for a particular letter, and then he is faced with a reading choice. Learner-readers pick up these reading choices gradually, and good readers may hardly be aware that they are making them most of the time. Here is your chance to get an overview of all the main reading choices, so that you know what a learner-reader has to master and what a structured reading programme has to cover.

First, we'll consider grapheme-phoneme links and reading choices. When reading, the student sees a letter or group of letters and must produce the sound which they represent.

Task 16.2

Write down any of the *single* 26 letters of the alphabet which represent more than one sound. There are ten letters listed in the answers. Cover the answers until you are ready to check.

Answers show the sounds of the letters, and an example of each sound in a word.

A

Vowels

a =	(ă) *pan*	(ā) *acorn*	
e =	(ĕ) *egg*	(ē) *equal*	
i =	(ĭ) *igloo*	(ī) *item*	
o =	(ŏ) *orange*	(ō) *open*	
u =	(ŭ) *up*	(ū) *universe*	
y =	(y) *yellow*	(ĭ) [or (ē)] *happy* (ī) *cry*	

Consonants

c =	(k) *cat*	(s) *city*
g =	(g) *gone*	(j) *giant*
s =	(s) *sun*	(z) *his*
x =	(ks) *fox*	(gz) *exam*

Single vowels

The first group of reading choices listed in the answer were the vowels. Each vowel has a long and a short sound. The diacritical markings we use to show these are the macron and the breve. The macron for the long sound, is the straight bar (¯) to indicate that the sound of the vowel continues (ē). It can go on as long as you have breath. (e̅‾). The long vowel sounds are written as (ā) (ē) (ī) (ō) and (ū).

The breve is the little dish-shape (˘) above the vowel to indicate a sound that is short, and finishes quickly. The short vowels sounds are (ă) (ĕ) (ĭ) (ŏ) and (ŭ). The word *breve* means short and is related to the word *brief*. So the short and long sounds for the vowels should have been straightforward.

The letter y when it is at the beginning of a word is acting as a consonant and makes the sound (y) as in *yellow*. But when it is at the end of a word the *y* is acting as a vowel and has the sound (ĭ) as in *happy* or (ī) as in *cry*, just like the letter *i* which it is replacing.

However, some of the sounds you make for the vowels may be slightly different according to your local accent. The *y* in the middle of a syllable is usually substituting for the letter *i* and so has the same sounds as the letter *i* (ĭ) in *physics* or (ī) as in *psychology*. But when *y* comes at the end of the word, there is a tendency to lengthen it a little and say 'funnee, happee', so, beside the letter *y* you may have written the sounds (y) and (ī) and either (ĭ) or (ē) for the sound in *happy*.

In received pronunciation the short *u* for instance is pronounced (ŭ) as in *cut*, but in Yorkshire and many northern areas of the country the *u* is pronounced like the *u* in *pull*, with the lips more rounded and pushed forwards.

The important point is that you can hear and discriminate between similar sounds. And if you are teaching, you should listen hard to your students' sounds.

Single consonants

There are only four single consonants which can represent more than one sound. The first is *c* which has the hard sound (k) in *can* and the soft (s) as in *cigarette*; *g* similarly can be hard as in *gate* where it makes the (g) sound and soft in *ginger* where both letters *g* have the (j) sound. The letter *s* has the unvoiced sound (s) at the beginning of words and in most other positions in a word: *sun*, *history*, and *hats*, but sometimes it has the voiced sound (z) as in *crabs* and *rose*. The letter *x* has two sounds, voiced and unvoiced. It is most commonly the unvoiced (ks) as in *fox*, but it has the voiced (gz) sound in *exam*.

If that was straightforward, consider now the letters which are found in pairs, the digraphs, firstly consonant digraphs.

Task 16.3

This time, list some consonant digraphs: two consonants which occur together, and represent one sound. Cover the answers until you are ready to check. Answers show the sounds of the letters, and an example of each sound in a word.

A

th	(th) unvoiced	*think*
	(th) voiced	*them*
sh	(sh)	*ship*
ch	(ch)	*chips*, (k) *chemist*, (sh) *champagne*
ph	(f)	*photograph*
ng	(ng)	*ring*
ck	(k)	*back*
ll	(l)	*hill*
ff	(f)	*staff*
ss	(s)	*cross*
zz	(z)	*jazz*

Consonant digraphs

A consonant digraph often consists of the letter *h* paired with another consonant. The *th* makes the voiced sound (th) as in *this* and *clothes*, and it makes the unvoiced (th) sound in *think* and *ninth*. The *sh*, either at the beginning or end of a word, has the sound (sh) as in *shop* and *wish*. The letters *ch* commonly has the sound (ch) as in *chips*, but also the sound (k) in Greek-based words such as *chemist* and *chorus*; but in words of French origin it can have a (sh) sound as in *chef* and *chauffeur*. These French-based words often have an exotic flavour to them. The *ph* is Greek of course, making the sound (f) as in *photo* and *phone*. The *ng* is the back of the throat sound (ng) as in *ring* and the *ck* just makes one sound (k) in *track*. The other double letters, *ff, ll, ss* and *zz* are consistent spelling patterns representing only one sound.

The answers given above are the main reading choices, each of which occurs in at least six English words. You may have thought of another sound which appears in a particular word but it does not yield enough examples to make it worthwhile to teach to pupils as a regular pattern. For instance the letter *c* makes the sound (ch) in *cello*, but this is an exotic foreign borrowing, and there are not enough words in English with that sound to count it as a regular reading choice. However, if we continue to enjoy Italian products such as ciabatta (chībata) bread, we may get used to this pronunciation of *c* as (ch).

Task 16.4

See how many vowel digraphs you can list by using the six vowels and *w*, pairing them up in various combinations. There are 20 in the answers below. Cover the answers until you are ready to check.

ay*	*tray* (ā)	au	*autumn* (or)
ey*	*key* (ē)	aw	*claw* (or)
oi	*coin* (oi)	ie*	*shield* (ē); *pie* (ī)
oy	*boy* (oi)	ei*	*receipt* (ē); *reins* (ā)
uy	*buy* (ī)	ue*	*argue* (ū); *glue* (o͞o)
ee*	*teeth* (ē)	oe*	*oboe* (ō)
oo	*spoon* (o͞o); *book* (o͝o)	eu	*eureka* (ū)
ea*	*dream* (ē); *head* (ĕ)	oa*	*goat* (ō)
ai*	*tail* (ā)	ui	*fruit* (o͞o); *build* (ĭ)
ou	*house* (ow); *double* (ŭ); *youth* (o͞o)	ow*	*snow* (ō); *brown* (ow)

Vowel digraphs

So we come to the vowel digraphs: pairs of vowels which together make one sound. The good news is that 12 out of the 20 vowel digraphs have just one sound and therefore are nicely predictable. In some of the cases, the sound represented by a vowel digraph is the long sound of the first vowel. This would apply to the digraphs that are starred *.

There is a mnemonic which is often chanted to encapsulate this idea: 'When two vowels go out walking, the first one does the talking', and this is a handy rhyme to tell learners, as long as they realize that it works for many, but not all, of the vowel digraphs.

Some of these vowel digraphs have more than one sound associated with them. The *oo* can give the sound (o͞o) in *moon* and *boot*, but the shorter sound in *book* and *foot*. In Scotland of course, and in some parts of Lancashire, things are simpler with just the one sound used for the *oo* in all those words.

Vowel modified by r

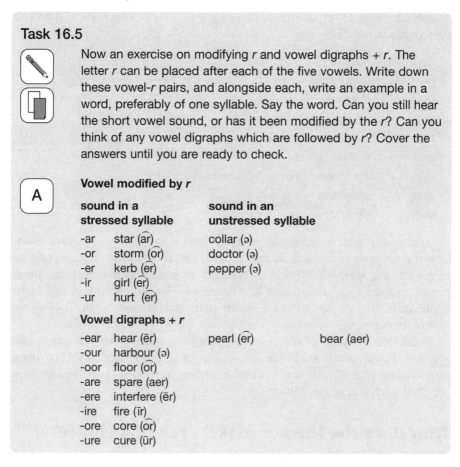

Task 16.5

Now an exercise on modifying *r* and vowel digraphs + *r*. The letter *r* can be placed after each of the five vowels. Write down these vowel-*r* pairs, and alongside each, write an example in a word, preferably of one syllable. Say the word. Can you still hear the short vowel sound, or has it been modified by the *r*? Can you think of any vowel digraphs which are followed by *r*? Cover the answers until you are ready to check.

A

Vowel modified by *r*

sound in a stressed syllable		sound in an unstressed syllable
-ar	star (a͡r)	collar (ə)
-or	storm (o͡r)	doctor (ə)
-er	kerb (e͡r)	pepper (ə)
-ir	girl (e͡r)	
-ur	hurt (e͡r)	

Vowel digraphs + *r*

-ear	hear (ēr)	pearl (e͡r)	bear (aer)
-our	harbour (ə)		
-oor	floor (o͡r)		
-are	spare (aer)		
-ere	interfere (ēr)		
-ire	fire (īr)		
-ore	core (o͡r)		
-ure	cure (ūr)		

The letter *r* in *ar* and *or* causes the sound of the vowel to change, producing (a͡r) in *dark* and (o͡r) in *storm*. But the *er, ir* and *ur* all have the same sound (e͡r) in received pronunciation. However in Scotland and other places where the *r* is always pronounced, the original short vowel sound can still be heard in these words. The *ar*, *er* and *or* can also produce the schwa sound when it comes at the end of a word. The schwa sound is written like a rotated e and represents the indiscriminate vowel sound (ə), almost a grunt, that comes at the end of *collar*, *pepper*, *doctor* and *harbour*. The rest of the modifying *r* groups are also given in the answer above with examples. Say them aloud to hear them clearly.

Note that *r* does not modify the preceding vowel in all cases. In words where the *r* is doubled, there is no effect on the vowel, which retains its short sound as in *mărry*, *bĕrry*, *sŏrry*, *cŭrry*.

Other letter strings

There are other letter strings of three or four letters which are linked reliably to a sound. They are:

igh	*night* (ī)	
ous	*famous* (ŭs)	
dge	*bridge* (j)	
tch	*match* (ch)	
ture	*picture* (chə)	
tion	*station* (sh'n)	
sion	*explosion* (zh'n)	*procession* (sh'n)
cian	*magician* (sh'n)	
eigh	*eight* (ā)	

In examining all of these single letters and letter groups, we have found that the links between letters and sounds are not as arbitrary and chaotic as might first appear. There is consistency in single consonants, in consonant digraphs and in common letter strings. The single vowels can cause more difficulty as they all have more than one sound, as do half of the vowel digraphs.

Therefore, if some of these graphemes have more than one phoneme, we are faced with a choice of sound when we are reading these graphemes, particularly if the word is unfamiliar. So let us consider how we deal with a reading choice.

How does the learner make a reading choice?

If the letters *ow* can be read with the sound (ō) or the sound (ow), how does the reader make that choice? Obviously he can try both choices and see which one fits the context.

What happens if there is no context, if the words are seen in isolation? Decide for yourself.

Task 16.6

Read the nonsense words below, deciding how you would pronounce each, or list alternatives if you can think of any.

Note your own thought processes as you decide.

Cover the answers until you are ready to check.

smay	jawk
laub	loik
conflue	eutronic
amphot	geef
poot	gread
troush	spow
chort	ceft

In some of these nonsense words there was a reading choice. How did you decide which one to say? Did you spot the letter/s that may cause a problem or did you use analogy to a word you already knew?

The first seven provided you with very little choice about how to pronounce them, but the second column may have created more uncertainty. Answers are given here, with an analogous word:

A

	'word'	analogy			'word'	analogy
1.	smay	stay	8.		geef	beef/genius
2.	jawk	hawk	9.		poot	root/foot
3.	laub	laud/daub	10.		gread	knead/bread
4.	loik	loin	11.		troush	flounder/soup
5.	conflue	glue	12.		spow	grow/now
6.	eutronic	euphoric	13.		chort	chortle/chorus
7.	amphot	amphor	14.		ceft	centre

Those in the second column were not quite straightforward. Number 8 could be (geef) as it looks like a short Anglo-Saxon word, but it could be pronounced (jeef), if you think of it having the soft *g* as in *gentle*. Number 9, *poot*, could be pronounced (put) if you think of it rhyming with *foot*, or (pōot) if you make the analogy to *boot*. There are choices for all of the others except for the final word, as the soft c rule is almost infallible.

Did you find that you were more attracted to a rhyming word to help you to decode? Analogy by rhyme is a powerful way of classifying words so we can pronounce them.

As you could see there, these grapheme–phoneme links are not just learned mechanically, by rote: we are constantly judging and making analogies with other words. A great deal of mental activity goes into matching the patterns of letters with similar ones that we have seen before. And that is just at the level of decoding letter strings in single words. But even at word level, reading consists of more than just decoding letters in short words. The learner–reader may come across words which are longer than she can cope with. What then?

How does the learner decode longer words?

What do literate people do when decoding unfamiliar longer words? Assume you now know the grapheme–phoneme links; how do you work out the pronunciation of longer words?

Task 16.7

Read these words, pronouncing them clearly. Be aware of how you tackled the words. Cover the answers until you are ready to check.

1 subalternate	5 pandemonium
2 vermiculose	6 thaumaturgist
3 circumduction	7 epithalamium
4 anthropophagy	8 ultimogeniture

Did you find you were checking your pronunciation by plodding through the word, syllable by syllable? That is usually the procedure most people adopt. Then you are just left with problem of where to put the stress. Here are the words, split into syllables, with the stressed syllable underlined. The meaning is added for the curious.

A

1.	sub - <u>alt</u> - ern - ate	of inferior rank
2.	ver - <u>mic</u> - ŭ - lose	worm-eaten
3.	cir - cum - <u>duc</u> - tion	a leading about, annulling
4.	an - thro - <u>poph</u> - ă - gy	cannibalism
5.	pan - dē - <u>mō</u> - nĭ - um	uproar (abode of all demons)
6.	<u>thau</u> - mat - <u>ur</u> - gist	a worker of miracles
7.	ep - ĭ - thal - <u>ā</u> - mĭ - um	a marriage song or poem
8.	ul - tim - ō - <u>gen</u> - ĭ - ture	inheritance by the youngest son

So if literate people use the methods of splitting a word into syllables in order to decode it, we must consider how we can begin to teach learner-readers such a technique.

Syllables

A new reader may be able to blend three of four letters into a word, such as *pet* or *stop*, but be completely overawed by a long word of six or seven letters such as *problem*. However if she is able to perceive this big word as consisting of two syllables, *prob* and *lem*, the task becomes easier: it becomes two items instead of seven, two syllables instead of seven letters.

A syllable is a beat in a word, and the number of syllables in a word can be tapped, clapped or counted on the fingers:

bis-cuit   di-no-saur   Hump-ty Dump-ty   wiz-ard   Tyr-an-no-saur-us rex.

Syllables carry the rhythm of the language. There is one vowel sound in every syllable, and several kinds of syllable.

It is therefore helpful to know more about syllables and about segmenting words into syllables. There are useful guidelines which can be learned and passed on. The ability to segment a longer, unknown word visually is a vital skill in learning to read accurately. Dividing a word into syllables makes it more manageable.

Two kinds of syllable form important building blocks in words: closed syllables and open syllables.

Closed and open syllables

Closed and open syllables have a single vowel. As you know, each vowel can have a short sound (ă) (ĕ) (ĭ) (ŏ) (ŭ), or a long sound (ā) (ē) (ī) (ō) (ū). If a single vowel is trapped inside a syllable it will have its short sound: *stop, let, tip, lick, on, at*. As you can see in these examples, the vowel sound is short if there is a consonant *after* the vowel in that syllable.

These are called **closed syllables** because the vowel is 'closed in' by the consonant that comes after it, and this gives the vowel its short sound. The following are closed syllables which fit this pattern:

vc	vcc	vc	vcc	vc	vcc	vc	vc
căb	stŏck	ăt	ălp	stĭm	lĕst	trĭb	strŭm

However if the position of the vowel is the last letter in the syllable, then it is called an **open syllable** and the vowel will be long, with the sound (ā) (ē) (ī) (ō) or (ū). The following are open syllables which fit this pattern:

v	v	v	v	v	v	v
cā	**stĭ**	**mū**	**drō**	**lē**	**trī**	**stū**
ca/ble	sti/pend	mu/sic	dro/ver	le/mur	tri/pod	stu/dent

Open syllables occur typically as the first syllable of a word, so there is an example of a word which contains the open syllable beneath each open syllable. Later we will examine how to split word into syllables so that we can identify the open and closed syllables in words.

The next task is to give you practice in recognizing and reading closed and open syllables, first in isolation.

Task 16.8

Write down these syllables, marking the vowel with a letter v above it, and marking any consonants after the vowel with the letter c.

Use the breve or macron sign to identify whether the vowel is short or long.

Then sort the syllables into two columns: closed syllables and open syllables.

Cover the answers until you are ready to check.

co	sim	gre	sig	pang	ho	fick	kin
ma	quib	hist	cro	stri	pre	imp	du

A

v	vc	v	vc	vcc	v	vcc	vc
cō	**sĭm**	**grē**	**sĭg**	**păng**	**hŏ**	**fĭck**	**kĭn**

v	vc	vcc	vc	v	v	vcc	v
mā	**quĭb**	**hĭst**	**crō**	**strī**	**prē**	**ĭmp**	**dū**

Closed syllables	Open syllables
sim	co
sig	gre
pang	ho
fick	ma
kin	cro
quib	stri
hist	pre
imp	du

Syllable division

Now let us find out how to divide a word into syllables. In order to segment a word into syllables, we need to identify the pattern of vowels and consonants in the word. We will deal mainly with words of two syllables where the 'rules' of syllable division are most reliable. You must do two things:

1. First, look for the vowels and mark them.
2. Then look at the letters between them.

These are the patterns you may find:

Syllable division vc/cv

This is the vowel-consonant-consonant-vowel pattern which occurs in words such as *bandit* and *rabbit*.

Step 1: Look for the vowels and mark them.

<table>
<tr><td>vccv</td><td>vccv</td></tr>
<tr><td>bandit</td><td>rabbit</td></tr>
</table>

You just need to notice and mark where the vowels are and the letters between them. Here you have the vccv pattern. This is a common pattern in English words, and the syllable boundary is between the two consonants.

Step 2: Divide the word into syllables between the two consonants. Now that you can see the syllables clearly, you can identify whether the syllables are closed or open, and mark the length of the vowel accordingly.

<table>
<tr><td>vc</td><td>cv</td><td></td><td>vc</td><td>cv</td></tr>
<tr><td>băn</td><td>dĭt</td><td></td><td>răb</td><td>bĭt</td></tr>
</table>

Now that the word is split into syllables, you can see there are two closed syllables; the vowel sounds will be short, so they can be read confidently as *ban-dit* and *rab-bit*.

Task 16.9

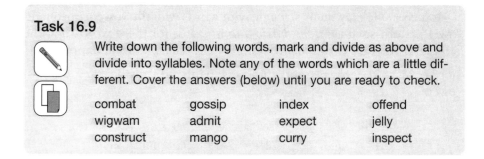

Write down the following words, mark and divide as above and divide into syllables. Note any of the words which are a little different. Cover the answers (below) until you are ready to check.

combat	gossip	index	offend
wigwam	admit	expect	jelly
construct	mango	curry	inspect

Task 16.9

A

VC	CV
cŏm	băt

VC	CV
gŏs	sĭp

VC	CV
ĭn	dĕx

VC	CV
ŏf	fĕnd

VC	CV
wĭg	wăm

VC	CV
ăd	mĭt

VC	CV
ĕx	pĕct

VC	CV
*jĕl	ly

VC	CCCV
* cŏn	strŭct

VC	CV
*măn	gō

VC	CV
*cŭr	ry

VC	CCV
*ĭn	spĕct

Most of those words obey the vc/cv syllable division pattern. The starred words are worth noting.

The words *jelly* and *curry* have *y* at the end, which acts as the second vowel. The sound of the *y* at the end of the word can be either (ĭ) or (ī), and the learner may have to try both before deciding on that final sound. (You may use the (ē) sound instead of (ī).) The words *construct* and *inspect* have a superfluity of consonants in the middle. In such cases, avoid splitting a consonant blend so the *str* of *construct* and the *sp* of *inspect* are kept together. The word *mango* has an open syllable as the final syllable which gives the final long vowel (ō). This is an unusual construction for an English word, and is a sign that it is a foreign import.

To summarize, the vccv pattern splits between the two middle consonants, to give two syllables, the first of which is a closed syllable and so the vowel sound is short.

Syllable division v/cv

If you find this pattern of vowels and consonants in a two-syllable word, it may cause problems.

If a learner is having trouble decoding a word with this pattern, tell him to split it after the first vowel. This is a pragmatic solution to a tricky problem: there are quite a lot of five-letter words in English with this pattern of vowel-consonant-vowel, for example: *comic, model, lemon, cabin, topic, visit*. On the whole, once a student has learned to decode words, s/he does not have difficulty in pronouncing these words correctly.

However s/he may really struggle with words with the vowel-consonant-vowel pattern such as: *item, basic, human*. It is for these words that the 'split after the first vowel' instruction is necessary. See what happens.

Step 1: Mark the vowels and the consonants and divide after the first vowel.

V	CV
i	tem

V	CV
ba	sic

V	CV
hu	man

Step 2: The syllables can now be read as ordinary closed and open syllables, giving the long or short sounds of the vowels:

v	cv
ī	těm

v	cv
bā	sĭc

v	cv
hŭ	mǎn

Task 16.10

Write down the following words, mark and divide into syllables as above. Cover the answers until you are ready to check.

basic	hotel	unit	navy
modem	student	virus	robot
bacon	evil	label	crony
hoping	saving	taming	ripen
trader	stroking	tuner	striving

A

v	cv
bā	sĭc

v	cv
hō	těl

v	cv
ū	nĭt

v	cv
nā	vy

v	cv
mō	děm

v	cv
stū	děnt

v	cv
vī	rŭs

v	cv
rō	bŏt

v	cv
bā	cŏn

v	cv
ē	vĭl

v	cv
lā	běl

v	cv
crō	ny

v	cv
*hō	pĭng

v	cv
*sā	vĭng

v	cv
*tā	mĭng

v	cv
*rī	pěn

v	cv
*trā	der

v	cv
*strō	kĭng

v	cv
*tū	ner

v	cv
*strī	vĭng

The v/cv division pattern works well for all these words. Knowing where
the syllable splits helps the reader to pronounce the word. If the reader
recognizes the vcv pattern and splits the word after the first vowel, he can
then read each syllable. He finds that the first syllable is an open syllable,
and thus gives the long vowel sound.

The starred words are the ones for which this rule is particularly useful. You may have spotted that these are words with suffixes, and to be
precise, vowel suffixes. This syllable division pattern is enormously valuable as a word-attack skill for such words, and there are hundreds of
similar words in English.

These two patterns, vc/cv and v/cv, provide us with a reliable way of segmenting and reading words of two syllables. Now you can practise both together.

Task 16.11

Look at the following pairs of words. Divide them into syllables using the vc/cv and v/cv rules, to see if the procedure gives the correct pronunciation.

holly	holy
navvy	navy
slimming	slimy
tacking	taking
backer	baker
mopping	moping
planner	planer
stripping	stripy
hopping	hoping
stacking	staking

As you can see from that task, those syllable division patterns can be very handy for decoding, and especially useful for proofreading one's own work. The student who has written *shoping* for *shopping* now has a means of checking her work to see that it reads correctly. Dividing words this way is a powerful proofreading technique to enable her to spot and correct her own mistakes.

Syllable division v/v

This syllable division pattern is a more unusual one, where the syllable split occurs between two vowels. It occurs where there are two vowels together, but they do not make a vowel digraph. Examples are words like *poet, diet, truant*.

The student again spots the vowels and marks them. When she sees the v/v pattern, she divides the word into syllables between the vowels:

Step 1:

v	v		v	v		v	v		v	v
di	et		po	em		fu	el		tru	ant

Step 2:

v	v		v	v		v	v		v	v
dī	ĕt		pō	ĕm		fū	ĕl		trū	ănt

Task 16.12

Here are some more of those words for you to try for yourself. Answers are not given, as they are all straightforward like the examples above. Take care with the last word, however. Why is it different?

poet	trial	dual	duel
duet	cruet	fluent	duo

The last word divided between the vowels, like all the rest, but this produced an open syllable at the end, giving a long vowel sound, dū/ō. This is not a usual English construction, and betrays its Latin origin.

Task 16.13

If you feel confident about these patterns, apply them to this mixed bag of words of two syllables. Remember that this is a word-attack skill to use when you can't decode a word, so do not read the word first. Do it like this:

Spot and mark the patterns vcv, etc.

Apply the rules about where to divide into syllables.

Mark the vowels long or short and read the word.

Write in columns according to the pattern vc/cv, v/cv, v/v.

Can you find the odd one out?

Cover the answers until you are ready to check.

commit	disgust	stoic	
robot	splendid	pretend	
cruel	robin	triumph	
context	stolen	motel	
trial	protest	poplin	dual

A

vc/cv	v/cv	v/v
com/mit	sto/len	sto/ic
splen/did	ro/bot	cru/el
dis/gust	pre/tend	tri/umph
pop/lin	pro/test	tri/al
con/text	mo/tel	du/al

The odd one out is *robin* because it has a vcv pattern, but does not divide after the first vowel. If it did, it would be pronounced (rō-bin). It is one of those vcv words which can be decoded easily by most children.

Most words of two syllables can be segmented and decoded successfully once the students get a feel for the patterns of vowels and consonants in words, and where the split should occur.

Syllable division with regular final syllables

Another strategy is to recognize that some words may have a group of letters at the end which form a regular final syllable. Examples of these regular final syllables are *ture, -tion*, and all the *-le* syllables, that is the *-le* with the preceding consonant: *-ble, cle, -dle, -fle, -gle, -kle, -ple, -stle, -tle*. When these occur at the end of a word, the trick is to segment them visually from the rest of the word and read the first syllable.

You do not need to mark the position of vowels or consonants when dealing with regular final syllables. It is useful to practise marking off the regular final syllable with a pencil, and spot whether the first syllable is closed or open. Mark the vowel in the first syllable long or short:

    fĭx / ture   mō / tion   răt / tle   tī / tle

Task 16.14

Divide the regular final syllable off from the end of these words, look to see if the first syllable is open or closed and mark the vowel accordingly.

picture	fracture	nature	future
mention	fraction	nation	motion
tumble	candle	mingle	trample
table	idle	bugle	staple

A

pĭc/ture	frăc/ture	nā/ture	fū/ture
měn/tion	frăc/tion	nā/tion	mō/tion
tŭm/ble	căn/dle	mĭn/gle	trăm/ple
tā/ble	ī/dle	bū/gle	stā/ple

These syllable-division rules are very useful for decoding words of two syllables and can provide good guidance for segmenting and decoding longer words.

Conclusion

Despite the complaints about the irregularities of the English language, reading is not a matter of learning every word. We have found that there are reliable strategies for decoding.

1. First, the reader needs to know the grapheme–phoneme links, and that includes grappling with a reading choice if one grapheme has more than one sound.
2. Second, understanding how to segment into syllables, so that longer words can be visually segmented and the resulting syllables read correctly.
3. Other decoding skills include spotting the morphological elements in longer words: prefixes, base words and suffixes, and these were dealt with in Chapter 14.

Our brains are constantly active when we are reading in context, regularly monitoring whether the words we are decoding are real words, and if they make sense in the context. Young readers, or those with literacy problems, will need help to improve their reading accuracy. Teachers can help by presenting new words in lists of rhyming groups, building them into a structured programme so that the most common and predictable choices are consolidated before the more esoteric and obscure ones. This helps students to make analogies and choices when reading. Accurate decoding at the word level is the best aid to reading comprehension.

Summary

Orthography

- Orthography = correct spelling of words
- English is ridiculed for orthographic inconsistencies
- Reason: origins of English from many languages
- Spelling became fixed on orthographic layers:
  Anglo-Saxon
  Romance
  Greek/Latin
- Good readers are aware of:
  patterns of letters within words
  possible choices of sound that the letters represent
  (as in homographs)
- 80 per cent of English orthography is regular

How does the reader decode English orthography?

- Grapheme–phoneme correspondence
- 26 letters consisting of: vowels and consonants
  - can produce vowel digraphs, consonant digraphs
  - vowels modified by r
  - other letter groups
- Many of these graphemes = more than one phoneme
  = reading choice
- Reader makes reading choice by analogy, especially rhyming
- Longer words require segmentation into syllables

Syllables

- Syllable = a beat in a word. Every syllable has a vowel
- Types: open syllables, e.g. bē
             closed syllables, e.g. bĕt
- Syllable division
- To segment a two-syllable word:
  locate vowels and consonants between them
  divide according to pattern
  vc/cv, e.g. ban-dit
  v/cv, e.g. ro-bot
  v/v, e.g. di-et
- and regular final syllables, e.g. -ble, -tion

CHAPTER 17

Orthography: spelling

What is spelling?

Having considered strategies for reading English orthography, let us now look at spelling. Spelling involves a process starting with the sounds of a spoken word and ending with the written letters on the page. Whether we say the words aloud as we write, or dictate them to ourselves in our head, we are moving from sounds to letters: from phonemes to graphemes. Additionally, if someone says 'How do you spell "eight"?' we need to be able to spell the word aloud e-i-g-h-t, using the names of the letters. The name of the letter is the only immutable thing about a letter. A letter's shape may change. For instance, the letter g may look like any of these:

g g *g* ɡ 9 ℊ *𝒢* ℊ
G G 𝐺 ɢ 𝐺 G 𝐺 𝒢

The sound which it represents may alter from word to word, but by referring to its name, there is no doubt which letter is meant.

Spelling is in some ways the opposite of reading. Reading begins with the sight of letters on the page: spelling begins with heard or remembered sounds. But of course spelling is not a simple reversal of the reading process.

The spelling system in English

If English were a transparent language, there would not be a problem with the spelling. Each sound would have just one spelling. But we have about 44 different sounds in English and only 26 letters to represent them. In addition, English has adopted the spellings from other languages that have become fixed from the time we adopted them. The spellings have become fossilized in orthographic strata (see Chapter 16), and this has resulted in several spellings for one sound.

283

Example: k

For instance the sound (k) occurs in most of the languages which have contributed to modern English. Simple words such as *cat, kitten* and *stuck* all originated from that bottom stratum of vernacular Anglo-Saxon and Germanic spelling so the sound (k) is spelled *c, k* and *ck* respectively. However in a Greek-based word, the (k) would be spelled *ch* as in *chemist* and *mechanic*. But if the word had a French connection, and the sound (k) came at the end, it may be spelled *–que* as in *unique* or a *cheque*.

So spelling requires a lot more thought and processing than just hearing a sound and writing the first letter that is linked to that sound. It requires a feel for similar words, and often a decision about a choice of spelling. Many young children or poor spellers seem to become stuck at the level of 1:1 transcription; one phoneme being represented by a single letter. This leads to such misspellings as *hed* (head), *mad* (made), *jint* (giant) and *sel* (cell). These spellers become disappointed and confused when their system lets them down.

The fact is that English spelling requires a lot of complex thought-processing. Good spellers have to make decisions about how to transcribe words all the time. Look at Task 17.1 in which one of the sounds in each word requires a choice of spelling. You have to make a spelling choice, in this case using homophones. Homophones are words which sound the same, but have different spellings according to meaning.

Task 17.1

Sound out the words in the left-hand column, and write down at least two spellings for each. Cover the answers in the right-hand column until you are ready to check.

Sound	Spellings			Sound	Spellings		
(sē)	see	sea		(wŭn)	won	one	
(rōd)	rode	road		(rīt)	right	write	rite	wright
(mād)	made	maid		(flē)	flee	flea	
(bēn)	been	bean		(thaer)	there	their	they're
(too)	too	two	to	(staer)	stare	stair	
(stēl)	steel	steal		(brāk)	brake	break	
(plān)	plane	plain		(nīt)	night	knight	
(rān)	rain	reign		(sĕnt)	sent	scent	cent
(rŭf)	rough	ruff		(throo)	threw	through	
(pēl)	peel	peal					

There you can see what is meant by a spelling choice: one particular sound which may be spelled in several different ways. In the majority of the words above, you have probably noticed that it was mostly the long vowel sound that required the alternative spellings, with just a few where a consonant sound was the culprit, as in (rŭf) and (sěnt). It is the spelling choices in English which make the spelling system seem chaotic.

Teachers and learners can gain confidence if they have more knowledge about the spelling system, and the rules and patterns that can be relied upon in most cases. So we will listen now to the sounds of English, and how we spell them.

The consonant sounds

We will consider first phoneme-grapheme correspondence in English, and then spelling choices. Let us start with the consonant sounds as these have the most reliable spellings.

Task 17.2

Starting with the list of 21 consonant sounds, say each sound and write the most common way of spelling that sound. The phonemes are written in brackets. You may just write one letter in most cases, but in some cases there may be an alternative choice when spelling that sound.

Cover the answers until you are ready to check.

1	(b)	13	(s)
2	(k)	14	(t)
3	(d)	15	(v)
4	(f)	16	(w)
5	(g)	17	(y)
6	(h)	18	(z)
7	(j)	19	(kw)
8	(l)	20	(ks)
9	(m)	21	(gz)
10	(n)	22	(ch)
11	(p)	23	(sh)
12	(r)		

These consonant sounds are the most straightforward to transcribe into graphemes, and in most cases, as you can see in the answers, they just have the one spelling you would expect. But look at the sounds where there were alternatives:

Task 17.2
continued

A

#	(sound)					
1	(b)	**b** bat				
2	(k)	**c** cat	**k** kilt	**ck** duck	**ch** chemist	**que** cheque
3	(d)	**d** dog	**ed** wagged			
4	(f)	**f** fox	**ff** cliff	**ph** graph	**gh** laugh	
5	(g)	**g** gate				
6	(h)	**h** hot				
7	(j)	**j** jet	**ge** cage	**dge** hedge	**g** ginger	
8	(l)	**l** leg	**ll** fill			
9	(m)	**m** man				
10	(n)	**n** net	**kn** know			
11	(p)	**p** pen				
12	(r)	**r** ran	**wr** write			
13	(s)	**s** sun	**ss** cross	**ce** face	**c** city	**sc** scent
14	(t)	**t** ten	**ed** packed			
15	(v)	**v** van	**ve** sleeve			
16	(w)	**w** wing				
17	(y)	**y** yellow				
18	(z)	**z** zip	**s** tins	**zz** buzz		
19	(kw)	**qu** queen				
20	(ks)	**x** fox				
21	(gz)	**x** exam				
22	(ch)	**ch** chip	**tch** match			
23	(sh)	**sh** shop	**ti** cautious	**ci** social		

Spelling choices: consonants

In most cases there are guidelines to govern which spelling choice a writer should make. A few examples are given here:

The sound (k)
The letter c is usually used, but *k* is needed before *e* or *i*. The letters *ck* are used at the end of a one-syllable word after a short vowel as in *pack, neck, stick, sock, duck*. Use *ch* for longer scientific or musical terms: *chromosome, chorus*. Use *-que* in words of French origin, for example, *cheque*.

The sounds (t) and (d)
Both of these sounds, at the end of a word, can be spelled *ed*. The sound (t) is spelled *ed* after a voiceless consonant, at the end of *helped, packed, switched*. The sound (d) is spelled *ed* after a voiced sound, at the end of *yelled, slammed, stayed*. When spelling these words, the learner has to think not only of sounds, but also of grammar. The letters *ed* form a suffix at the end of a verb in the past tense. To spell these correctly needs at least an awareness that the word (hĕlpt) consists of the base word *help* with the suffix *-ed* added on at the end. Similarly with (yĕld), the learner must recognize the morphemes *yell* and *-ed* embedded in that word, and then she can spell them correctly.

The sound (s)

The spelling of this sound depends on its position in the word, its grammatical function and the language from which the word is derived. The sound (s) is nearly always spelled with the letter *s* at the beginning of the word (*sun, serpent*). The *s* is used at the end of words if it is a suffix used to form a plural (*cats, gates*), or a suffix used to form the third person singular from of the verb (*helps, packs*). The ss is used for the (s) sound at the end of a short word, following a short vowel (see the 'Floss' rule below) as in *class, mess, kiss, moss* and *fuss*. The letters -*ce* are used at the end of a word where the sound (s) is part of the main word and is not a suffix (face, prince, chance). The letter *c* is used for the sound (s) in words derived from French. The *c* is always followed by *e, i* or *y*.

The sound (j)

Most of the time, the sound (j) is spelled *j* if it occurs at the beginning of a word or syllable (*jest, justice, re-ject, en-joy*). The letters -*ge* are used at the end of a word (*change, huge, engage*). However if the (j) has a short vowel sound before it, giving the sounds (ăj) (ĕj) (ĭj) (ŏj) or (ŭj) in a short word of one syllable, the (j) is spelled *dge* (*badge, hedge, bridge, dodge, fudge*). In words of French origin, the sound (j) may be spelled with a *g* if it is followed by the letters *e, i* or *y* (*gentle, giant, gyrate*).

The 'Floss' rule

It is worth mentioning the 'Floss' rule as it applies to several of the sounds above. It refers to consonants that double or have an extra letter when they occur at the end of a short word (one syllable) after a short vowel. The consonants in 'Floss' are a reminder of the first three:

(f) **ff**, (l) **ll**, (s) **ss**.

The same rule applies to several consonant sounds:

-**ff**   staff, off, cliff, cuff

-**ll**   shall, smell, mill, doll, full

       and the irregular-sounding -**all**, ball, fall, small

-**ss**   pass, mess, hiss, toss, fuss

-**ck**   pack, neck, stick, lock, luck

-**dge** badge, ledge, fridge, lodge, fudge

-**tch** batch, fetch, stitch, blotch, hutch

These choices can be learned as spelling rules, but are best learned as rhyming groups, or as words with the same pattern.

The vowel sounds

It is the vowel sounds in English which cause most of the spelling choices and problems, as you realized in the homophone task earlier. In particular, it is the long sound of the vowel, which produces the greatest number of spelling choices of any sound.

Spelling choices: long vowels

Historically, there have been many changes that have influenced the vowels more than any other sounds: the Great Vowel Shift, regional differences in pronunciation and imported words.

Task 17.3

See how many ways you can find to spell the long vowel sounds: (ā), (ē), (ī), (ō), (ū). There are several different ways of spelling each of these five sounds. You should be able to think of at least three examples of your chosen spelling in words, to prevent you from choosing one-off irregular spellings.

Cover the answers until you are ready to check.

A

Sound	Open syllable	Inside a syllable					End of a word		
(ā)	**a** a-corn	**a-e** cake	**ai** train	ei neighbour			**ay** day	ey grey	
(ē)	**e** e-quals	**ee** teeth	**ea** heat	ie chief	ei receive	e-e delete	**ee** tree	ey money	[y] happy
(ī)	**i** i-tem	**i-e** time	**igh** night	y-e type			**y** cry	ie tie	
(ō)	**o** o-pen	**o-e** hope	**oa** soap				**ow** snow	oe toe	
(ū)	**u** u-nit	**u-e** tube	eu euphoria				**ew** stew	**ue** argue	

This table contains all the spellings of the long vowel sounds. Each of these spellings will have at least six words containing that sound and spelling in English. Those in bold are the most commonly used spelling choices, and the others are found less frequently.

The table demonstrates that the spelling of a long vowel sound depends to a large extent on where the sound is in the word: for example, the sound (ā) is spelled just *a*, if it occurs in an open syllable; *ay* if it comes at the end of a word; and if the sound (ā) is heard in the middle of the syllable, it is most likely to be spelled *a-e* (made, fame, tape) or *ai*. There are two spellings for the (ā) which are not in bold: the *ei* and ey spelling are less frequently used.

Other sounds

Besides the consonant sounds and vowel sounds, there are several other sounds which have spelling choices. They are (er), (oi), (sh'n) and (ŭs).

Task 17.4

See how many ways you can find to spell these four extra sounds: (er), (oi), (sh'n) and (ŭs)

Write down as many as you can think of. You should be able to think of at least three examples of each spelling you choose. Cover the answers until you are ready to check.

A

Sound	Spelling and examples			
(er)	**er** kerb	**ir** girl	**ur** turn	**ear** learn
(oi)	**oi** coin	**oy** boy		
(sh'n)	**tion** action	**sion** permission	**cian** magician	
(ŭs)	**us** crocus (noun)	**ous** dangerous (adjective)		

You may have found the tasks above quite difficult because you were being asked to concentrate on the spelling of a particular sound, as that is probably not the way you normally classify spelling patterns. We tend to use analogy when thinking about spelling, and the tasks would have been easier if you had been required to find a rhyming word with similar spelling for *cake*, *train* and *night*, etc. Alliteration and rhyme are powerful ways of filing words according to their sounds and the spelling of a word is more predictable when a larger unit such as a rhyming chunk can be identified. In task 17.4 above, classifying the spelling according to sound, demonstrates the range of spelling choices that are available for a particular sound, which is useful information for the student or the educator. We must remember that these spellings cannot be mixed and matched at random, as George Bernard Shaw mischievously implied when he suggested that the word fish could be spelled *ghoti* (the sound (f), *gh, as in* laugh; (ĭ) *o* as in *women*; and (sh) *ti* as in *initial*).

You have seen from this survey of sounds that spelling choices are restricted by the position of the sound in the word, the word's original language, its grammatical function and analogous words. The tables in the tasks above display the spelling choices for the consonants, the long vowels and some other sounds. This is a representative list of most English spelling choices, but it is not comprehensive. These choices may seem daunting, but they do represent some patterns and consistency, and provide guidelines for spelling. They may convince us that English orthography is not an entirely random lottery, and that for most sounds there are only a few possible ways of spelling them.

We have covered here the concept of a spelling choice (a spoken sound which can be spelled in more than one way). In English there are a fairly large number of choices, causing foreign language learners and weak spellers a great deal of puzzlement, anxiety and frustration. However, if the student knows that there are only two or three possible ways of spelling a particular sound, at least s/he can try them to see which looks right. This leads to increased control and confidence in spelling.

The awkward squad

However, the critics of English spelling and the spelling reformers will make us aware of two other difficult areas of English spelling: the schwa sound and the irregular words. To this list can be added the confusibles: words which sound almost the same, but have different meanings and therefore are a speller's minefield. All three of these will be considered now.

Schwa

The schwa sound is represented by (ə), which is the unstressed sound that is represented by the letter *a* in *literacy*, the *e* in *happen*, the *o* in *petrol*, the *er* in *teacher*, the *our* in flavour. The sound is an indistinguishable vowel sound, barely more than a grunt, which is heard in many unstressed syllables. If we were to make a list of all the ways we can spell the schwa sound, it would become very long and unwieldy, and would be no good as a list for a learner who is trying to collect together the alternative spellings. We must find another way of resolving this particular spelling difficulty.

The next task will help you to think how you do this yourself.

Task 17.5

In the left-hand column (overleaf) are the sounds of some words. Pronounce them and then write the word correctly. Think how you did it, or cast your mind back to the time when you had to learn these words. Cover the answers in the right-hand column until you've finished.

Task 17.5	Sound of word	Spelling	Word spelling
continued	(pĕtrəl)	o	petrol
A	(dĭzməl)	a	dismal
	(mȇrmə)	ur	murmur
	(fȃrmə)	er	farmer
	(kəlĕct)	o	collect
	(tăblət)	e	tablet
	(dūbĭəs)	ou	dubious
	(əlŏng)	a	along
	(ĭnjə)	ure	injure
	(ănkə)	or	anchor
	(vĭkə)	ar	vicar

Once you had worked out the sounds of the word, you would be able to spell it without much thought, but was this always so? Some people with a very good visual memory may have had the letters of the word etched on their brain in the right order, having only seen it once. It is more likely that when, as a young reader, you first read the word *petrol*, you attacked it and sounded it out as two separate and equally stressed syllables pĕt-rŏl. After that you would have mulled it around in your mind to try to make sense of it. The context of course would help, and when you realized what the word was, you would say it with the correct stress, and normal pronunciation. However, that process of learning to decode the word would stand you in good stead when you came to spell it. You may have thought '(pĕtrəl) really looks like pĕt-rŏl', using exaggerated pronunciation to help you spell the word. Such exaggerated pronunciation is commonly used by many people when spelling words such as Wednesday (Wĕd-nĕs-dā), February (Fĕb-roo-ă-rĭ), independent (ĭn-dē-pĕn-dĕnt) or chocolate (chŏk-ō-lāt). It is the technique which gives us the useful link between reading and spelling. If teachers can help learners to learn words for spelling by using such exaggerated pronunciation, they will be conveying a valuable technique, and the best means of tackling the spelling of the ubiquitous schwa (ə).

Irregular words

There are some English words which seem to flaunt all the spelling guidelines that have been devised. These are the words such as *although*, *answer*, *autumn*, *climb*, *cough*, *could*, *debt*, *dough*, *eye*, *once*, *people*, *said*, *shoe*, *sugar*, *talk* and *who*.

These words just need to be remembered. Some of them may be susceptible to exaggerated pronunciation (answer, autumn, climb, people) and can be remembered in that way. A learner may prefer a visual mnemonic for some, e.g. eye, climb:

Oral mnemonics, based on the letters in the word, may help for some: for example, the *ould* in *could*, *would* and *should* is remembered by some children as 'Oh you Lucky Duck'.

For some kinaesthetic learners who have written the word many times, the word might be 'in their hand'. They prefer to check the spelling by writing in order to remember the hand movement for the sequence of letters.

These are some of the ways that tricky words are learned. Most competent readers depend on visual memory from having seen the word spelled correctly on several occasions.

The confusibles

However, there are some words which seem designed to trip up the unwary speller. These confusibles are usually homophones which sound the same or similar. The decision about which spelling to use depends entirely on visual memory, and the ability to link a particular spelling with the precise meaning. Lists of these tricky words occur in spelling books or in lists in a spelling dictionary. They are weasel words because they may look familiar, and so will not be picked up by a computer spell-checker. They are dependent on visual memory, and the writer's linking of spelling and meaning. They are just the sorts of words for which a spelling dictionary is really useful.

Task 17.6

Just for interest, here are some of the words which are often confused and misused. How is your visual memory? If you are unsure about any of them, the answers are in the dictionary!

accept	except	eerie	eyrie
elicit	illicit	affect	effect
entomologist	etymologist	ail	ale
faint	feint	air	heir
aisle	isle	hangar	hanger
altar	alter	lightening	lightning

Task 17.6
continued

ascent	assent	loath	loathe
bail	bale	lumber	lumbar
baton	batten	mare	mayor
beer	bier	naval	navel
berth	birth	plaintiff	plaintive
bizarre	bazaar	pray	prey
bridal	bridle	prize	prise
brooch	broach	choir	quire
collage	college	serial	cereal
cornflour	cornflower	stationary	stationery
council	counsel	straight	strait
draft	draught	surplice	surplus
due, dew	Jew	whore	hoar

How do we learn to spell a word?

It seems that, between listening to a word and writing it down, several processes occur:

Sound–letter transcription: The writer listens to the sound of the word and, for a simple word, or for a young child learning to spell, the first thing he does is to transcribe the word sound by sound: the sounds (k)(ă)(n) are spelled *can.*

Analogy: After that, knowledge of analogous words helps, especially words which alliterate with, or rhyme with the target word. By seeing words in groups, the learner is encouraged to notice patterns and make analogies.

sh	tr	-ake	-eam	-ew
ship	trip	bake	team	new
shop	trap	lake	beam	stew
shot	trot	cake	dream	grew
shelf	tramp	wake	cream	flew
sharp	track	flake	steam	blew

Morphemes: We also recognize morphemes in words: we hear the final *ing* or *able* or *ist* at the end of a word (*resuming, drinkable, pyrotechnist*) and realize it is a suffix; or we perceive that the *pre* or *con* at the beginning of a word (*preconditionally, contemporary*) may indicate a prefix; so then we can concentrate on spelling the base word.

Spelling rules: We may even have learned some spelling rules and find we have to apply them, as in the drop the *e* rule in *debatable*, or the doubling rule in *shopping*. (See Chapter 14, 'Grammar 2: Morphology'.)

Visual memory: But finally, having written what we think, having reread the word, we sit back and look at the whole word again, trying to see if it looks right, trying to remember if we have seen it spelled that way before.

As literate adults we are able to process all this information about phoneme-grapheme links, analogies, morphemes and visual memory simultaneously or selectively as we spell words and as the situation demands. Most of the words we have to spell are so well practised that they are automatic. But it is necessary to lead children or weak spellers through these steps methodically in order to help them become competent spellers.

Some schools of thought will admit only of the last procedure (visual memory) as being relevant to spelling. They believe we spell by just remembering the words we have read: 'The more you read, the better your spelling will be' is the mantra. But there are some good readers who are very bad spellers, and the two processes cannot be seen as automatically affecting each other. We know that many dyslexic students use only the strategy of trying to remember the shape of the word, and it leads to very inaccurate and inflexible spelling. As they try to copy a word straight from their visual memory, with no reference to the sounds in the word, letters are often missed out or written in the wrong order. If these students do not have the skills of phonics or analogy, they have no means of checking their spelling.

So teaching techniques must include teacher-knowledge of spelling patterns and of these strategies for encoding words. Visual matching with a remembered word may be the last strategy of the competent speller, but we must not encourage it to be the first strategy of a weak speller.

Conclusion

The easiest spelling system would be a transparent one, in which one letter made one sound. But English is an old-established language, affected by incomers bringing with them different languages, accents and their own ideas of how to transcribe speech into written language on the page. Our grammar is relatively simple (we do not have to assign a gender to every noun, for instance), but our spelling is complex.

The orthography is complicated to learn and to teach, but it is hoped that the discussion in this chapter has pointed out the patterns and consistencies that make it easier. If you are a good reader and speller of English, congratulate yourself!

Summary

- Spelling:
  Speech sounds represented as written words
  sounds $\longrightarrow$ letters
  44 phonemes $\longrightarrow$ graphemes

- Spelling choices:
  One sound with more than one spelling
  Consonant sounds – usually one main spelling, usually predictable
  Short vowel sounds – one main spelling, usually predictable
  Long vowel sounds – several choices, depending on position in word

- Spelling strategies

- Hearing the sound

  Transcribing sounds

  Use of analogy

  Recognition of morphemes
  (prefix/base word/suffix)

  Applying spelling rules

  Checking with visual memory

- Writing the word

- Dyslexic students may try to spell from a faulty visual memory.
  They need to be taught spelling patterns and rules as part of a structured, multi-sensory programme.

- The English spelling system: tricky, but not chaotic.

CHAPTER 18

Punctuation

Introduction

When teaching reading, we concentrate of course on the letters and words in the first place and we may forget even to mention the other little marks and squiggles that occur in a text. It is only when we hear a reader who is blithely ignoring those little dots that we realize the importance of punctuation in making sense of the passage.

The National Literacy Strategy defines punctuation as 'a way of marking written text to help the reader's understanding'. Tom McArthur in *The Oxford Companion to English Literature* (1992) tells us that punctuation 'is the practice in writing and print of a set of marks to regulate texts and clarify their meanings, principally by separating or linking words, phrases, and by indicating parentheses and asides'. So punctuation has a linking function in that it bundles meaningful bits of text together. The young reader learns to stop at a full stop and take a breath, thus linking the words in one sentence into an idea, and separating it from that in the next sentence. In a sentence such as 'They bought a newspaper, two magazines, a video and a bar of chocolate' the commas in a list help to join related items and separate them from each other.

The purposes of punctuation are, according to David Crystal (1995), four-fold. First, punctuation displays the grammatical structure of the text to enable stretches of written language to be read coherently. Sentence end-markers and indentation of paragraphs would be significant here.

Second, punctuation gives the reader a clue about prosody, the rise and fall of the voice, and the stress on words and syllables which gives each language its particular characteristic intonation and rhythm. Question marks and exclamation marks indicate the emphasis and intonation of spoken language. Even a single word would be spoken differently depending on its punctuation. The word *gone* followed by a question mark would be spoken with rising intonation: 'Gone?' If it were followed by an exclamation mark, 'Gone!', it would be uttered more loudly than the rest of the text and would imply shock, triumph or a similar strong emotion.

The third purpose of punctuation is to highlight semantic units and contrasts, such as the balance implied by the use of a colon: 'The air was heavy: the water still'. Line divisions and stanzas indicate poetry.

The fourth purpose is a semantic dimension which can be seen on the page rather than heard in the voice reading it. This is illustrated by the use of 'scare' quotes to highlight that a word has a special sense, or capital letters to imply a Very Important Point. This latter was greatly loved by A.A. Milne's character Pooh Bear to show the importance of things in his small world: 'A Very Special Present', 'A Bear of Very Little Brain'. Punctuation marks can also be thought of as the traffic signals in written language: they tell us to slow down, notice this, take a detour or stop. Good punctuation is the sign of a thoughtful writer. It is like good manners: a courtesy designed to help readers to understand a story without stumbling.

The history of punctuation

The word punctuation comes from the Latin meaning a point, and is related to the word 'punctilious'. In early written texts, no spaces were made between words, so the first punctuation occurred when points were put between words, and these can still be seen in carved Latin inscriptions on some tombs:

DE ▲ MORTVIS ▲ NIL ▲ NISI ▲ BONVM

St Jerome in the fifth century used punctuation in Latin translations of the Bible. Another key figure was Alcuin in the eighth century, who was an Anglo-Saxon tutor at the court of the Emperor Charlemagne. He was responsible for a new spelling and punctuation system for biblical and liturgical manuscripts. In the 1400s–1500s, two Italian printers from Venice, who were both called Aldus Manutius – they were grandfather and grandson – developed marks similar to the present day full stop, colon, semi-colon and comma. In Elizabethan times, the critic George Puttenham included advice on punctuation as a means of marking text for sense and meaning. But these punctuation marks had mainly a declamatory function to indicate on the script how it should be spoken aloud, including pauses to take breath. However, in the seventeenth century this method was replaced by the syntactic approach of the playwright and grammarian Ben Johnson, who marked the text according to grammar and meaning, as in modern punctuation.

Punctuation down the centuries has been rather erratically applied. Caxton was haphazard in those early printed texts. Dickens apparently was very punctilious about it and would proofread the scripts of his novels, with careful attention to the punctuation. William Wordsworth, on the other hand, left punctuation almost entirely to his editor.

Most writers hardly think about basic punctuation. They just put it in as they write, aware of the pauses and prosody of the spoken language. But the more esoteric aspects of punctuation require a little more thought.

When children are first learning to punctuate, they are told to say the words aloud and listen for pauses and the fall of the voice at the end of a sentence. Consideration of the rise and fall of the voice provides a good indicator of full stops and commas, but it is not the whole story.

Task 18.1

Try this traditional punctuation task. Here is a passage with the punctuation missing. Harry Potter fans will probably recognize that it is from Chapter 3 of J.K. Rowling's *Harry Potter and the Chamber of Secrets*. Think in detail about where you would put the spacing and the punctuation marks. What helps you to decide? How many different kinds of punctuation did you use?

The passage with its original punctuation is reproduced overleaf.

Cover it until you are ready to check.

> blimey im tired yawned fred setting down his knife and fork at last i think ill go to bed and you will not snapped mrs weasley its your own fault youve been up all night youre going to degnome the garden for me theyre getting completely out of hand again and she pulled a heavy book from the stack on the mantelpiece george groaned mum we know how to degnome a garden harry looked at the cover of mrs weasleys book written across it in fancy gold letters were the words gilderoy lockharts guide to household pests there was a big photograph on the front of a very good looking wizard with wavy blond hair and bright blue eyes as always in the wizarding world the photograph was moving the wizard who harry supposed was gilderoy lockhart kept winking cheekily up at them all mrs weasley beamed down at him oh he is marvellous she said he know his household pests all right its a wonderful book mum fancies him said fred in a very audible whisper dont be so ridiculous fred said mrs weasley her cheeks rather pink all right if you think you know better than lockhart you can go and get on with it and woe betide you if theres a single gnome in that garden when i come out to inspect it

Task 18.1
continued

A

'Blimey, I'm tired,' yawned Fred, setting down his knife and fork at last. 'I think I'll go to bed and –'

'You will not,' snapped Mrs Weasley. 'It's your own fault you've been up all night. You're going to de-gnome the garden for me, they're getting completely out of hand again.'

And she pulled a heavy book from the stack on the mantelpiece.

George groaned.

'Mum, we know how to de-gnome a garden.'

Harry looked at the cover of Mrs Weasley's book. Written across it in fancy gold letters were the words: *Gilderoy Lockhart's Guide to Household Pests*. There was a big photograph on the front of a very good-looking wizard with wavy blond hair and bright blue eyes. As always in the wizarding world, the photograph was moving; the wizard, who Harry supposed was Gilderoy Lockhart, kept winking cheekily up at them all. Mrs Weasley beamed down at him.

'Oh, he is marvellous,' she said, 'he know his household pests, all right, it's a wonderful book ...'

'Mum fancies him,' said Fred, in a very audible whisper.

'Don't be so ridiculous, Fred,' said Mrs Weasley, her cheeks rather pink. 'All right, if you think you know better than Lockhart you can go and get on with it, and woe betide you if there's a single gnome in that garden when I come out to inspect it.'

There were at least ten different kinds of punctuation mark, including full stops, commas, speech marks, dashes, hyphens, ellipses and apostrophes, as well as indentation for paragraphs, capital letters for names and italics for a book title. J.K. Rowling's punctuation here is quite restrained and is lacking in the exclamation marks which another author may have included.

As you did the task you would be aware that you were orchestrating all the skills for punctuating: reading it aloud to try to hear the sentence breaks and conversation; checking the names in the passage for capital letters; being aware of abbreviated forms; as well as imagining conventional layout for the page. And you did not even have to think about the spelling. Imagine how difficult the task of punctuating is for a student who is struggling to spell the words as well.

Is punctuation important?

Those who are sticklers for correct punctuation are often criticized, but their critics are rebuffed with an amusing story about a panda, retold by Lynne Truss (2003):

> A panda walks into a café. He orders a sandwich, eats it, and then draws a gun and fires two shots in the air.
>
> 'Why?' asks the confused waiter as the panda makes towards the exit. The panda produces a badly punctuated wildlife manual and tosses it over his shoulder.
>
> 'I'm a panda,' he says, at the door. 'Look it up.'
>
> The waiter turns to the relevant entry and, sure enough, finds an explanation.
>
> '**Panda**. Large black-and-white bear-like mammal, native to China. Eats, shoots and leaves.'
>
> So punctuation does matter.

The next section will cover most aspects of punctuation as a reminder to you of the majority of the conventions, and as a ready reference for most of the queries that will come your way.

Frequency of use of punctuation marks

The list of punctuation marks in Table 18.1 records their frequency in a wide range of English texts from ICE-GB, the British Corpus of the International

Table 18.1 Frequency of punctuation marks in British text

Commas	19 485	(41.9%)
Periods	18 632	(40.1%)
Dashes	1 347	(2.9%)
Opening parentheses	2 090	(4.5%)
Closing parentheses	2 118	(4.6%)
Semi-colons	743	(1.6%)
Question marks	810	(1.7%)
Colons	806	(1.7%)
Exclamation marks	444	(1%)

Source: ICE-GB.

Corpus of English. The corpus is a computer database of language materials, begun in 1991, with the aim of containing 100 million running words of British English. The written component, when it totalled approximately 400,000 words, was analysed to find the frequency of punctuation used.

As you can see from the figures, the largest percentage of punctuation marks used by far are the comma and period (or full stop), which account for over 80 per cent of all punctuation.

This chapter will deal with 17 aspects of punctuation:

- full stops
- commas
- semi-colons
- colons
- apostrophes
- question marks
- exclamation marks
- hyphens
- parentheses
- square brackets
- dashes
- ellipses
- quotation marks
- capital letters
- italics
- paragraphing and indentation
- referencing

The first 13 are marks which are placed within the text. The last four are ways of presenting the text, but they can also be considered under the heading of punctuation.

As you read the heading for each punctuation type, cover the text below it, and try to jot down any uses of that particular piece of punctuation. The number of uses described in the text is indicated by the number after the heading.

However, the lists are certainly not exhaustive, and you may find other uses that are not mentioned. You may find that you know a great deal about punctuation already.

The full stop (.) 5

The first mark that children usually learn is called the full stop in Britain, but in the US and amongst scholars and printers it is also called the period. It is used in the following ways:

At the end of a sentence

The word *period* originally meant a periodic sentence – that is, the span of the whole sentence – but eventually came to mean the mark at the end of it. It's the place where the reader can stop to draw breath, and is therefore a clear indication when reading aloud that the voice drops, and that the utterance should have made sense.

For initials

Another use for the full stop is in initials: J.R.R. Tolkien, J.K. Rowling; B.A. for Bachelor of Arts; the abbreviations H.R.H. for His/Her Royal Highness, N.A.T.O. for North Atlantic Treaty Organization, T.U.C. for the Trades Union Congress and Y.M.C.A. for the Young Men's Christian Association. It must be said however that in modern plain typography, and in order to increase typing speed, the full stops are being omitted from many of these abbreviations.

In abbreviations

Full stops are used in abbreviations such as 'Gen.' for Genesis (in biblical references), 'Rev.' for Reverend, 'Inc.' for incorporated. In those examples, the full stop is used at the end of the first syllable of the word. But in a contraction such as 'Dr', 'Mr', 'Mrs', and 'St', a full stop is not needed, as the final letter of the word is included in each of these contractions.

In times and dates

A full stop is used in the time of day: 8.30 am, 16.40; and dates: 20.05.99.

In Internet addresses

In Internet and email addresses the full stop is obligatory and crucial. It is called a 'dot' when quoting an address. So www.bbc.co.uk is spoken as 'www dot bbc dot co dot uk', and fredbloggs@hotmail.com is given as 'fred bloggs at hotmail dot com'. Leave out the dot and the chances of a successful communication are nil.

The full stop is still the most important punctuation mark. It is obligatory at the end of a sentence and in Internet addresses but the use of the full stop in other circumstances is declining.

In summary

Use a full stop for:
1. end of sentence
2. initials: J.R., B.A., H.R.H., N.A.T.O., T.U.C., Y.M.C.A.

3. abbreviations: Med. *but* Dr Mr Mrs
4. times and date: 8.30 a.m, 16.40, 20.05.99
5. Internet and email addresses

The comma (,) 8

The comma is the most frequently used punctuation mark. It is the punctuation mark of the shortest duration, giving the lightest pause for breath. The word comma comes from the Greek and means 'a clause'. It is used to mark a group of words off from others in the sentence and is a highly flexible mark, separating a larger sentence into meaningful groups. It is used in the following ways:

To clarify meaning

Each the following sentences uses the comma to clarify meaning in a slightly different way:

> If you want him to come, ask him yourself.

Here it is used to clarify meaning by creating a pause.

> Waking up, his son, Paul, saw the tidal wave.
> Waking up his son, Paul saw the tidal wave.

In the sentences above, commas are used to avoid ambiguity. In the first, Paul is the name of the son, but in the second Paul is the father.

> Further violence often defeats its object.
> Further, violence often defeats its object.

Similarly, the first sentence of this pair is unclear. Without the comma we may be referring to more violence, rather than making another, further point in the discussion about violence, which is made clear by the use of the comma in the second sentence.

> By the end of 1916, 273 deaths had occurred.

A comma is needed between numbers to aid clarity. The collocation of the two numbers would be confusing without a pause between them, which the comma provides.

In lists

A common use of the comma is in lists to separate the items, which are usually nouns, adjectives or sometimes verbs.

Nouns

The comma is used after each item, but is not usually needed before the word *and*. So it would be used like this:

She bought oranges, apples, bananas and pears.

In the sentence 'Jack, Jill and Michael went up the hill', Jack, Jill and Michael are going happily up the hill together, whereas in the following sentence, 'Jack, and Jill, went up the hill', the two commas are used to put Jill into parentheses, and so it was Jack who went up the hill, with Jill as a companion.

Adjectives

Commas are needed too in lists of adjectives: 'They were big, shiny, juicy apples.' As with a list of nouns, a comma is not needed before *and* as in 'There were big, tall and imposing pillars in the hall'.

Verbs

The same applies to lists of verbs: 'She turned, looked, screamed', but the comma is dropped if the word *and* is inserted: 'She turned, looked and screamed'.

For place names

When using place names in a sentence, commas are needed:

At the corner of Oxford Street and Regent Street, London, pickpockets abound.

The book was set in Dallas, Texas.

When delivering, take care to distinguish Beeston, Leeds, from Beeston, Nottingham.

Commas here are needed both before and after London, Leeds and Nottingham, as these cities are almost a parenthetical clarification of the main place in the sentence.

Similarly, commas would be used in a run-on address: 'He has lived at 4, Town Street, Horsforth, Leeds, for five years', though the comma after the number 4 is optional here and frequently omitted nowadays.

In letters

At the beginning of letters, the greeting is followed by a comma: 'Dear Sir', 'Dear Mr Smith', 'My dear James'.

At the end of the letter, the valediction is also punctuated by a comma whether it be 'Yours faithfully', 'Yours sincerely', 'With best wishes' or

'With love from', but it is worth noting that there is no full stop after the name at the end of the letter.

For dates and numbers

Dates will take commas when used in a sentence: 'Sunday, 30th June 1998, was a very hot day.'

Large numbers will also take commas in groups of three, for example, '1,374,980' although these are now sometimes being dropped in favour of the continental practice of a space in the same position.

To segment sentences

Commas may be used parenthetically to explain or qualify another word in the sentence:

The witness, a middle-aged woman, stepped forward.

Her mother, panting as always, rushed up the stairs.

Between clauses

Commas are used between clauses, but in the following sentence, a comma would not be needed: 'John felt ill and went to bed early', because the subject of both clauses is the same.

However, in the next two sentences a comma is needed to form a slight pause, as the subject of each clause is different and we need a little more time to adjust to this:

John felt ill, but nobody cared.

If you behave like that, I shall leave.

In complex sentences

In complex sentences, which contain subordinate clauses, the subordinate clause is separated off by the use of commas as in the examples:

Because I was ill, he went away.

He ran to the station, but, when he arrived, the train was just leaving.

Although we love him dearly, we were glad when Monday arrived.

The director, who was present, agreed to the project.

The commas tuck the subordinate clause out of the way, making the main clause obvious, and so the sense of the sentence is more transparent.

In summary

The most frequent use of the comma is to break up sentences into meaningful units. Use it for:

1. clarification of meaning
2. lists
   a. nouns
   b. adjectives
   c. verbs
3. place names
4. letters
5. dates and numbers
6. segmenting sentences
7. between clauses
8. complex sentences

When we are teaching, the full stop and the comma are the most important items of punctuation, and children in Year 4 are expected to start using commas in their own writing. However, the next item, the semi-colons, would not be required in the writing of a primary school pupil.

The semi-colon (;) 4

The semi-colon is made up of a point and a comma, and comes somewhere between them. It has more weight than a comma and is used when a comma is not clear enough, or to provide contrast when there are other commas in the sentence. It has the following uses:

In lists with longer items

The semi-colon separates component parts in a list, if the items consist of several words or contain internal commas:

> The listed children's books can be purchased from: W.H. Smith, Fargate; Waterstones, Orchard Square; Blackwells, Mappin Street; or Rhyme and Reason, Hunter's Bar.

The semi-colon allows them to be grouped in a clear and obvious way.

In complex sentences

The other use of the semi-colon is to separate and coordinate parts of a complex sentence.

Like most human beings, she was born; she married; she had children; she died.

He worked hard; he played hard; indeed, he lived hard.

In the examples above, each component is a clause, and could be punctuated as a series of sentences, but the sense of connection between them would be lost. The semi-colon allows pauses, but also continuity.

For balance and antithesis

In the following two sentences, there is the feeling of balance and antithesis, so the semi-colon is appropriate punctuation:

Many disliked him; she disliked the uniform.

As a player, he commanded admiration; as a manager, he attracted derision.

Between connected clauses

The two sentences that follow contain a connective, and in this case the semi-colon comes before the connectives *moreover* and *therefore* to give a complete sentence, but one which definitely has two component parts:

William was a brave man; moreover, he was intelligent.

The dog is frightened; therefore, you cannot expect him to be friendly.

In summary

The semi-colon is easiest to use in an appropriate list. Its other uses require a feel for style, rather than set rules, and are only needed when more sophisticated punctuation is being used.

The semi-colon is used to:

1. separate longer items in a list
2. identify and coordinates parts of a complex sentence
3. create balance and antithesis
4. connect clauses

The colon (:) 4

The colon comes from the Greek, meaning a part of a body, and it is also linked to part of a dance. It is a division of prosody, marking a breathing space at the end of a principal clause. It has an anticipatory function. Think of it as an actor's pause before a declaration, as it often appears before an announcement, a list, a quotation or a summary.

Before an announcement, list, summary or quotation

Announcement

For example:

> Today they face a further threat to their survival: starvation.

List

This is probably its most used function – to anticipate a list:

> You will need the following: a pen, a pencil, a rubber, a protractor and a ruler.
>
> They put in their order: a high-spec computer, a laser printer and a scanner.

Summary

For example:

> His speech amounted to this: jobs will be lost.

Quotation

A colon comes before a quotation:

> I told them: 'Do not in any circumstances go onto the railway line'.
>
> The proverb is: a stitch in time saves nine.

Note that when quoting a proverb, it does not start with a capital letter.

In logical propositions

The colon may be also be found in logical propositions such as 'Sandy is a woman: all women are unpredictable: therefore Sandy is unpredictable'.
When using numbers, colons are necessary to express a ratio

> Dyslexic boys to girls occur in the ration of 3:1.
>
> The ratio of adults to children should be 2:10 for this activity.

For time

We are of course familiar with the colon used in displaying the time divisions 'hours:minutes:seconds' on digital clocks, stop watches or timers: 1:20, 13:50, 3:17:21.

In summary

The colon is used in:

1. announcing a list, a quotation or a summary
2. logical propositions
3. ratios
4. time

The apostrophe (') 3

The apostrophe was introduced into English from French in the sixteenth century. It indicates omission or possession.

Omission

This high mark sits perkily above the line of the lower-case letters, flying like a kite to indicate that letters have been missed out. The contracted form is usually more colloquial than the full form: so 'is not' becomes *isn't*. 'He is' or 'he has' can both be contracted to *he's*. The old town crier's way of giving the time, 'It's four of the clock and all's well' has been preserved in our *o'clock*. Some words in a spoken utterance lose the beginning as in *'fraid I can't come*, or *fish 'n' chips*, and transcriptions of dialect too are often peppered with apostrophes as letters and parts of words are omitted: *Is th' summa' wrong wi' 'e?*

Forms of words which were previously abbreviations using the apostrophe, such as *'flu* for influenza, *'fridge* for refrigerator and *'phone* for telephone, are now frequently spelled without the apostrophe as they are seen to be legitimate words in their own right.

The apostrophe may also indicate the omission of numbers in dates: *the winter of '45*.

Possession

The apostrophe is also used to show possession. This is probably linked to the Old English genitive (possessive) case which used the inflexional ending *-es* to express 'of the'. The *e* is dropped in Modern English, thus justifying the apostrophe.

The apostrophe *-s* to show possession is straightforward enough when it refers to a singular noun: *Noah's ark*, *Mozart's Requiem*, *the girl's brother*, *the man's car*.

The *children's toys* obviously belong to the children, so *'s* comes after the word children. Problems often occur when the *'s* is added to a noun ending in *s*. *The boys' coats* should really be *the boys's coats* if we are meaning the coats of several boys, but the final *s* has been dropped (for the sake of euphony, because it's hard to say), leaving just the apostrophe at the end of the word. Similarly we have *the girls' toilet* and *the dogs' dinner*.

After a sibilant

A further difficulty for writers is whether to use the apostrophe after a word which ends in a sibilant (a letter giving a hissing sound such as *s, x, z*).

Rex's bone, Buzz's gun, with the *'s* seems right but so too does *for conscience' sake*, without the final *s*. Is it *St James'* or *St James's*? Are they *Keats'* poems, or *Keats's* poems? People still argue fiercely about such points. Usage varies and probably depends on the pronunciation which seems most euphonic and acceptable. Would what's written reflect what you say? Would you say *Charles Dickens house* or *Charles Dickens-es house*? Probably the best guide is to follow what would sound best in speech.

The guidelines are clearer with names from the ancient world where the extra final *s* is omitted as in *Archimedes' screw, Achilles' heel*. The same is true of Jesus as in *Jesus' disciples*.

Trade names ending in s seem to be more susceptible to the whims of fashion in typography. We may expect to see *John Lewis', Woolworth's, Boot's*, but all of these now miss out the apostrophe altogether in their store signs. The Scottish publishing company founded by W. and R. Chambers in 1859, published *Chambers's Encyclopaedia*, with the *'s* added to the name. But by 1969 there was no *'s* in sight when *Chambers English Dictionary* was published.

In the case of the *hostess's privilege* and the *hostesses' concerns*, it is only in the written form that you can see that the former refers to the one hostess, and the latter to more than one. Similarly, the *baby's rattles* and the *babies' rattles* sound exactly the same when spoken, and only the written form reveals whether one baby or more is being referred to.

Pronouns

Another area of confusion occurs because of an *s* in the possessive pronouns, *yours, his, hers, its, ours* and *theirs*. There is obviously a sense of possession here, but none of these takes an apostrophe.

mine	ours
yours	yours
his	theirs
hers	theirs
its	theirs

The exception is the indeterminate pronoun *one* which does take the apostrophe -*s* as in *a place of one's own*.

The tricky word is *its*. 'Its' is used as a pronoun in *The cat licked its paw*, and there is no apostrophe just as there wouldn't be in the *his* of *He licked his finger*. The confusion arises because of the use of the contraction *it's* which is short for *it is* as in *It's a nice day* or *it has* as in *It's gone away*. In the contraction *it's*, the *'s* indicates omission.

To indicate plurals of letters, figures and symbols

To avoid ambiguity when citing letters, figures or symbols, the apostrophe may be used, unusually, to indicate a plural:

His name contains two f's and his phone number four 8's.

Too many I's render a letter egotistical.

Such symbols as θ's are used by mathematicians.

The college staff had two Ph.D.'s, three M.A.'s and two former MP's.

Misuse of the apostrophe

A common misuse of the apostrophe is in the so-called 'greengrocer's apostrophe' where an ordinary plural *s* acquires an apostrophe, giving us *apple's*, *carrot's* and *strawberry's*. It is so named because it frequently occurs on greengrocers' boards, and in shop notices such as 'We sell fresh pie's'.

In summary

The apostrophe is used to indicate:

1. omission
2. possession
3. plurals of letters, figures and symbols.
   (But its misuse is also widespread.)

Once children have started to use the apostrophe it seems to emerge from every nook and cranny wherever there's the hint of an *s*. The apostrophe can be troublesome to teach and to correct in a student's work, and needs to be approached carefully but confidently, teaching only one of its functions at a time.

The question mark (?) 3

The squiggle that is a question mark may have originated from a form of the letter q of the Latin word *quaere*, 'to question'. For children we can explain that it is the shape of a round bracket, finishing off the question, with a line leading down to the full stop. So it indicates both a question and the end of the sentence. It is used in the following ways:

In direct questions

Its primary use is to show that a preceding word, phrase or sentence is a direct question: 'Why?', 'On the boat?', 'Do you want more potatoes?' It is spoken with rising intonation at the end of the question. Questions often start with a question word or the reversal of the subject and verb so from the statement 'He is' we can form the questions 'Is he?', 'Who is he?', 'Where is he?'

It is not used in indirect speech, because a reported question is part of a statement: 'I asked him where he went for his holiday'.

In tag questions

A speaker or writer may often use tag questions to turn a statement into a question, and to gain the attention of the listener: 'It's there, *isn't it?*', 'He did it, *didn't he?*', 'It's true, *don't you think?*'

In rhetorical questions

The rhetorical question is a stylistic device often used in advertising or by politicians. It does not expect an answer. 'Do you want thicker, healthier hair?' may catch your eye in a shampoo advertisement. The rhetorical question from a politician 'Do we want lower fares and trains running on time?' may be a prelude to a new transport policy. We use rhetorical questions in conversational speech: 'Why should I care?', 'Why bother?' and these all take a question mark, even though they are not expecting an answer.

In summary

Questions marks are used at the end of:

1. direct questions
2. tag questions
3. rhetorical questions

The exclamation mark (!) 1

The exclamation mark may have come from the Latin /yo/ spelled *io*, reconfigured with the *i* placed above the *o* to give our modern mark. The Latin word was an exclamation of joy. The alternative explanation is that it is a pointer or a dagger. It can be used after a word, phrase or sentence, either as an exclamation of joy: 'Great!', 'How lovely!', 'What a beautiful day!' or in a more combative and fiercer tone of voice, as an imperative: 'No!', 'Go away!', 'Give it to me!' It can also be used for sheer astonishment: 'Gosh!' or 'It can't be the same man!'

Advertisements often rely on imperative sentences with exclamation marks: 'Buy now! Pay later!'

A question mark and exclamation mark may even be used together, in which case the question mark comes first as in: 'Where on earth has she gone?!'

The hyphen (-) 7

A hyphen is a short mark in the middle of the line of print. It is shorter than a dash and has two main functions: to divide words, and to compound them. Hyphens are used in the following ways:

To divide words

The hyphen can divide words, for instance if a longer word will not fit on a line. This often occurs in newspapers where the narrow columns provide only short lines of print.

> They quoted the latest stat-
> istics.

If a word is to be split into syllables, hyphens are used: *con-cen-tra-tion*, *Wed-nes-day* and so on. The same device can be used to indicate a stammer or gasping or sobbing: *'Boo-hoo, I d-don't w-want to s-s-see him'*.

If a writer wishes to indicate that a person is speaking deliberately slowly, enunciating every word clearly, hyphens can be used to separate syllables, but the longer dash is used between words as in: *You – are – on – the – wrong – bus – for – the – Mon-u-ment*.

To separate vowels

In words with a prefix which ends in a vowel such as *pro* and *re*, a hyphen is used if the base word begins with a vowel and may therefore cause confusion for instance between *co-op* and *coop*. Examples are: *co-operative*, *co-educational*, *pre-empt*, *re-employ*, *re-edit*. However, it is now common practice to spell many previously hyphenated words without the hyphen.

To form compound words

The most frequent use of the hyphen is in order to compound words, linking two or more words into a collective union. It can be done to create nouns: we may have a *get-together*, a *knees-up*, a *heart-to-heart* or a *girls-night-out*. Or it can be used to create adjectives: a *four-star hotel*, *rosy-red cheeks*, chicken which is *finger-lickin' good*. (These adjectives are dealt with in more detail later, as they form a large group).

A hyphen can also be used to anticipate a word in the sentence with which it is meant to be compounded, as in: 'Do you want a four- or five-star hotel?'

Words which in earlier times were compounded have now achieved whole word status and have dropped the hyphen. *Today* and *tomorrow* are good examples of this.

Shakespeare's coinages

Shakespeare was a great coiner of new words. His lexicon can throw up *halfe-blowne*, *pale-visag'd*, *pell-mell*, *ill-tuned*, *smooth-fac'd*. And these were just from one play, *King John*.

Other examples from Shakespeare are:

Arch-heretique	canker-sorrow	sinne-conceiuing
baby-eyes	faire-play	kindred-action
bare-pickt	giant-world	ore-look'd
thin-bestained	Basilisco-like	vile-concluded
breake-vow	heauen-mouing	widow-comfort

We have continued this way of forming new words in modern times. Probably the majority of hyphenated words are descriptive, and are created to form adjectives.

Compound adjectives

labour-saving	good-looking	
steel-making	terror-stricken	
hard-working	red-hot	
worldly-wise	pitch-black	never-ending

Look at the examples above. Vast numbers of these have been created in recent years. They are often ephemeral in nature, used for an apt description of the moment, later to be dismantled. But some of them, such as *labour-saving*, *heart-broken* and *good-looking*, are now achieving whole-word status without the hyphen.

Hyphenated prefixes

Similarly, many prefixes which are hyphenated in British English such as *by-product*, *off-chance* and *up-grade* are much more likely to be written as continuous words in American English. As spell checkers on computers often default to the American spelling setting, our spelling is becoming more international, and these hyphenated words may therefore become written as a continuous word, like their American equivalent, thus accelerating the role of change in the language. Below are some examples of compounded prefixes which still use a hyphen in most cases:

a-	a-fishing
by-	by-product
off-	off-chance, off-licence
ex-	ex-convict, ex-president
vice-	vice-president
anti-	anti-personnel

To clarify meaning

Hyphens are used to clarify meaning. Look at these pairs of examples:

twenty-odd people	twenty odd people
extra-marital sex	extra marital-sex
re-cover	recover

Using the hyphen in *twenty-odd* people makes it clear that it is the number of people that is being discussed. Without the hyphen we may be speaking of twenty strange individuals. Similarly the hyphen in *extra-marital sex*, could lead to the divorce courts, or in *extra marital-sex*, to an increase in a married couple's love life. The hyphen is needed in *re-cover* as in reupholstering a chair, to prevent confusion with the word *recover*, to get better from an illness.

To link nouns

The hyphen can be used to link two proper nouns: *a London–Paris flight, the Clinton–Gore administration, Arab-Israeli talks*, and of course hyphenated names, *Jones-Morton, Wedgewood-Benn*.

It can also link two nouns to describe a person or thing: *an actor–manager, player–manager, city-state, spin-doctor, mother-in-law, steel- maker*.

There are hyphenated combinations where one element is a capital letter; as in *U-boat, X-ray, B-movie*.

Hyphenated words are used to show onomatopoeic or nursery words: *tick-tock, clip-clop, topsy-turvy*.

To refer to word fragments

When referring to affixes in a piece of writing, the hyphen is used to indicate the status of the prefix or suffix as a word fragment:

He misspelled the suffix *-ful* in *helpful*.

In *omnipresent* the *omni-* means all.

The problem of forming plurals

Forming plurals with these hyphenated words can be an area of difficulty. The answer is to think about the meaning and do it sensibly. With many of the words, the usual plural *-s* can be added to the end of the compound. We talk about 'flower-pots' and the children being great 'show-offs', but we cannot sensibly do the same with 'court-martial' and 'man-of-war' as it is the first noun which has to be made plural, giving us 'courts-martial' and 'men-of-war'.

In summary

Hyphens are used to:

1. divide words
2. separate vowels
3. form compound words
4. to form adjectives
5. with prefixes
6. clarify meaning
7. link nouns
8. refer to word fragments
   (forming plurals may be tricky)

Parentheses ( ) 1

Parentheses usually refer to round brackets. The brackets come in pairs and so we use the plural form spelt with *-es* to describe them. The singular is *parenthesis*. Something is written or spoken in parenthesis if it is an aside, or an addition to the main thrust of the sentence: 'Our new manager (he's just arrived) would like to meet you'.

The examples given below show how this aside can be an extra thought, an explanation, or an insertion of a title, reference or statistic:

He is a surgeon (admittedly he doesn't look like one) and a fine pianist.

The new professor (an incredibly long-legged blonde) rose to give her inaugural lecture.

My friend (soon to be my brother-in-law) will pay for the next round.

In her book (*Overcoming Dyslexia*) Margaret Combley describes how ...

In his use of compound words (see Chapter 8) Shakespeare....

We can send two representatives and additional observers (who can participate, but not vote).

The commonest causes of death are heart disease (31.9 per cent) and malignant cancers (17.6 per cent).

Square brackets [ ] 2

Square brackets can be used as a means of parenthesis, but their use is more specific.

For insertion

First, they may be needed to insert into a quotation words which weren't originally there, but which are needed for clarity: 'The two [Grant and McKinley] were summoned before the committee'.

For [sic]

Second, they may be used to comment on the choice of word or spelling in an original document by using [sic] in square brackets, the Latin word meaning *thus*. This is used by writers and editors to distance themselves from a dubious or erroneous usage in the original document, perhaps also to draw attention to it in a mocking way:

At Roman banquets the guests wore garlics [sic] in their hair.

She wrote that her techer [sic] had authorized it.

In summary

Square brackets are used for:

1. insertion
2. [sic]

The dash (–) 1

The dash is sometimes used as a more flamboyant, or stronger, way of expressing something in parenthesis. It is used in the same way that round brackets would be employed:

Was it because she knew – or suspected – more than she was admitting?

It can also be used to indicate hesitation between words in speech (see hyphen).

The ellipsis (. . .) 2

The word comes from the Greek meaning 'coming short'. It is a grammatical term to describe a sentence such as: 'I cycled to Oxford, and Mary as far as Reading', where the word *cycled* is omitted, but understood after the word Mary: 'I cycled as far as Oxford and Mary cycled as far as Reading'. Similarly, 'She said he'd come', is an elliptical sentence short for 'She said he would come' or 'She said he had come'.

Information can be left out for economy or effect or the rhythm of the language. In punctuation the word *ellipsis* has come to refer to three dots, which signify that something is missing. Ellipses can be used to indicate the following.

Missing words

This is particularly used in quotations so the line:

> There has been, as far as we can tell, no loss of life

maybe quoted as

> There has been ... no loss of life.

The ellipsis indicates something missing from the original quotation, but expresses what is required.

An incomplete sentence

The device of ellipsis as punctuation at the end of a sentence is used to leave the reader 'hanging in the air':

> The enemy came slowly nearer, then ...

It is also a device used by teachers to motivate in creative writing.

In summary

Ellipsis in punctuation is used to indicate:

1. missing words
2. incomplete sentence

Quotation marks ("" or '') 1

Quotation marks are sometimes referred to as 'speech marks' and can come in double or single form. If made by typewriter or computer, the double ones look like the number 66 at the beginning of a quotation and like 99 at the end. In handwriting they are usually just pairs of short straight lines. If you look at recently published novels or texts you will probably find that those published for the American market use double quotation marks (the Chicago style) and the British use single marks (called the Oxford and Cambridge style), but styles do vary.

Quotation marks have been used only since the nineteenth century, so are one of the newest forms of punctuation. The National Literacy Strategy requires that children be taught to use double pairs for speech. In this case single marks would be used for a quotation within a speech as in:

"Did I hear you say, 'The car turned over,' or am I imagining it?"

For clarity, when a dialogue or conversation is taking place, each speaker's utterance begins on a new line and is indented. The simplest layout is shown in the sentence:

"Let's go," he said.

A comma concludes the speech, within the quotation marks. A full stop finishes the sentence.

When the speech is broken by information about the speaker, the punctuation looks like this:

"Freddy," said one man, "your father's got away."

The sentence spoken maintains its normal punctuation, and a comma is placed after *said one man*, to punctuate the pause.

If the speaker were at the beginning of the sentence, the punctuation would be:

Jane screamed, "Get it away from me!"

She ran to Shane and whispered, "You can hide in the cupboard," as the front door opened.

All the examples here would usually be found with single quotation marks in print in Britain, but students in school would be expected to use double marks.

Using a dash

Speech can be conveyed by the use of a dash. James Joyce felt that quotation marks were messy, and introduced direct speech with a dash, using the layout as below.

– Don't do it.

– Why not?

– Oh, please yourself. But you'll get hurt if you do.

– Why, thanks! That's really considerate of you.

There are several ways of dealing with speech in a narrative, and modern punctuation is to keep the text as uncluttered and clean as possible, whilst conveying the meaning accurately.

We come now to some aspects of punctuation which do not require special marks or squiggles but which are, nevertheless, ways of visually identifying some aspects of the way text should be read and understood. They are capital letters, italics, indentation and paragraphing and the presentation of titles of books, articles, etc. in referencing.

Capital letters 12

The word capital comes from the Latin meaning *head*. Capital letters come at the head of a sentence, and are of greater height and usually different form from the lower-case letters.

Students need to know the correct use of capital letters, so they are listed here in categories. Capital letters are used for:

Beginning a sentence

The first word in a sentence is capitalized, after a full stop, but also after an exclamation mark or a question mark, as in the examples:

That's no way to treat a lady! Even if she's no lady.

What are you thinking? I'll give a penny for your thoughts.

Proper names

Proper names take capital letter in initials, first names and surnames: *W.H. Smith, John Brown*; in an epithet like *William the Conqueror*, or a trade name such as *Rolls Royce*, *Ford* or *Tesco*.

Official titles

Official titles take a capital when they refer to a particular person or thing.

Commonwealth   Member of Parliament (MP)   Senator   Queen Elizabeth
Prime Minister (PM)   HMS Sheffield   President Bush

Historical epochs

For example:

Middle Ages, Jurassic Period, the Renaissance

Nationalities and Languages

For example:

French, German, Australian

Place names

For example:

Ramsey Street, Oxford Road, Staines, Middlesex.
County of Yorkshire, England, Wales.
Red Sea, Atlantic Ocean, River Nile.

Religious names

In religious life when we refer to our own deity, the name begins with a capital letter, as does the personal pronoun when we use it for a particular deity. Hence we refer to God with 'He', 'Him' or 'His', using capitals.

God, Jesus, Holy Ghost, The Almighty
The Talmud, The Koran, Methodist, Shrove Tuesday

The calendar

Capital letters are used for:

1. days of the week: *Sunday, Thursday*
2. months of the year: *May, July, September*

The date, of course, is written using a capital letter for the day of the week and the month: *Thursday, 1st January 2004.*

Exclamations

These take a capital letter:

O! Oh!

The exclamation /ō/, however spelled, takes a capital letter.

'I' pronoun

The personal pronoun I is the only one which is always written with a capital.

Speech

At the beginning of any direct speech a capital letter is used to head the first word:

She asked, 'Do you come here often?'
I asked him point-blank, 'Then why do it?'

Titles of books, periodicals, etc.

The titles of books and periodical are capitalized, and this will be dealt with at the end of this chapter.

In summary

Capital letters are used for:
1. beginning a sentence
2. proper names
3. official titles
4. historical epochs
5. nationalities and languages
6. place names
7. religious names
8. the calendar
9. exclamations
10. personal pronoun
11. speech
12. titles of books, periodicals

Italics 4

In ordinary handwriting we may underline some words that need to stand out. When using a computer, these words are put in italics, or italicized. The letters are sloped to the right.

Italics were first used in 1501 by the Italian printer Aldo Manuzio. This is the man who changed his name into Latin and called himself Aldius Manutius. He and his grandson were famous for several printing innovations, of which this was one. Italics are used for the following:

Emphasis, importance and antithesis

Italics have elocutionary use and indicate how something is to be spoken aloud. She *hates* him, is clearly for emphasis. The *p*'s picked out in *P*retty *p*rincesses *p*icking *p*urple *p*lums, indicate the alliterative pattern.

The contrast between the italicized words in the following sentences show the balance of antithesis in the sentence:

You may like it, but *he* dislikes it intensely.

The word is spelt *human* not *humane*.

Foreign phrases

For example, *status quo, femme fatale, hors d'oeuvres*.

To him the *status quo* was sacred.

Quotations

Quotations can be italicized:

The exact quotation is to *fresh woods and pastures new*, not *to fresh fields* ...

Titles of books and periodicals

Titles of books and periodicals look clear and neat when italicized.

I see in *The Times* that X died yesterday.

Harry Potter and the Philosopher's Stone was J.K. Rowling's first book.

In summary

Italics are used for:

1. emphasis, importance, antitheses

2. foreign phrases
3. quotations
4. titles of books

Paragraphing and indentation

The word paragraph comes from the Greek meaning a stroke or line drawn, which is the mark used to separate the written speeches of the various characters in Platonic dialogue.

A paragraph contains one or more sentences with a single purpose. In the hierarchy of a book's structure the book is broken into chapters, each with its own subject. The chapter may, (in a book of information, or academic text) be divided into sections, each with its own subheading. After this, the paragraph carries the theme of argument as each paragraph has a different purpose. The shortest unit of meaning is the sentence.

There is a maxim 'Look to the paragraphs and the discourse will take care of itself'. But paragraphs are interrelated, and the smoothness of the transitions between them is often maintained with conjunctions and phrases such as *therefore, in these circumstances, although, on the other hand* and *finally*. These maintain the momentum and flow of the argument from paragraph to paragraph.

The national press, particularly the tabloids, are known for writing very short paragraphs, often only one sentence long. This gives them their punchy and fast-moving style.

Indentation is the practice of starting a line a little way in from the margin. The word comes from the Latin *dens* a tooth, and means 'to make a tooth-like incision'. It stems from the practice of scribes leaving a space at the beginning of a page for the illuminator to draw in the illuminated letter. Traditionally, the first word of each paragraph was indented, but with modern layout, this is often no longer the case, and block paragraphing is used with a blank line between the paragraphs to distinguish them from each other.

Quotations which are more than a few words long are usually indented so they stand out from the rest of the text. For example:

One of the most popular poems collected in many anthologies is that written by Dylan Thomas, in anger, on the death of his father. It begins:

Do not go gentle into that good night,
Old age should burn and rave at close of day;
Rage, rage against the dying of the light.

Titles of books, periodicals and referencing

This final section contains useful information for students who must make reference to academic sources. Academic essays require references to books, articles or journals, and this section deals with a way of referring to these in a text, as well as how to list references at the end of an essay.

Use of capitals in titles

Titles of books and periodicals are written with a capital letter at the beginning of each word, except the words *a*, *an* and *the*. Most people also do not capitalize conjunctions such as *and*, *but*, *because*, or prepositions such as *to*, *for*, *from*, *at*:

> *Did She Fall or Was She Pushed?*
>
> A *Study of the Language of Apes*

Alternatively, titles can be written uniformly in small capitals:

> THE MIDNIGHT FOLK by JOHN MASEFIELD
>
> TELL ME I'M OK REALLY by ROSIE RUSHTON

Use of a determiner

Here are some pointers if you need to refer to a newspaper. When you are writing, capitalize *A* or *The* in the title if it appears in the original title in the masthead of the paper. So you would refer to *The Times*, *The Guardian*, *The Times Educational Supplement*, all with the word *the* capitalized. But if referring to the latter by its abbreviation it would be *the* TES.

Referencing

Look at the four ways of referencing, below. The information needed for a reader to trace the article is the author's name, date of publication, title and publisher. The essential elements are set out here, but presentation may be affected by the house style of individual publishers.

Italics are used for the name of the entire work, the actual book or journal to which you are referring. The order is: surname, initials, date, title (*italics*), place: publisher.

Here are ways of referring to four different kinds of publication:

For a straightforward single author of a book:

Fowler, H.W. (1926) *Modern English Usage*. London: Oxford University Press.

For a publication with editors:

Snowling, M.J. and Thomson, M.E. (eds) (1991) *Dyslexia: Integrating Theory and Practice*. London: Whurr.

For a chapter within an edited book:

Augur, J. (1985) Guidelines for Teachers, Parents and Learners. In M. Snowling (Ed.) *Children's Written Language Difficulties* (pp. 147–171). Windsor: NFER-Nelson.

For an article within a journal:

Bradley, L. and Bryant, P.E. (1983) Categorizing sounds and learning to read – a causal connection. *Nature* 301, 419–421.

Much academic writing uses the Harvard system of referencing. When referring to an author in the text, merely give the surname and date of the publication:

Children's errors in forming irregular verbs have been examined in detail (Pinker, 1999).

All references are then listed fully, as above, in alphabetic order of author at the end of the text. The essential elements are set out here, but note that presentation may be affected by the house style of individual publishers. Indeed, see the simplified Whurr house style in the Bibliography on pp. 331–2.

Conclusion

Much of this section on punctuation may have seemed very prescriptive, but it is important to remind ourselves that punctuation is as much an art as a science. When considering punctuation and layout, the main rules are to err on the side of simplicity and consistency, making sure that whatever you do aids your meaning and intention, as a courtesy to the reader.

If you are an educator, you will have succeeded if the students you teach can use basic forms of punctuation and layout clearly and with confidence.

Summary

- Punctuation separates text and bundles meaningful sections of text together. There are 11 types of punctuation that consist of marks placed in the text:

  Full stop, comma, semi-colon, colon, apostrophe, question mark, exclamation mark, hyphen, parentheses, ellipsis and quotation mark. Of these, the comma and full stop are the most frequently used.

- Other aspect of punctuation concern presentation of the text: the use of capital letters, italics and indentation.

- Conventions for punctuating the references required in academic writing are also described.

Postscript

This book has dealt with the two sides of the language coin: spoken and written language. Our premise is that successful written communication is based on mastery of the spoken form, and that knowledge about the subject of language leads to more effective communication. In addition, it is empowering for those of our readers who help others to speak, read or write to know about all aspects of language so that they may be able to identify the points of difficulty.

Language is the most important tool developed by humans. By using it to label and order our world, we have refined our thinking and communication. The use of language is an essential part of being human. The importance of this tool in evolutionary terms is underlined when we consider how speech is produced. The speech organs are the same as those used to breathe and swallow, and peak efficiency in breathing and eating has been sacrificed in order to develop speech.

Part 1 provided a reminder of the biological basis of spoken language, and a description how the brain and organs of speech work to produce the sounds of English. These sounds are the building blocks of words which, between infancy and adulthood, increase to a lexicon of tens of thousands of items in the average person's memory. Our innate sense of universal grammar ensures that we learn to utter these words in a form and sequence that will carry meaning in English. With these processes in place, we are able to produce an infinite number of unique utterances to inform, instruct or convey to the listener the full range of human emotions.

In one respect, language is a constantly evolving process; where some words change their function or meaning, others drop from use altogether, and others are newly coined. Language can thus be fluid, ever-changing, colourful, vibrant and full of energy. On the other hand, some language must be handled with the utmost care and precision, as a few carelessly spoken words can make or break a business, put lives at risk or bring down a government.

Part 1 explained spoken English language and its many forms and varieties, in a descriptive way. Part 2 dealt with the written form of the language, a relatively new human achievement. The invention of writing created great opportunities for expanding communication, enabling us to convey ideas to others in a different place and at a different time. Writing also converted the ephemeral spoken form into a permanent written record, which could be more closely examined, leaving it open to analysis and scrutiny. English spelling has had a chequered history, and did not bear such examination well. The orthographic system has its consistencies and its difficulties, its admirers and critics. The task of mastering it can be confusing and formidable for a learner who is faced with reading and spelling the words, writing the sentences and putting in the punctuation. In dealing with spelling and grammar the information had necessarily to become prescriptive so as to reflect the writing conventions and notions of correctness that are taught in our schools and accepted by most writers.

We hope that in this book we have furnished readers with enough information about spoken language and the conventions of written language for them to analyse their own speech and writing, and become more aware of the use of language around them. The interactive tasks were designed to pull the reader into the conversation about language, and to share the authors' delight in its patterns and idiosyncrasies.

As with any complex human activity, things can go wrong with any of these language processes, which may result in cases of students with speech and language problems, dyslexia or related difficulties. For those readers who are teaching or supporting such students we hope we have provided enough information to increase your professional knowledge, and even inspired you to delve further into this fascinating area of human activity.

Bibliography

Aitchison J (1987a) Teach Yourself Linguistics. London: Hodder & Stoughton.
Aitchison J (1987b) Words in the Mind. Oxford: Blackwell.
Aitchison J (1996) Cassell's Dictionary of English Grammar. London: Cassell.
Ayto J (1990) Dictionary of Word Origins. London: Bloomsbury.
Barber CL (1964) The Story of Language. London: Pan Books.
Bloom L, Lahey M (1978) Language Development and Language Disorders. London: Wiley.
Bloomfield L (1933) Language. New York: Holt, Rinehart & Winston.
Borwick C, Townend J (1993) Developing Spoken Language Skills. Staines: The Dyslexia Institute.
Bragg M (2003) The Adventure of English. London: Hodder & Stoughton.
Bryson B (2001) Troublesome Words, 3rd edn. London: BCA.
Byrne M (1987) Eureka! A Dictionary of Latin and Greek Elements in English Words. Newton Abbot: David & Charles.
Chomsky N (1957) Syntactic Structures. The Hague: Mouton.
Chomsky N (1965) Aspects of the Theory of Syntax. Cambridge, MA: The MIT Press.
Chomsky N (1972) Language and Mind. New York: Harcourt Brace Jovanovich.
Chomsky N (1986) Knowledge of Language. New York: Praeger.
Cruttenden A (1974) An experiment involving comprehension of intonation in children from 7 to 10. Journal of Child Language 1: 222.
Crystal D (1985a) Linguistics (2nd edition). Harmondsworth: Penguin Books.
Crystal D (1985b) The Cambridge Encyclopaedia of Language. Cambridge: Cambridge University Press.
Crystal D (1988a) Rediscover Grammar. London: Longman.
Crystal D (1988b) The English Language. Oxford: Pelican Books.
Crystal D (1995) The Cambridge Encyclopaedia of the English Language. Cambridge: Cambridge University Press.
Crystal D, Crystal H (2000) Words on Words. Harmondsworth: Penguin Books.
De Villers P, De Villers J (1979) Early Language. London: Fontana.
DfEE (Department for Education and Employment (1998) The National Literacy Strategy. London: DfEE.
Diack H (1975) Standard Literacy Tests. St Albans: Hart-Davis Educational.
Fowler HW (1926) Modern English Usage. London: Oxford University Press.
Gimson AC (1962) An Introduction to the Pronunciation of English. London: Edward Arnold.

Gowers E (1962) The Complete Plain Words. Harmondsworth: Pelican Books.
Greenbaum S, Quirk R (1990) A Student's Grammar of the English Language. London: Longman.
Greenfield S (1997) The Human Brain: A guided tour. London: Weidenfeld & Nicolson.
Grice HP (1975) Logic and conversation. In Cole, P, Morgan JL (eds), Speech Acts. New York: Academic Press.
ICE-GB (International Corpus of English: Great Britain) http://www.ucl.ac.uk/english-usage/ice/
ICE-GB corpus (CD-ROM) available by email: icecup@ucl.ac.uk
Jarvie G (1993) Bloomsbury Grammar Guide. London: Bloomsbury.
Jones P (1997) Learn Latin. London: Duckworth.
Lyons J (1977) Chomsky. London: Fontana.
McArthur T (1992) The Oxford Companion to the English Language. New York: Oxford University Press.
McCrum R, MacNeil R, Cran W (1986) The Story of English. London: Faber and Faber.
Maciver A (1939) The New First Aid in English. Glasgow: Robert Gibson & Sons.
Manser M (1988) The Guinness Book of Words. London: Guiness Publishing Ltd.
Nash O (1959) Very like a whale. In: Smith PG, Wilkins JF (eds), The Sheldon Book of Verse. Oxford: Oxford University Press.
Partridge E (1947) Usage and Abusage. London: Hamish Hamilton.
Partridge E (1986) A Dictionary of Catch Phrases, 2nd edn. London: Routledge & Kegan Paul.
Partridge E (1999) You Have a Point There. London: Routledge.
Pinker S (1994) The Language Instinct. London: Penguin Books.
Pinker S (1999) Words and Rules. London: Weidenfeld & Nicolson.
Quirk R (1968) The Use of English. London: Longmans.
Rees N (1996) Dictionary of Word and Phrase Origins. London: Cassell.
Room A (1999) The Cassell Dictionary of Word Histories. London: Cassell.
Rowling JK (1998) Harry Potter and the Chamber of Secrets. London: Bloomsbury.
Sheridan R (1775) The Rivals.
Todd L (1995) Cassell's Guide to Punctuation. London: Cassell & Co.
Truss L (2003) Eats, Shoots and Leaves: The zero tolerance approach to punctuation. London: Profile Books.
Wells JC, Colson G (1971) Practical Phonetics. London: Pitman.
Williams B (2003) School reports. In: Foster J (ed.), Wordspinning. Oxford: Oxford University Press.

Index